IN MEMORIAM INSI VODVLLI F ET L IVLI APOLLINARIS
CIVIVM TREVERORVM EQVITVM ALAE AVG ALIORVMQ
QVORVM INSCITA SVNT NOMINA SED QVORVM RELIQVIAE
IN GALACI SEPVLCRIS IACENT

In memory of Fred Broadhurst

Lancaster's Roman Cemeteries

Edited by
Peter Iles and David Shotter

2009

Lancaster's Roman Cemeteries

This volume is No. 4 in the New Series of Resource Papers published by the
Centre for North-West Regional Studies at Lancaster University
Text and Illustrations Copyright © Peter Iles, David Shotter and the individual authors 2009.
All rights reserved.
The moral rights of the authors have been asserted.

Designed, typeset, printed and bound by
4word Ltd, Bristol

British Library Cataloguing in Publication Data. A catalogue record for this book is available from the British Library

ISBN 978–1–86220–233–7

Cover: Impression of Roman Lancaster by David Vale M.B.E.

Frontispiece: memorial stone to Insus, son of Vodullius (photograph: Ross Trench-Jellicoe)

Contents

List of figures

Note: the map background used in figures 1.2, 1.3, 2.1 and 5.2 is based on the street pattern of 1892, prior to alterations for modern traffic.

List of Plates

List of Contributors

Andrew Bates is a Project Officer with Oxford Archaeology North

Dr Fred Broadhurst[†] was a retired Senior Lecturer in Geology at the University of Manchester

Denise Drury, formerly a Project Officer with the Lancaster University Archaeological Unit, is now a Senior Project Manager with Archaeological Project Services in Lincolnshire

Ben Edwards is the retired County Archaeologist for Lancashire

Christine Howard-Davis is Finds Manager at Oxford Archaeology North

Elizabeth Huckerby is Environmental Manager at Oxford Archaeology North

Dr Paul Holder is Head of Stock Management and Logistics at the John Rylands University Library, University of Manchester

Vix Hughes, until recently a Project Officer with Oxford Archaeology North, is now a Project Officer with Oxford Archaeology South

Peter Iles is Specialist Adviser (Archaeology) for Lancashire County Council

Dr Jacqui McKinley is a Senior Project Officer and Specialist Osteoarchaeologist at Wessex Archaeology

Peter Noble is a Senior Archaeologist in the University of Manchester Archaeological Unit

Dr Charlotte O'Brien is Environmental Laboratories Manager, Archaeological Services, Durham University

Stephen Rowland is a Senior Project Manager at Oxford Archaeology North

Dr David Shotter is Emeritus Professor of Roman Imperial History at Lancaster University

Emily Somerville is Conservation Officer for Social History and Decorative Arts at Lancashire County Council

Jenny Truran is Conservation Officer for Social History and Decorative Arts at Lancashire County Council

Dr Andrew White recently retired as Curator of Lancaster City Museums

John Zant is a Project Officer at Oxford Archaeology North

[†]It is with great sadness and regret that we have learned of the death, on 1 October 2009, of our fellow contributor Fred Broadhurst; out of respect to him this book is dedicated to his memory

Acknowledgements

Putting together a multi-authored volume is never a straightforward matter, and the editors would like to express their gratitude to those who have contributed directly to the writing of this book (who are listed above on p.ix), and to those others who participated in the discussion sessions that preceded the writing up – Stephen Bull (of the Lancashire County Museum Service) who, with Edmund Southworth, was also responsible for the securing of the grant-funding which ensured that the memorial stone of Insus was brought into public ownership and displayed close to its original site, as well as facilitating the publication of the present book; also Rachel Newman and Jamie Quartermaine of Oxford Archaeology North; Mike Nevell and David Power of the University of Manchester Archaeological Unit; and Ben Edwards, Andrew White and Fred Broadhurst. We are especially grateful to Rachel Newman for her invaluable help and advice during the editorial process, to Anne Shotter for reading through the complete manuscript, and to Dr Jean Turnbull, Co-ordinator of the Centre for North-West Regional Studies at Lancaster University, and her successor, Dr Sam Riches, who have taken the manuscript through the publication process.

Both Oxford Archaeology North and the University of Manchester Archaeological Unit have supplied text-illustrations and photographic images, and we are also grateful to Ben Edwards, Heather Dowler (Assistant Curator of Lancaster City Museum), Emily Somerville and Adam Parsons (of Oxford Archaeology North) for the images that they provided. We are also grateful to Mary Vale for permission to use the impression of Roman Lancaster drawn by her late husband, David Vale M.B.E., to John Ketteringham who facilitated this, to the York Museums Trust for permission to use their photographs of tile tombs, to the editor of *The Lancaster Guardian* for permission to use their photographs of the memorial stone, and to the Portable Antiquities Scheme for permission to use their photograph of the Beckfoot cremation. Where appropriate, other photographs are acknowledged where they appear in the book.

For chapter 2, the author would like to thank Andrew White, both for the provision of an initial list of burial sites, and also for commenting on some of the conclusions reached.

For the work described in chapter 3, the authors wish to thank Dalesmoor Homes (77–79 Penny Street), CityBlock Ltd (81 Penny Street) and Fairclough Homes (the Streamline Garage site) for facilitating and financing the archaeological works, Rachel Newman for editing the chapter, and Anne Stewardson for preparing the illustrations.

For the work described in chapter 4, the authors wish to thank Hattrell and Partners for commissioning the archaeological work and David Bissell (Plant Hire) for the machinery used on site. Thanks are due also to Richard Gregory, who digitised the figures, and Derek Trillo (of G.ten Photography and Design) for post-excavation photography of the memorial stone. Finally, thanks are due to Anthony Birley, Stephen Bull, Ben Edwards, Paul Holder and Roger Tomlin for their advice and comments during the preparation of the report on the memorial stone; also to Dot Boughton, Finds Liaison Officer for Lancashire and Cumbria, for providing a German-language summary.

Preface

Yet even these bones from insult to protect,
Some frail memorial still erected nigh,
With uncouth rhymes and shapeless sculpture decked,
Implores the passing tribute of a sigh.

Thomas Gray 1751, *Elegy Written in a Country Churchyard*

In November 2005, Lancaster's Roman dead briefly achieved national press, television and radio coverage, following the discovery of an almost-complete memorial stone erected in honour of a Treveran cavalryman, named Insus, the son of Vodullius. Subsequently, much time and effort have been expended by Lancashire Museums to ensure that the stone should become available for conservation, study and eventual display in north-west England. It is especially gratifying that, as a result of that effort, Insus' memorial stone has not only been restored to its former glory, but that in recent months it has been placed on permanent display in Lancaster City Museum.

Another equally important result of the interest and the effort was the successful application for funding not just to repair the stone and to put it on display, but also to facilitate a publication which would discuss the significance of the memorial stone itself, and draw together all of the surviving evidence – antiquarian and more recent – for Roman burials in Lancaster. The present book is the result of that, and all who value Lancaster's Roman past are deeply indebted to Lancashire Museums – in particular, to its Director, Edmund Southworth, and Stephen Bull, the Curator of Military History and Archaeology – and to the Heritage Lottery Fund for their generous help; without their assistance, this report might not have seen the light of day and, more importantly, this very fine – indeed, unique – stone might have been lost to the region for good.

Whilst it is true to say that the discovery of the memorial stone was the catalyst, it would not do to underestimate the desire that had been building to bring at least some of the results of many years' work to a wider audience. Lancaster has been the site of a series of small developer-funded excavations over recent years, and whilst the reports exist within the Lancashire Historic Environment Record, few have been examined outside the understandably limited remit of their individual projects. Fewer and fewer academic journals now accept such reports, a situation that has its roots in the considerable costs of developing, publishing and sustaining them.

Amongst day-to-day practitioners in archaeology, the opportunity to step back and consider the wider picture is increasingly a luxury. There is thus a tendency to rely more upon those with particular research interests – both professional and otherwise – to draw out a deeper understanding than can be obtained by those who are forced to move from site to site and task to task by commercial or other external considerations. It is important, therefore, that new information is made available to as wide an audience as possible, so that an informed debate can occur and a better understanding of our heritage can be developed.

The bulk of this book is devoted to two recent excavation-campaigns, which took place on adjacent sites – those conducted on the site of the Streamline Garage (on the west side of King Street) by the Lancaster University Archaeological Unit (now Oxford Archaeology North) and on the site of the Arla Foods Depot (north of Aldcliffe Road) by the University of Manchester Archaeological Unit. These pieces of work are fully reported in chapters 3 and 4, together with relevant contributions by specialists. Also included are an assessment of the current state of our knowledge of the Roman fort at Lancaster and its associated civilian settlement (chapter 1), and an attempt to draw together all the reports of funerary material found between the eighteenth and twentieth centuries, which are contained in a variety of antiquarian and casual publications (chapter 2). In the latter case, our purpose has been to establish the nature, dates and findspots of a considerable number of reported finds – with varying success, although hopefully achieving a new level of certainty in a number of instances. In its turn, although only one formal cemetery area has emerged clearly – namely that to the south of the area of known Roman settlement – the exercise has facilitated the formulation of hypotheses as to where others may lie.

Finds made in this southern cemetery area, which of course include most prominently the memorial stone for Insus, provide a picture of extended use stretching from prehistory to the third and fourth centuries AD. However, apart from the memorial stone itself, which indicates a considerable individual expenditure, the finds from this cemetery area present a picture characterised by a paucity of grave-goods and by basic simplicity – even casualness – of treatment of the human remains; this represents a great contrast to the evidence from Brougham in Cumbria. Nor, apart from the memorial stone itself, is there any clear evidence of military participation in this particular cemetery. The final chapter of the book presents a discussion of these and other related contextual matters; two appendices then provide full accounts of the Burrow Heights figures, which are significant in our understanding of the possible nature of commemoration of the dead in the vicinity of Roman Lancaster, and the conservation of the memorial stone to Insus.

Zusammenfassung

In dem hier vorliegenden Band *Lancaster's Roman Cemeteries* werden sämtliche Information zusammengetragen, die uns nach heutigem Wissenstand für eine Bearbeitung der romano-britischen Grabstätten in Lancasters Stadtmitte behilflich sein können. Zu Beginn der Analyse steht eine Erörterung, die sich mit Lancaster als römischem Garnisonsstandort im Nordwesten Englands beschäftigt. Die Erörterung soll vor allem einen Einblick in die Entwicklung des römischen Militaerstandortes auf dem Burgberg (Castle Hill), die Lune überblickend, verschaffen: von Lancasters erstem römischen Kastell, welches wahrscheinlich unter Quintus Petillius Cerialis (71–74 n. Chr.) errichtet wurde, bis hin zu der Anfang des 4. Jahrhunderts erbauten grösseren Anlage, welche nach den Plänen der 'Saxon Shore' Forts ihre Vorgänger ersetzte. Diese Abhandlung beschäftigt sich ausserdem mit der Entwicklung der zivilen Siedlung ausserhalb der Kastellmauer, welche sich anfangs entlang Lancasters späterer Church Street befand (die Strasse, die aus dem Kastell nach Osten hin herausführte) und sich später nach Norden gen Lune und ca. 300m in südlicher Richtung ausbreitete.

Dem Essay schließt sich eine Erörterung aller sowohl antiquarischen als auch neueren schriftlichen Quellen an, die von entweder prähistorischen oder römischen Gräbern in der Umgebung berichten. Diese Quellen, die sich zum Teil recht stark in ihrer Qualität und Genauigkeit unterscheiden, werden auf ihre Glaubwürdigkeit hin untersucht um herauszufinden, welche römischen Fundstellen der Wirklichkeit entsprechen und wo genau sie sich befinden. Das Ergebnis dieser Unteruschung ist, dass viele der bisher als prähistorisch angesehenen Fundstellen in der Gegend um die Stadt Lancaster nun als romano-britisch angesehen werden müssen. In der hier vorliegenden Veröffentlichung wurde außerdem versucht, ihre genaue geographische Lage festzustellen, aber nur die Lage ein einzigen Bestattungsplatzes – jener welcher am südlichen Ende der Siedlung an der römischen Ausfallstraße liegt – konnte mit Sicherheit bestimmt werden.

Die dieser Erörterung folgenden zwei Kapitel beschäftigen sich mit den wichtigsten Ergebnissen der Grabungen, die zwischen den 90er Jahren und 2006 stattfanden und von Lancaster University Archaeological Unit (now Oxford Archaeology North) und Manchester Archaeology Unit (2005) durchgeführt wurden. In diesen Grabungskampagnen wurde schwerpunktmäßig der Friedhof am Südende der Siedlung untersucht. Dieser Bestattungsplatz wurde vom 2. Jh. n. Chr. bis ins frühe 4. Jh. n. Chr. benutzt und die Anzahl der Brandgräber überwiegt deutlich der der Flachgräber. Es wurden keinerlei Hinweise auf Scheiterhaufen gefunden und die meisten Brandgräber enthielten nur wenige Beigaben; häufige Funde waren Sandalenbeschläge aus Eisen und Überreste des Leichenschmauses, die nicht vom Scheiterhaufenfeuer 'verzehrt' worden waren. Der weitaus wichtigse Fund war der extrem gut erhaltene Reitergrabstein des aus Trier stammenden Soldaten Insus, der vor seinem Tode in der Ala Augusta gedient hatte. In der Umgebung des Grabsteins wurden keinerlei Grabbeigraben gefunden und deshalb gehen wir davon aus, dass der Stein sehr wahrscheinlich ein Zenotaph war. Diese zwei Kapitel enthalten sowohl vollständige Berichte der Grabungskampagnen als auch die relevanten Berichte der jeweiligen Spezialisten.

Das letzte Kapitel ist den Bestattungsplätzen im Raum Lancaster im Allgemeinen gewidmet: es werden Vergleiche mit anderen romano-britischen Friedhöfen im Nordwesten Englands angestellt, unter anderem Beckfoot, Birdoswald, Brougham und Low Borrowbridge (Cumbria). Die Erörterung in diesem Kapitel trägt hauptsächlich die Ergebnisse der Diskussionen zusammen, die die Autoren mit anderen Wissenschaftlern in zwei Fachseminaren geführt haben. Das Ergebnis der Seminare war, dass wir zwar auf der einen Seite in den letzten Jahren unser Wissen über die Bestattungen im Raum Lancaster enorm vergrößern konnten, dass es aber auf der anderen Seite auch noch viele Lücken gibt, vor allem was den römischen Friedhof bei Brougham (Cumbria) angeht, und ob die Bestattungen in Lancaster vielleicht bestimmten militärischen Einheiten zugesprochen werden können.

Den Erörterungen schliessen sich zwei Appendices an: Appendix I beschreibt eine Wallanlage, die drei Meilen südlich von Lancaster nahe der römischen Ausfallstraße entdeckt wurde und welche vielleicht die Überreste eines substantiellen Mausoleums darstellen könnte. Appendix II gibt uns einen Einblick in sowohl die Säuberung, Konservierung und Reparatur des Reitergrabsteins in Lancashire Museums' Conservation Studios, als auch in seine Auffindung und Werdegang bis hin zu seiner Ausstellung in Lancasters City Museum.

CHAPTER 1

The Roman Site at Lancaster

By David Shotter

In common with many sites in north-west England, a Roman fort was once assumed to have been established at Lancaster during the campaigns of Cnaeus Julius Agricola (AD 77–83; Campbell 1986). However, it now appears that, as at many other northern military sites, the early history of Roman Lancaster was, in chronological terms, considerably more complex than was previously supposed (Shotter 2001a; 2001b).

When the Romans came to Britain in AD 43, they are now thought by many to have met with less opposition than was once generally believed; we are still discovering more about pre-Claudian political and economic contacts between Rome and some British leaders. Indeed, recent work has shown that the site at Silchester (Hampshire), the central place of the tribe of the Atrebates (*Calleva Atrebatum*), was effectively on the way to becoming a Romanised site *before* Claudius' troops set foot in Britain (Clarke and Fulford 2002). Moreover, at the time of the Roman invasion, eleven British leaders evidently submitted to Claudius (*ILS* 216). Thus, although the opposition mounted by Caratacus was troublesome, and at times even ferocious, it did not, in terms of the overall numbers involved at least, amount to a widely-embraced anti-Roman movement.

Amongst those who submitted were two northern leaders, Cartimandua and Venutius, both of whom are described by the Roman historian, Cornelius Tacitus, as 'Brigantians' (Tacitus *Annals* 12.40,3); of the two, Cartimandua was plainly more enthusiastically pro-Roman. For the time being, however, a marriage-alliance between the two, probably insisted upon by Rome, ensured that at least the northern flank of the Roman advance was protected by Brigantian 'neutrality', or even support. Although the individual areas of political and economic strength of the two Brigantian leaders are not known for certain, it is likely that Cartimandua's lay in and to the east of the Pennines, with the *oppidum* at Stanwick perhaps representing her principal centre (Richmond 1954; Turnbull 1984). Venutius' main strength may have lain in the North West, in the territory known later as that of the Carvetii, with a chief centre possibly located at Clifton Dykes, near Penrith (Higham and Jones 1985; Edwards 2006).

It is evident that harmony did not last long between the two Brigantian leaders, and it seems likely that a cause of the deteriorating relationship was Cartimandua's refusal in AD 50 to entertain a request for sanctuary made to her by Caratacus, preferring instead to hand him over to the Roman authorities (Tacitus *Annals* 12. 36, 1–2). Tacitus is very imprecise in his accounts of events in the 50s and 60s, but it seems that, as the relationship between Cartimandua and Venutius broke down, so the pro-Roman stance of the Brigantes became more fragile, necessitating Roman military intervention (Carrington 1985). Tacitus provides little detail of chronology and locations of such activity, but finds of pre-Neronian *aes*-coins, especially contemporary copies of issues of Claudius, in coastal and valley locations in the North West, suggest that Roman forces probably operated on two fronts (Shotter 1994): some troops marched overland from their bases in the north Midlands, whilst others were taken by ship, perhaps from the Dee estuary, to be disembarked in the wide river-estuaries that characterise the north-west coast (Shotter 2002). As these troops effected rendezvous, they proceeded to penetrate Brigantian territory along the valley-routes.

It is probable then, that the Lancaster area saw Roman troops for the first time in the course of operations such as these. However, it is likely that these early activities did not result in permanent Roman military dispositions in what is now Lancashire and Cumbria, the troops probably returning to winter-quarters at their home-bases further south. Eventually, in AD 69, taking advantage of the confusion created by the Roman civil war which followed the death of Nero (Tacitus *Histories* 3.45), Venutius drove his former wife from power, leaving her to be rescued by her Roman 'patrons'. This turned the territory of the Brigantes into a hostile neighbour of the fledgling Roman province of *Britannia*. The conquest of the North had, therefore, become a matter of urgent necessity (Fig. 1.1).

In the North West, the combined land-and-sea assault was probably utilised again; the chronology of this has now been shown, according to the dating of timbers in the earliest fort at Carlisle, to have commenced in the early 70s under the governors, Vettius Bolanus and Petillius Cerialis (Birley 1973;

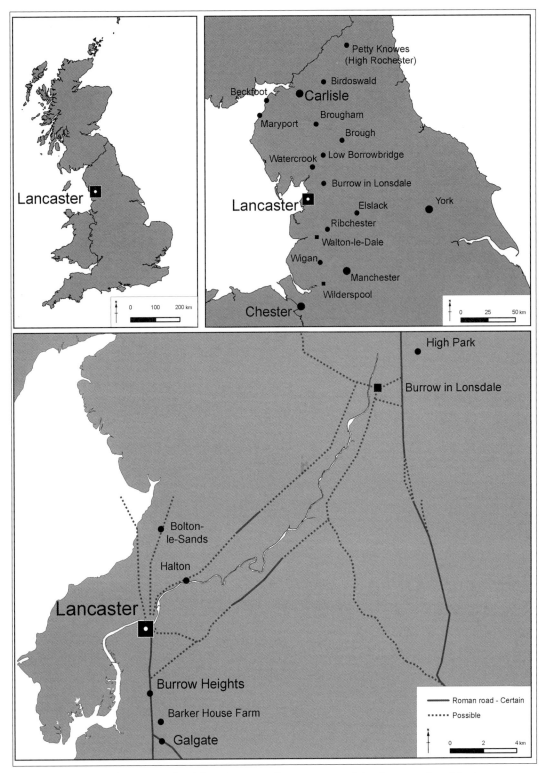

Figure 1.1 North-West England: location map, showing some of the sites mentioned in the text

Caruana 1997; Shotter 2000a; McCarthy 2002, 73). Artefactual evidence from the fort on Castle Hill suggests that it was then that a permanent military establishment was first constructed in Lancaster, although it should be noted that no evidence of either pre-Roman settlement or earlier Roman temporary structures has ever come to light on the hill. The importance of the site derived from its position, commanding both a disembarkation place and a crossing-point of the River Lune, as well as constituting

a link in a line of forts that extended from the north Midlands and Cheshire, through Preston, and on up the Lune valley, towards Carlisle.

Excavations at Lancaster over the years (Jones and Shotter 1988; Shotter and White 1990; Shotter 2001a) have shown that the first fort, which assumed the conventional 'playing-card' shape, was constructed of turf and timber, and sat across the crown of Castle Hill, probably occupying approximately 2.25 hectares (Fig. 1.2). Excavation in the 1970s revealed the remains of a substantial turf-and-clay rampart, which was still 3 metres wide at its base and 1.5 metres in height, with a well-defined battered front face (Jones and Shotter 1988, 26–58). Although legionaries may well have been involved in the construction of the fort, its first garrison, as has been demonstrated by the recent discovery of the memorial stone of Insus, the son of Vodullius (see below, pp.79ff), was evidently an auxiliary cavalry-unit, an *Ala Augusta* (probably the *Ala Augusta Gallorum Proculeiana*; Holder 1982, 107 and 109; Shotter 1988a, 214f; Shotter and White 1990, 27–30), which may have seen substantial recruitment of horsemen from the tribe of the Treveri in modern Germany.

Over the next half-century, the fort underwent modifications – enlargement, rebuilding in stone and probably reorientation (*RIB* 604; Shotter and White 1990, 21f); whilst the early fort appears to have faced east, its larger stone-built successor was probably turned through 90 degrees, leaving its north gate as its main approach. This north gate gave access to a river-crossing (perhaps a ford, in the first instance), whilst the east gate had led out on to what is now Church Street, intersecting a north-south roadway which later became known as Penny Street/ Cheapside, above what is now Stonewell. It is likely that also from the east gate (adjacent to the location of Covell's Cross and the Judges' Lodgings) a road swung northwards, presumably

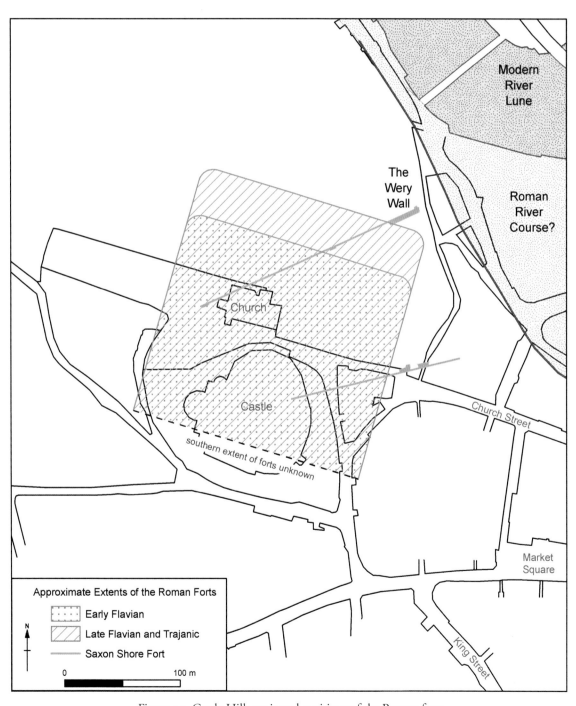

Figure 1.2 Castle Hill: projected positions of the Roman forts

towards a beaching-point on the riverside. There is no requirement to assume that there was a 'formal harbour' in the Roman period – at least, not until the later years.

We know something of the fort's subsequent history: there is reason, on the evidence of coin-loss (Shotter 1990, 118f), to believe that it lost all or part of its garrison, temporarily at least, at the time of the Antonine advance into southern Scotland in the mid-second century. By this time, the *Ala Augusta* appears to have been moved to Chesters on Hadrian's Wall (Holder 1982, 107), and at some point – either before or after the Antonine interlude in Scotland – Lancaster received as its garrison another Gallic cavalry-unit, the *Ala Gallorum Sebosiana*; this unit had been at Carlisle in the Flavian period (Tomlin 1998, 74f [*Tab. Luguval.* 44]; *RIB* 2411, 88 and 2465, 1–2, Shotter and White 1990, 27f), and has recently been attested at Inveresk in the Antonine period by the discovery in 2007 of another cavalryman's tombstone at Carberry (Tomlin 2008, 372f). The *Ala Sebosiana* was still in garrison at Lancaster in the mid-third century, when it was recorded as having been involved in rebuilding-work on the bath-house and *basilica* (*RIB* 605); the former of these structures was discovered in the 1970s outside the eastern rampart of the fort (Jones and Leather 1988a, 72–6), whilst the latter was presumably a *basilica equestris exercitatoria*, normally attached to the headquarters (*principia*) of cavalry-forts.

This rebuilding work requires some comment: the two buildings concerned were of major significance, and are described on the dedicatory inscription as having been rebuilt 'from ground-level' after having 'collapsed from old age'. Does this imply that the fort had suffered decay during a period of abandonment, or had the damage occurred during hostilities? It is worth noting that the dedication-stone has been dated to AD 262–5 (Birley 1936, 5); this was during the period when the western provinces of the Roman Empire were involved in a civil war in which they broke away from the central government, setting up a rebel-organisation, the independent 'Empire of the Gauls' (*Imperium Galliarum*). This rebellion was initiated in 260 by Postumus, whose name was subsequently erased from the inscription, and brought to an end in 273 by the 'legitimatist' Emperor, Aurelian. Civil wars, as we know only too well today, engender great bitterness, and it is possible that Lancaster's bath-house and *basilica* required rebuilding after an episode of *civil* strife; a unique third-century dedication to *Dea Gallia*, found in 2006 at Vindolanda, may provide another example of the voluble expression of sympathies in such a context (Tomlin and Hassall 2007, 346f; Birley 2008, 185).

In the closing years of the third century, the Emperor, Diocletian (AD 284–306), initiated a major reform of the Roman army, which rearranged existing units into two types of force: the élite troops, including legions and auxiliary cavalry, became 'mobile field-armies' closely associated both physically and in terms of loyalty with the emperor(s) of the day, whilst the remainder, mostly troops of lower status, were organised as 'border-soldiers' (*limitanei*) and posted in individual provinces. This 'root-and-branch' reform involved the splitting up of many of the former individual units, and presumably the loss of some unit-names.

It is likely that the *Ala Sebosiana*, if it survived the end of the Gallic rebellion, will have been incorporated into the field-armies, although it is possible that some of its troopers may have remained in Lancaster, where they appear to have been joined by a Unit of Bargemen (*Numerus Barcariorum*; *RIB* 601; Shotter 1973). Whilst the principal duty of these men and their shallow-draughted barges was probably lighterage in Morecambe Bay, we should remember that the altar, which is our sole evidence for them, was dedicated to the war-god, Mars, by men who are described as 'soldiers' (*milites*).

The presence of such a unit at Lancaster seems to emphasise the growing importance in the later years of the Roman period of coastal defence and maritime communication (Mason 2003, 149ff); this is also significantly reflected in the complete rebuilding of the fort in the early fourth century on the northern and eastern slopes of Castle Hill. The style adopted is similar to that of the 'Saxon-Shore forts' of south-east England, such as Portchester Castle (Hampshire), which were notable for the strength of their defences. Indeed, the 'Wery Wall', the single fragment of this new fort to have survived above ground (Jones and Leather 1988b, 80–2), has been shown by excavation to have been the remains of the core of a polygonal bastion for the mounting of a heavy catapult or ballista, similar to the half-round bastions that survive at Portchester (Plate 1.1) and Pevensey. Little is known of the internal arrangements of this fort, but, at approximately four hectares, it was clearly capable of holding more than a small military garrison, and presumably had a principal function of defending the integrity of a mooring- or beaching-area on the River Lune. Although the history

Plate 1.1 Portchester Castle, Hampshire: south wall with half-round bastions (photograph: David Shotter)

of this fort is poorly understood, artefactual evidence from it suggests that, like Birdoswald on Hadrian's Wall (Wilmott 2001), it survived well into the fifth century – if not beyond.

As at most Roman forts, a civilian community developed rapidly outside the fort-walls (Sommer 1984; Shotter and White 1990, 32–40; Fig. 1.3). Typically, the populations of such settlements might contain local craftsmen and service-providers, attracted by the prospect of business with the military in the fort, those retired soldiers who stayed on in the locality, using their gratuities to establish homes and businesses for themselves and their wives, and also the girl-friends and families of serving soldiers who, prior to the early third century, were not permitted officially to marry. By analogy with other such sites, it would be reasonable to suppose that, for a variety of reasons, some inhabitants will have come from considerably further afield. In any case, it is likely that the populations of such settlements will, in time, have exhibited a very 'cosmopolitan' appearance.

Although the physical extent of such small towns is not often clear – generally having no walls, they probably grew as need dictated – we can be certain that they were lively, noisy and, having in mind the variety of activities that they probably contained, smelly too; they will have become particularly busy on market-days,

as people came in from the rural hinterland to buy and sell. In this way, a relatively broad group of local people will have been drawn into a Romanised lifestyle (Dio Cassius *Roman History*, 56.18, 2–3).

The town that developed outside the fort at Lancaster is not particularly well-known in terms of extent, but elements of it have emerged through excavation over the years (Drury, in prep). It is, for example, clear that Lancaster's house-building 'boom' in the eighteenth century uncovered much structural and artefactual evidence, particularly in an area around Church Street and Penny Street. By analogy with other such sites, we can be certain that Roman Lancaster's extramural settlement will have contained provision for religious buildings, metal-working, textile-manufacture, tanning, 'fast-food' outlets, bars and brothels. What is known of Church Street suggests the presence of timber- and stone-built properties, with their gable-ends facing on to the street – indicating that street-frontage space was at a premium. Such buildings probably consisted of a shop or workshop on the street-frontage itself, with living-accommodation behind. Examples of such accommodation are visible today at the site of Vindolanda. Recent work on the site of Mitchell's Brewery (on Church Street), for example, showed evidence of bronze-working on the street-frontage; next door, there was some evidence that was

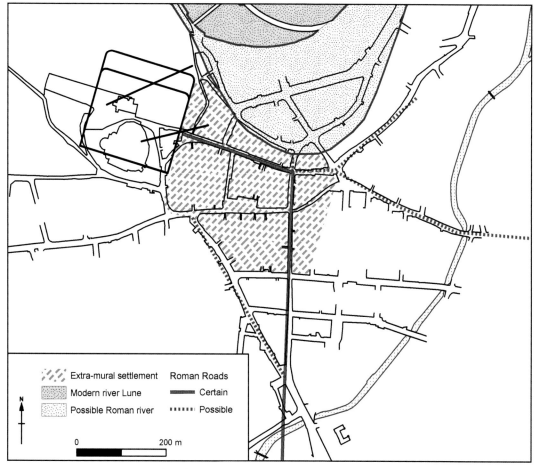

Figure 1.3   Plan showing the likely extent of the extramural settlement

consistent with the presence of a temple (Howard-Davis *et al.* in prep). It was also in this area that the fort bath-house was located; this will have provided social and leisure facilities for both soldiers and civilians.

Excavation has also shown that extramural buildings were not restricted to this eastern side of the fort; to the north of the fort, in the northern Vicarage Field, evidence has been found at various times of what appears to have been a substantial courtyard-house, with its own private bath-suite which was approached through an impressive entrance flanked by columns (Wright 1959, 106–8; Jones, Leather and Shotter 1988, 61–71) and which exhibited evidence of internal painted decoration. Whilst, to date, the building has revealed no clues as to its purpose, it is hard to resist the suggestion that it was an official residence of some kind. It is possible, in view of its position overlooking the river, that it was in some way connected with 'customs and excise'. By chance, in the late eighteenth century, an altar was found, built into the fabric of the Castle, which had been dedicated to the god, Mars Cocidius, by an 'appropriate' official, Lucius Vibenius, *beneficiarius consularis* (*RIB* 602), part of whose job may have been concerned with the supervision of tax-collection.

We know relatively little of Lancaster's rural hinterland in the Roman period; fieldwork and aerial reconnaissance in the Lune valley have revealed evidence of farmsteads, although how they related to the economic and social activity of the fort and town is hard to say (Shotter and White 1995, 58–76). It is certain, however, that a cavalry-regiment will have had a sizeable requirement for food for the men and their mounts, as well as bedding for the latter. The writing-tablets from Vindolanda certainly suggest that some, at least, of such requirements will have been met locally.

The farmers, like the townspeople, will probably have represented a mixture of backgrounds – some of local origin, others probably former Roman soldiers who had purchased farmland on their retirement from active service. An example of the latter is provided by the retired *decurio* ('cavalry-centurion'), Julius Januarius, who, around the turn of the second and third centuries, was evidently farming land around Bolton-le-Sands and who invoked the help of Ialonus, perhaps the deity of the River Lune, in his efforts to secure a good harvest (*RIB* 600). Such a man will obviously have been Romanised; however, a rather different picture is provided by a small farm, recently excavated at Barker House Farm, on the site of Lancaster University (OA North 2004; see further below on p.7). On this site, which can be dated as active during the Roman period, there was no sign of obvious economic interaction with the fort and town, despite the fact that it lay just four miles to the south of the fort, and closely adjacent to the Roman road approaching Lancaster from the south. Clearly, the evidence from Barker House Farm and that from Bolton-le-Sands send contrasting 'messages' regarding the relationship between the fort and town on the one hand, and the inhabitants of the rural hinterland on the other.

Finally – and appropriately in the context of the present volume – we come to the subject of death: Roman law precluded the burial of the dead, with the exception of infants, within the limits of a settlement (Philpott 1991, 101). Obviously, in the case of an unwalled settlement, such as that at Lancaster, the positioning of burial-areas may have been a rather uncertain matter. Lancaster has produced cemetery-evidence in three main areas – Cheapside/Stonewell, Westfield War Memorial Village and the southern ends of King Street and Penny Street (see below in chapter 2). The first and last of these clearly respect known Roman roads, whilst the evidence from Westfield War Memorial Village (to the west of Castle Hill) is dubious in nature (see below on pp.17ff). Of these, it is the area at the southern end of the town that has yielded the bulk of the surviving evidence, and it is this area that provides the principal focus of the present volume.

CHAPTER 2

Early Evidence for Burials in Lancaster

By Peter Iles

That Lancaster was settled in the later prehistoric period is taken for granted; indeed, by the Bronze Age there must have been a sufficiently large settled population to explain the urnfield on Lancaster Moor – on land that was later to become Williamson Park, the Moor Hospital and St Martins College (Harker 1865; 1877; Harrison 1896). Where these people actually lived is, however, more of a mystery and so is what happened during the latter part of the Iron Age and into the Roman period. This problem has been recognised for a long time, just as late prehistoric settlement has proven difficult to recognise in the county as a whole (White 1987, 15; Haselgrove 1996, 62). Recent work on a site at Lancaster University (OA North 2004) has, along with survey work at High Park, near Kirkby Lonsdale (Jecock 1998), shed some light on this matter.

The latter involved the detailed survey of a well-preserved landscape retaining settlement and farming features of Neolithic to post-medieval date, located in an area above modern arable limits and which had been preserved through the medieval period by its status as a deer park. The phasing of the individual sites suggested two things: first, that there was a well-organised and densely-settled landscape hereabouts in the later prehistoric and Romano-British periods; and second, that sites there that would have been classified by their surface morphology into the Bronze Age must in fact have been of later Iron Age or Romano-British date (Jecock 1998, 31). There is no reason to suspect that this particular area was unique during these periods and we should expect both a similar density of occupation and the continued use of 'traditional' settlement styles on suitable sites elsewhere. Where these settlements and field systems are not seen, it seems more likely that this is due to their destruction by medieval and later agriculture than to their original absence from the landscape.

Excavation in advance of development at the south end of Lancaster University revealed an almost-aceramic settlement containing at least two round houses of typical pre-Roman type, but confirmed the continuance of the use of this traditional type of dwelling by producing Radiocarbon dates from the first to fourth centuries AD (OA North 2004, 20 and 33–4). This settlement is not the only one where the longevity of

house styles and site types has been demonstrated, and this is an issue that needs to be addressed across the whole North West (Alistair Vannan *pers. comm.* 2009; Hodgson and Brennand 2007, 50–2).

What have the above discoveries to do with Roman cemeteries in Lancaster? The answer is that it fed concern about the attribution of burials in the southern part of the city centre. As well as the Lancaster Moor urnfield (noted above), a series of cremation burials has been recorded from Queen Square to Penny Street Bridge (Fig. 2.1). As will be seen, details of some of these are vague, and it is even possible that one or two have been recorded twice, but there seems to have been a reasonably dense cluster of sites to the south of the presumed area of the Roman town. A small number of these sites were originally identified as Roman; there have been three sites investigated in modern times that certainly were of that period, whilst others are described in such a manner as to give us reasonable certainty that they are of prehistoric date. Some, however, are more doubtful and it seemed a particular coincidence that recent work was revealing only Roman, and not prehistoric, burials – although it is true that the most recent work on the former Arla Foods Depot site (see below in chapter 4) revealed some prehistoric activity. Were we, therefore, actually seeing the overlap of two burial grounds, a later prehistoric and a Roman site, or were some of the earlier discoveries misidentified? Of course, it is conceivable that both are true and that we have a Roman cemetery continuing an earlier tradition. Examination of all the reported evidence for earlier discoveries may help towards clarifying the matter.

The Lancashire Historic Environment Record (HER) lists more than twenty separate sites, which have been or could be taken to represent either prehistoric or Roman burials (Fig. 2.1; Table 2.1, below). In order that the record should be complete, this table includes both the historical discoveries that are the main concern of this chapter, but also more modern discoveries that are fully discussed in chapters 3 and 4. It is certainly possible that there are others that have been missed (and it would be appreciated if any omissions or new information were communicated to the author), but in at least one instance a site claimed as a burial site by later writers cannot be confirmed by reference to the

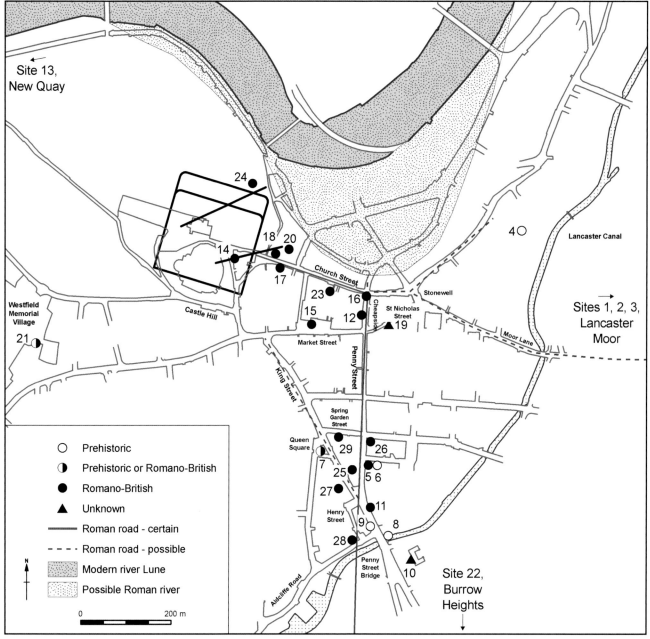

Figure 2.1 Distribution map of known burial sites

original report. In this case, during the construction of a railway station at Lancaster – whether this was Lancaster Castle Station or Green Ayre Station is unclear – the discovery of Roman material, including a 'unique' face-pot, is reported by Watkin (1883, 186); this is taken by Braithwaite (1985, 113, Fig. 9.4, 123f) as having been a cemetery site, and by Philpott (1991, 30) to have included a cremation, despite there being no reference to human remains in Watkin's description. It is worth pointing out, however, that the unique 'Face Pot' in question is compared by Braithwaite (1985, 113, Fig. 9.4) to those of the Danube region, but a more compelling comparison with its 'Toby Jug' style is perhaps with that found at Trier (Braithwaite 1985, 116f, Fig. 11.2). In the context of a wider discussion of Roman Lancaster it would be tempting to construct links between this item and the two Treveran memorial stones (below).

Prehistoric or Roman?

Shotter and White (1990, 5) list nine of the entries in Table 2.1 as prehistoric sites, that is, sites 1 (as two sites), 2, 3, 4, 6, 7, 8 and 9. White (1997) lists only three 'satisfactory' Roman burial sites: 5, 25 and 26, as well as the tombstone, site 12 and tile tomb, site 20. Re-examination of the records is, however, illuminating. The urn from **Site 3** is described as Roman by Harrison (1894, 185):

… about thirteen and a half inches in height, and ten inches in diameter, tapering to five inches at the bottom. The inner diameter at the top was three inches, and of the outer lip five and a half inches. The urn was not well burnt, a light red colour when found; but on washing a piece, it was a dark slate colour. The lower half was quite plain and smooth. The upper half had four slightly indented rings,

Table 2.1 *Prehistoric and Romano-British Burials Recorded in Lancaster*

Site No.	Location	NGR	Summary	References
1	Lancaster Moor in the area of Williamson Park	SD 48886134	Prehistoric urnfield – six urns found 1863–5, one urn 1872.	Harker 1865; 1877; Harrison 1896, 15; Jackson 1935, 100–1
2	St Martins College (formerly Lancaster Barracks)	SD 487608	Six prehistoric urns and a stone 'ornament' found in 1877.	Harker 1865; 1877; Harrison 1896, 15; Jackson 1935, 100–1
3	Lancaster Cemetery, Quernmore Road	SD 492618	Cinerary urn, found June 1894 with some fragments of bone.	Harrison 1894, 185; *Lancaster Guardian*, 9 June 1894
4	Alfred Street	SD 48076193	Bronze Age urn and accessory vessel, found 1893.	Shotter and White 1990, 5; Fox n.d., 40
5	Church of St Thomas, Penny Street	SD 47756143	Complete black burnished ware cremation vessel of mid-second century date.	White 1997, 9; Lancaster Museum LM92
6	Church of St Thomas, Penny Street	SD 47756143	Collared urn, probably later Bronze Age.	Shotter and White 1990: 5; Lancaster Museum LM271
7	Queen Square	SD 47636146	Cinerary urn found 1847 with burnt bones and 'the skull of a child'.	Simpson 1852, 121; Watkin 1883, 185
8	Nr Penny Street Bridge	SD 47786128	Bronze Age cinerary urn found *c.*1900.	Penney 1975, 92
9	Corporation Arms, Penny Street	SD 47746130	'Late Celtic' Cinerary urn found 'in the early part of the last century' (*c.*1800 or *c.*1900?).	Penney 1975, 92
10	South-east Lancaster, not far from Queen Square	Possibly either SD 47836123 or SD 48586073	'Some more urns' found in 1876.	Watkin 1883, 185
11	East side of Penny Street, almost opposite Henry Street	SD 47746134	Flask-shaped vase half-full of calcined bones. Roman.	*Lancaster Guardian*, 23 May 1857
12	Pudding Lane (now Cheapside); probably *ex-situ*	SD 47726175	Tombstone of Lucius Julius Apollinaris, found in 1772.	Baines 1836, 4, 486; Watkin 1883, 184; *RIB* 606; Edwards 1971, 23–26
13	Rubbish tip at the western end of New Quay Road; *ex-situ*	SD 46136198	Stone fragment inscribed ...]ELICI[....]O PATRI...	Shotter 1976, 22; Hassall and Tomlin 1978, 473; Hassall and Tomlin 1986, 436; Shotter and White 1995, 93–4; *RIB* 3186
14	A cellar on Castle Hill	SD 47446187	A monumental stone, found in 1830, reported as recording the death of a son or daughter of Julian Probus.	Baines, 1836, 4, 489; Simpson 1852, 120; Watkin 1876, 115; Watkin 1883, 184–5
15	Town Hall, Market Square	SD 47616173	A large slab with 'lines of letters on it' found in 1874 and presumed to have been a tombstone.	Watkin 1883, 184
16	Cheapside	SD 47736179	Bones and other finds, 1812.	*Lancaster Gazette*, 12 September 1812; Simpson 1852, 119; Watkin 1883, 185
17	South side of Church Street, possibly the former Cooperative Stores site	SD 47626182	Pottery 'recently found' including 'a cinerary urn'.	Watkin 1883, 188

Table 2.1 *Continued*

Site No.	Location	NGR	Summary	References
18	Upper part of Church Street, probably 78–80 Church Street	SD 47536188	Various remains found in 1776 including 'a large human skull'.	Baines 1836, 4, 486–7; Watkin 1883, 171–2; Edwards 1971, 26–7
19	St Nicholas Street	SD 47786173	Two skeletons and Roman pottery found 1854.	*Lancaster Guardian*, 15 April 1854
20	Lancaster, possibly Church Street	SD 47566189 ?	Tile tomb found 1752.	Lukis 1883, 240–1; White 1997, 9
21	Westfield War Memorial Village	SD 47006169	Six skeletons, an iron ring and pottery found 1934–5.	*Lancaster Guardian*, 12 October 1934; Spence 1935; Chandler 1982, 11–14
22	Burrow Heights, Scotforth	SD 47145852	Possible Roman mausoleum nearby, from finds made in 1794.	Baines 1836, 4, 487; Watkin 1883, 180–1; Edwards 1971, 27–32
23	Mitchell's Brewery site, Church Street	SD 47656180	Two cremation burials and an inhumation.	Howard-Davis *et al.* in prep
24	Mitre Yard, St Marygate	SD 47486203	Portion of bone veneer, possibly bier decoration.	Webster J. 1988, 149–50, no.26
25	92–94 Penny Street	SD 47706142	Roman cremation urn lower portion of a black burnished ware vessel.	Ellis 1986–7, 32; White 1997, 9
26	77–79 Penny Street, 81 Penny Street, 99–101 Penny Street	SD 47746148	Complete profile of a third-century black burnished ware vessel, some cremated bone and sherds from similar vessels.	Salisbury and Coupe 1995; LUAU 1996; White 1997, 9; OA North 2003a; 2003b
27	Streamline Garage Site, King Street	SD 47676138	Roman cremations, inhumations and pottery.	LUAU 2001a
28	Arla Foods Depot, Aldcliffe Road	SD 47706127	Memorial stone to Insus, single fragment of burnt bone.	UMAU 2007
29	Electricity substation site, Spring Garden Street	SD 47676149	A number of fragments of Roman pottery and flecks of possible burnt bone.	OA North 2008

made when on the potter's wheel, and a small raised ring just under the neck. Between the third and fourth rings was a cross or check pattern marking. …

All the other cinerary urns from Lancaster Moor and the Bowerham Barracks (**Sites 1 and 2**) are easy to assign to the Bronze Age, however, and Harrison's Roman interpretation is by no means infallible. It may be worth noting at this point that, whilst prehistoric cremations appear to be placed in technically crude but often well-decorated vessels, the Roman equivalents are commonly placed in almost-undecorated domestic pottery utensils, with black burnished ware of Romano-British manufacture apparently being preferred over more decorative imported wares. The shape and fabric described are not that of a typical prehistoric urn, but equally the red surface would be odd for a Roman reduced ware; perhaps the explanation is that it was a colour-coated ware or one exposed to such heat that its

surface has become oxidised (see discussion of the Streamline Garage Site finds, chapter 3 below).

The prehistoric urn found in 1893 in Alfred Street (**Site 4**) has not been traced. It is listed by Shotter and White (1990, 5) and is mentioned by the rather uncritical Fox (Fox n.d., 40), who notes that it was found during the excavation of a sewer and was badly damaged during recovery. It was said to have been associated with an incense cup. Unfortunately, the former give no reference and that provided by the latter is incorrect, as it is to Watkin's 1883 work that could not, of course, mention the discovery.

The date of the Queen Square urn (**Site 7**) is more open to debate and yet, if it was Roman, it could be of great significance in confirming not only a much larger extent for the cemetery, but also that the line of King Street is likely to be Roman. The vessel has not been traced during this study – it was noted as being in the possession of a Miss Heaton in 1852 (a Lancaster inhabitant who was amongst those who collected Roman material during the nineteenth century). Simpson states that it is Roman and 'about eighteen inches high, of unburnt clay and the bulge is marked with lines'. It is then said that 'In 1840 a similar urn to the above was found in digging the foundation of St Thomas's Church' (Simpson 1852, 121). The original report in the *Lancaster Gazette* of 21 November 1840 notes that 'labourers employed in excavating at the new church of St Thomas, in this town, turned up an ancient earthenware vase. It was rude manufacture and filled with human bones'. A later article in the same paper would suggest that the main structure of the church was well on the way to completion at this time and the excavations must, therefore, have been for some ancillary or associated works, perhaps the construction of the surrounding garden and walls. Watkin repeats the descriptions of Simpson, but adds that 'the nature of the material would seem to imply a British rather than a Roman origin' (Watkin 1883, 185).

Unfortunately, there are two urns in the Lancaster City Museum that have been credited as being the St Thomas vessel and thus the model for the Queen Square find. Object LM92 (**Site 5**; Plate 2.1) is a virtually complete black burnished ware vessel some 260mm high and 224mm in diameter, which has lost much of its outer surface and appears generally grey and sandy, rather than black and polished. The widest part of this vessel is decorated with a band of diamond cross-hatching. The acquisition record for this item is vague, and notes only the 'Old Lancaster Exhibition' of 1908. The catalogue for this exhibition is available in the City Reference Library (Anon. 1908) and a rapid examination showed no obvious mention of an urn from St Thomas Church, either Roman or prehistoric. 'Vessels of Roman Pottery' are mentioned (Anon. 1908, 58), and appear to have been exhibited by the Reverend J.H. Hastings and Miss A. Johnson amongst others, whilst 'British Cinerary Urns' are credited to the Storey Institute Committee, with no mention made of Miss Heaton (Anon. 1908, 59). J.H. Ostridge of the Ordnance Survey saw this vessel at the Lancaster Museum in the 1950s where it was on display with the note, 'found when digging the foundations of St Thomas's Church (*c.* 1840)' (Ostridge 1954). There is no doubt that Ostridge would have been able to determine the difference between a Roman vessel and the other, prehistoric, candidate, below.

This second vessel, listed as object LM271 (**Site 6**; Plate 2.2), seems to have a better provenance. Its acquisition card notes that it was found 'digging foundations of St Thomas' Church, Lancaster in 1840' and that the donor was the Reverend J.H. Hastings of the Manor House, Halton. The Reverend John Harold Hastings is noted as aiding in the compilation of the volume in the Victoria County History series dealing

Plate 2.1 Romano-British urn (site 5), possibly from the Church of St Thomas (photograph: Peter Iles, by courtesy of Lancaster City Museum)

with the County Palatine of Lancaster, and to have been the Vicar of the church of St Wilfrid, Halton, from 1903 (Farrer and Brownbill 1914, 125). The vessel in question is of a typical orange-buff material, with a darker orange core visible through a deep surface scratch. It measures

Plate 2.2 Prehistoric urn (site 6), possibly from the Church of St Thomas (photograph: Peter Iles, by courtesy of Lancaster City Museum)

about 185mm high and about 170mm at its widest diameter, and has incised and impressed decoration. The collar is inscribed with a zigzag line, dividing the area between two incised lines top and bottom into a series of upper and lower triangles. Each of the triangles is further filled with diagonal lines, those above slanting top left to bottom right, those below sloping bottom left to top right. Below the collar is a line of impressed dots, a band of diamond cross-hatching with areas of vertical 'herringbone' decoration, and a second line of impressed dots. This is presumed to be the object noted by Penney (1975) as the Bronze Age urn found in 1840 at the church of St Thomas.

Dr Andrew White, who was for many years the curator of both objects, takes the black burnished ware urn (Site 5) as that discovered in 1840 (White 1997), but it could be argued that the prehistoric urn (Site 6) would perhaps better fit the original descriptions of 'earthenware' and 'rude manufacture'. Neither of the two known vessels approach the stated height of the Queen Square urn (18 inches = *c.* 450mm) and such a large vessel would seem more likely to be a prehistoric urn than a black burnished ware vessel, though both types can reach this size. Equally (but perhaps less plausibly) we could take Simpson's 'unburnt clay' to mean that the pot showed no evidence of burning on its exterior; that is, that it was not soot-blackened rather than being a badly-fired prehistoric pot. Certainly, the simple description of 'the bulge marked with lines' is more reminiscent of the simple cross-hatched band of the Roman item than the complex patterning of the prehistoric vessel. The loss of the exterior burnishing from the Roman vessel, too, could lead to its description as 'rude' though one still has difficulty with the word 'earthenware'. It is also tempting to follow the 'Roman' line when noting that the modern discovery nearest to Queen Square, in Spring Garden Street, was also of Roman pottery and possible cremated bone (OA North 2008, 10–11; see below on p.20). In discussion, Dr White has also made the point that there were known problems with the attributions of the Bronze Age material in the City Museum (Andrew White, *pers. comm.* 2009) and that on balance he prefers the Roman vessel as the one that was found in 1840. Unless further evidence comes to light it is felt that it would be wise to reserve judgment on the urns from the church of St Thomas, and to state that the Queen Square urn may have been either Roman or prehistoric, with the odds perhaps tending to favour the earlier date.

The same lack of certainty applies to **Site 10**, the discoveries of 1876. Watkin (1883, 185) notes the recovery in this year of 'some more urns' not far from the Queen Square or Penny Street finds, 'in making some excavations for the War Department'. The urns are not described, nor is the site located specifically, but the site of the militia barracks just 300m away at White

Cross, just south of Penny Street Bridge, must be a reasonable possibility, as these were constructed in 1854 and occupied by the military until 1881. It is certainly possible, however, that this site is a duplication of the 1877 discoveries at Bowerham Barracks noted by Harker, Harrison and Walker (Site 2 above); in this case, they would be firmly dated to the prehistoric period. This site is, however, some 1,200m, or about two-thirds of a mile, from Queen Square as the crow flies; whilst still 'not far' from the first find spot, it is four times the distance to the White Cross barracks.

Sites 8 and 9 come with their own problems: a Bronze Age urn (Site 8) is noted in Stephen Penney's short gazetteer (Penney 1975) and by Taylor (1903, 41). It has not been mentioned elsewhere; neither has the vessel itself been traced. Penney simply notes that it was found near Penny Street Bridge in *c.* 1900, whilst Taylor is more explicit, saying that it was reported by Alice Johnson (*c.* 1850–1943) as having been 'dug up under a cottage near Penny Street Bridge' in about 1900.

It is certainly possible that Site 8 is the same vessel that we record as Site 9. This second urn is described as 'late Celtic' in Alice Johnson's unpublished notebook (Penney 1975; he interpreted this as possibly Bronze Age). In the same short report he also notes the existence of Site 8 and we must presume he believed them to be separate. He states that the discovery was made 'during the construction of the Corporation Arms in Penny Street … in the early part of the last century'. This seems remarkably similar to the discovery of Site 8, as we know that the demolition of several buildings at the southern end of Penny Street and close to the Penny Street Canal Bridge, to allow the construction of a new building to house The Corporation Arms and The White Cross, occurred around 1900. This building is still extant, standing immediately north of the canal bridge, between Penny Street and Henry Street; having been known for some time as 'The Farmer's Arms', it has recently been refurbished to form 'The Penny Street Bridge'. Map evidence indicates a pre-1900 Corporation Arms on the same site, and suggests that the buildings there probably pre-date 1778 and may even have been extant in 1610, so works to form the inn may have occurred much earlier. It is thus possible (if less probable) that, if Penney is quoting from Johnson, that '… last century' was meant to suggest *c.* 1800 or even *c.* 1700 for the discovery. Without more detail, however, we are forced to take these two sites as separate prehistoric finds, despite the reasonable possibility of duplication and their location immediately adjacent to the known line of the Roman road, very close to the 2001 and 2005 Roman finds (see below in chapters 3 and 4).

The last of the historical urned burials, **Site 11**, was encountered in 1857 whilst excavating to form a coal depot on the eastern side of Penny Street almost opposite Henry Street. The exact site has not been determined, but it seems likely to have been at the northern end of the Alexandra Buildings, just south of the former Gardners Tiles site (below). The vessel, encountered at a reported nine feet (2.7m), was a two-handled flask, some fifteen inches (380mm) high and of a light brown colour. It 'bore no embossment but was of a very elegant shape and half-filled with calcined bones …[and it] is no doubt of Roman workmanship' (*Lancaster Guardian*, 23 May 1857). The depth of nine feet seems rather excessive for a burial, or for an excavation for a coal yard and it seems possible that this has been misreported. Another alternative is that the ground level has been raised up somehow, perhaps by spoil dumping from the adjacent Lancaster canal. It should be noted, of course, that there is considerable variation in the depth of cover over Roman deposits in the town, and on the nearby Arla Foods Depot site the upper Roman layers were at least 1m below the modern surface, with the base of the deposits more that three times that deep (see chapter 4, below).

It is noteworthy that no traces of the Roman road or of burials were reported during the construction of the Lancaster Canal in the late 1790s, or for that matter during the building of the nineteenth-century Springfield Hall or the later Royal Lancaster Infirmary that lie on the road line just south of the canal. However, in the 1990s, a number of Roman coins were shown to Lancaster Museum, which it is thought had been recovered during the construction of the hospital in the early 1890s (Shotter 2000b, 141f). It seems likely that some of these coins may have been part of a hoard.

Tombstones

The stone in memory of the Treveran, Lucius Julius Apollinaris, a cavalryman in the *Ala Augusta* (*RIB* 606; **Site 12**), is clearly of Roman origin. Its discovery in 1772 on what is now Cheapside is noted by West (1778, 24; Plate 2.3), Baines (1836, 4, 486) and Watkin (1883, 183–4); the stone itself is well described by Edwards (1971, 23–5) and implications of the text (it bears no sculpture to compare with other tombstones) are discussed by Edwards and in chapters 4 and 5. It was found, broken, and lying face-downwards on a bed of sand about a yard and a half (1.35m) below the surface on the west side of the street and approximately one third of the way down the slope (that is about halfway between Market Street and Church Street) in digging a cellar. Shotter and White (1990, 33) suggest that it was not *in situ*, no associated burial having been reported at the time (but see the discussion of the latest memorial stone find in chapter 4 below) and one must suspect that the stone had been brought here for reuse, from a cemetery no longer current. There is ample precedent for reuse of gravestones in Roman times (for

Plate 2.3 The tombstone of Lucius Julius Apollinaris (*RIB* 606), from an annotated sketch in the papers of Father Thomas West (photograph: Peter Iles, by courtesy of the Lancashire Record Office, RCHY 3/10/1)

example *RIB* 1641, 1642, 1667) as well as more recently (Edwards 1971, 18–23 and Plate Ib). Further rescue recording at 1 Penny Street in 1975 (White 1975a) and at Cheapside in 1984 (Watson 1987) failed to produce any other evidence for a cemetery in this area. If it were *in situ* it would indicate a formal burial that was in the south-west quadrant of the junction between the road from the fort's east gate (which formed the main road of the extramural settlement) and the main north-south road. Such a site appears to be unusually close to the known area of the settlement and thus at risk of accidental defilement, and in a location that would perhaps be put to a more practical use. It is possible, however, that this is a burial site that has been subsumed into the expanding town such as those discussed later (below on pp.14ff).

A second inscribed fragment bearing the ends of two lines of text was found *ex-situ* on a late nineteenth-century waste-tip at New Quay in 1976 (**Site 13**, Shotter 1976, 62) and initially identified as part of a tombstone. It was subsequently reinterpreted as a fragment of a dedication slab (Hassall and Tomlin 1986, 436; Shotter and White 1995, 93–4), but the original theory still has supporters; Tomlin has recently suggested that it may be read as a tombstone dedicated '*to Felix, a son most dutiful to his father*' (*RIB* III.3186, forthcoming). It is interesting to note that a series of Roman coins has also been recovered from this site (Penney 1982, 55-6) and it would be fascinating to try and link these objects with contemporary reports of development, to see if its original site may be discovered. **Site 14** is a third memorial, recovered 'in 1830, whilst digging a cellar on Castle Hill' (Baines 1836, 4, 487). This was reported as recording the death of a son or daughter of one 'Julian Probus' (*sic* Baines 1836, 4, 489; Simpson 1852, 120). The full text of this 'imperfect inscription' does not seem to have been reported at the time, but Watkin (1876, 115; 1883, 184–5) describes it more fully and shows that it was in fact a stone from Birdoswald fort (*RIB* 1919), and not originally from Lancaster.

A final potential tombstone (**Site 15**), noted by Watkin as found in 1874 (1876, 184), was said to have been 'a large slab about four inches thick, with "lines of letters on it"…'. This second-hand report notes the find spot as having been the old Town Hall in the Market Square. The brief description given means that we cannot be certain of its identification as a tombstone, nor that it was found *in situ*. It is equally possible that this was a completely different type of inscribed stone and, even if it was a tombstone, given its location well away from a known road line, it may well have been another discarded and reused fragment. Conversely, it could be considered with other sites (Site 12 above; Site 22 below) to be further evidence of an earlier cemetery. Discussions with David Shotter (*pers. comm.* 2009) suggest that it is possible that a portion of this stone is that fragment recorded above as site 13.

Possible Deposits in the Extramural Settlement

A number of sites through the town are also noted for the discoveries of bones or other burial materials and, whilst they may have some merit as the sites of individual burials, may also represent domestic and other remains from the extramural settlement. Simpson (1852, 119) notes such a site in Pudding Lane (later renamed Cheapside), which was first reported in the *Lancaster Gazette* of 12 September 1812 (**Site 16**). The first report is short and notes '… two small Roman mill stones, many pieces of antique earthenware, and a small quantity of human bones'. These finds are also reported by Simpson, but an unfortunate error converts the mill stones to milestones, although the error is corrected by Watkin (1883, 185) – two new milestones would have been a remarkable discovery here in the close vicinity of the fort, and they are not mentioned elsewhere. Millstones or querns are, in contrast, commonly reported from the extramural settlement at Lancaster (see, for example, Penney 1981a, Plate XV) and are taken to be a good indicator of domestic activity in the close vicinity. Watkin, however, also takes the opportunity to reinterpret the pottery as 'probably … cinerary urns'. No evidence for this is given, and the original phrase 'antique earthenware' would not appear to support the black burnished ware vessels commonly used for this purpose; the conclusion must therefore be based on the discovery of the bones. It is unfortunate that we are given no further details of the bones, as we would expect to find animal bones in the sort of midden deposit the other finds seem to indicate, and thus have to accept their identification as human. It is possible, of course, that this is indeed a domestic deposit and that the bones are those of an infant buried close to a dwelling (see chapter 5 below). Such a theory might perhaps be supported by the emphasis on the small quantity of bones, although we would really expect that the size of the bones – and they would have been very small – would also have been noted, and on balance it seems more likely that this is an adult burial or cremation deposit.

It is also possible that this interpretation of a 'cinerary urn' as a domestic vessel may also apply to the items 'recently found' on the south side of Church Street (**Site 17**, Watkin 1883, 188). This vessel was also associated with domestic material, 'ordinary red ware, a quern stone, a large amphora', as well as some material that may well represent the remains of stamped mortaria (for example, Webster P.V. 1988, item 10 on 104–5). Again, however, the evidence is simply not available to dispute the original report, which must therefore be taken at face value.

Earlier probable discoveries from the extramural settlement, which are described by Baines (1836, 4, 486–7) and Watkin (1883, 171–2), occurred in 1775 whilst sinking cellars for the house of Daniel Wilson at the top of Church Street (**Site 18**). Edwards (1971, 26–7) notes that this house is the fine bow-fronted building on the north side of Church Street, immediately east of its junction with China Street, now divided and numbered 78 and 80. The material described in these reports, which derived from Father West's observations (Father Thomas West, Lancashire Record Office RCHY3/7/54; Watkin 1883, 171–2), was assumed to indicate 'a supposed Roman burying place' and to have extended both northwards behind the house and southwards to the other side of the street. Ashes, burnt wood, bones, coins, pottery, building materials, and so on are described as having been found in a deposit 'from a foot to about five feet thick', but these could comfortably be a part of the remains of the civilian settlement outside the fort. Watkin also reaches this domestic conclusion, which is supported by more modern excavation and recording, including that undertaken in the garden to this property (Ellis 1987), and elsewhere along Church Street (see, for example, Penney 1981b; Shotter and White 1990, 33–40).

West, however, also mentions a single 'large human skull' as part of this deposit (Watkin 1883, 171), which needs to be considered. No doubt we can accept the identification of this object, but why was it there and where was the rest of the body? That it was (presumably) intact would suggest interment, not cremation, but it is noted as being part of a deposit including '… burnt bones, [and] ashes …'. Could it represent the unrecovered remains of a victim of a fire? No doubt, if this was the case there would have been other recognisably human bones recovered, but of course they may have been lumped in with the other 'bones' mentioned. Unburied bodies following a disaster are not unknown; examples are recorded at Wroxeter (Wacher 1974, 374), Caerwent (Nash-Williams 1930, 230), and Hockwold (Salway 1981, 696). There could, of course, be a more sinister reason. At the settlement next to Housesteads fort, the excavation of a building in 1934 found the skeletons of a male and a female, the former with a sword-point still embedded in it, deliberately concealed between two floor levels (Crow 1995, 69f). It is usually assumed that these bodies represented criminal activity. The quantity of material from this site, and its relationship to the supposed locations of the various forts (Fig. 1.2) may indicate that we are seeing the infilling of a ruined building on the very edges of the extramural settlement or, indeed, that this is dumping over the defences of the earlier forts. Both would suggest a date following the construction of the Saxon Shore type fort in the fourth century (above, p.4).

Two human skeletons were found in 1854 during sewer excavations along St Nicholas Street (**Site 19**), in an area now subsumed into the St Nicholas Arcade shopping centre (*Lancaster Guardian*, 15 April 1854). The remains were described as being six feet below the soil and laid 'near to each other, but in different directions across the road'. Whilst Roman pottery was recovered at the same time, it was not certainly associated with the burials, as the columnist uses the phrase 'near to the place' rather than describing the finds as together or adjacent. It is, of course, possible that these are late Roman inhumations and that they could be associated with a burial area on the route eastwards towards Lancaster Moor, but this is by no means the only option. It is probable, given the reported different orientations of the skeletons, that these were not burials in a well-regulated cemetery; indeed, there is no way of knowing the time-gap between the two burials – it is assumed that two reasonably contemporary inhumations would be laid roughly parallel. This does not help to date them beyond suggesting a later, rather than earlier, origin and there are examples of Romano-British inhumation cemeteries where burials were intercut, overlapping and at many angles, such as Cirencester (McWhirr *et al.* 1982, see, for example, Figs 30–3). Given the probable

Anglo-Scandinavian occupation of this part of the city and the existence of St Nicholas Street from at least 1360 (White 1993a, 29), there is no reason for burials in this area not to have been of post-Roman date. Indeed, it is even possible that the nearby medieval friary (founded 1260, see White 1993a, 38–40) has attracted pious but impecunious or otherwise ineligible burials to this edge of its precinct rather than to its church or cemetery proper between Sulyard Street and Moor Lane. In this case, however, we may have expected the burials to be roughly orientated with the precinct boundary and thus to each other – the hurried nature of such impromptu burials may, of course, have made this more difficult.

Finally, a note must be made of the possibility of some burials within the area of the former Mitchell's Brewery (**Site 23**), on the south side of Church Street, which was excavated between the later 1980s and 2000 by the Lancaster University Archaeological Unit. The excavations on this major site have yet to be published (Howard-Davis *et al.* in prep), and draft specialist reports have kindly been made available for this work. The first is a short report on two fragments of skull, part of a tibia and a coccyx recovered in 1992 from the fill of a large Roman pit in the area of Roman buildings behind Church Street, interpreted as an adult male, perhaps 30 years old (Potts in prep). The other report (McKinley in prep) relates to two urned cremation burials recovered in 1999, one from the area between Anchor and Chancery Lanes, the other from the main site behind the area of Roman buildings, and describes the remains of two older adult females. Discussions around these two discoveries indicate that the first is assigned to the third or fourth century from an assessment of the pottery and that the other is given a similar date on stratigraphic grounds. Neither of these two burials is reported to have been sealed by later deposits in the settlement.

Taken with evidence from Sites 12 and 15 (above), White's suggestion of an earlier cemetery area that was subsumed into an expanding settlement in the early second century (White 1975a, 30) is not completely ruled out, and such remains have been identified elsewhere (McCarthy 2002, 78). An area of late burial following 'retreat' into the fourth-century fort seems more probable (Charlesworth 1978, 116; LUAU 2001a, 6; Shotter 2001a, 27; Howard-Davis *et al.* in prep; Zant *et al.* in prep). The chief problem with the former theory is that ceramic and numismatic evidence gathered over the years suggests that the settlement along Church Street commenced from an early date (Shotter and White 1990, 75ff) and that some, if not all, of these burials would appear to have been within the early settlement bounds.

As noted, a phase of later burial seems more probable, but is not without its problems. The extent of later Roman settlement is difficult to determine as in many areas the latest Roman deposits have been destroyed by post-medieval developments, particularly cellaring (see, for example, White 1974, 16–20; Bellis and Penney 1980; Penney 1981a, 33; Shotter 2001a, 20). As a consequence, the presence of a phase of abandonment and then of burial, as noted at Botchergate in Carlisle (McCarthy 2002, 85–6), has yet to be confirmed and without the early Lancaster material being re-discovered, we can offer only possibilities.

The Tile Tomb

A more spectacular find, that of a tile tomb, was reported by Samuel Peele in 1753 and communicated to the antiquarian William Stukeley (**Site 20**, Lukis 1883, 240–1). There is no contemporary drawing but a tile tomb found at York was illustrated in 1736 (*Eboracum*, Plate X; Plate 2.4) and the tiles from a similar tomb at Dringhouses are held in the collection at the York Museum (Plate 2.5). The tile tomb from Lancaster is described by Peele as made of roof tiles fastened together with a great mass of mortar, with huge stones outside this; it contained a human skull and some other bones. The tiles bore the incuse stamp ALSB, standing for the *Ala Sebosiana* (*RIB* 2465.2), an auxiliary cavalry unit forming Lancaster's garrison from the second half of the second century until at least the middle of the third century (see

above, chapter 1). The particular form of the inscription appears to have been identical with that found on tile fragments recovered in 1973 outside the north-east perimeter of the fort (Shotter 1988a, 186–8). Such tombs are both impressive and rare and it would seem likely that the person so entombed would have been of some importance.

It may be significant that Samuel Peele also sent coins of Valens and Honorius to William Stukeley at the same time and, if they were recovered from the same site, this could suggest a burial of the late third or fourth century. Shotter (1988a, 212f) certainly argues for the presence of the *Ala Sebosiana* at least as late as the 260s, although the fact that we have no mention of them at Lancaster after this date is a difficulty (Shotter and White 1990, 22f; Birley 1936, 5). The use of tiles bearing the stamp of the *Ala Sebosiana* do not make it certain, of course, that the person for whom they provided a coffin was necessarily a member of that unit (see discussion, chapter 5). It is unfortunate that the site where the discovery was made is not specifically named, but is only described:

> 'The discovery happened in a garden in this town, on digging up the ground for new foundations … The very great rains which have fallen this winter had such an effect upon the earth that the whole sepulchre tumbled out, fast and firmly cemented, as if the same had been one intire piece' (Lukis 1883, 240–1).

Plate 2.4 Drawing of the tile tomb from York, 1736 (photograph by courtesy of York Museums Trust – Yorkshire Museum)

Plate 2.5 Roman Tile Tomb from Dringhouses, York (photograph by courtesy of York Museums Trust – Yorkshire Museum)

Andrew White notes that, in the 1750s, Lancaster was not expanding outwards except in two directions, to the north onto the Green Ayre, and north-westwards on the banks of the Lune at St George's Quay. He suggests that either of these is possible as a location, but the building could have simply been the infill of former garden ground within the built-up area, and could just as easily relate to upper Penny Street (Andrew White, *pers. comm.* 2009). As well as these possibilities, the description of the tomb tumbling out of the ground could perhaps be taken to suggest a significant slope to the land – this is, of course, by no means certain – and as such perhaps the east side of the fort alongside St Marygate or the north side of Church Street, on the steep slope down to the river, may be the strongest possibilities.

The Bone Veneer

One further piece of evidence from the excavations of 1973 outside the north-eastern perimeter of the auxiliary fort deserves mention here (**Site 24**). A fragment of decorated bone veneer was recovered, probably from Mitre Yard T6 or T7 (Jones 1988, 59–60; Webster J. 1988, 149f and no. 26), of a type that has been recorded at other sites, including Lydney, Silchester and, most recently and in large quantities, at Brougham (Greep 2004, 274). It is clear that such bone veneers had a number of uses, which are now known to have included the decoration of furniture and of funeral-biers. The discovery of such material at Brougham in the excavations carried out in 1966–7 by the late Dorothy Charlesworth and their subsequent publication (Cool 2004) have served to highlight the use of bone and antler veneer in the funerary context, a fact which was not appreciated at the time of the preparation of the report on the excavations of 1973 in Lancaster.

The fragment from Lancaster represents one of the most complex forms of this type of bone-carving,

designated in the Brougham report as Type E2.1 (Greep 2004, 280). Such carvings

'consist of rectangles with deeply incised parallel grooves, the upstanding ridges between being cut in a crenellated pattern. Narrow crenellated strips (*c.* 2mm wide) were made separately and inserted into the channels resulting in an offset chequerboard pattern' (Greep 2004, 282).

Greep also makes the point that such complex carving 'would have demanded skill and time to manufacture'; this in its turn would mean that it would have been expensive.

The piece from Lancaster is approximately 62mm by 45mm, and has 29 crenellations in one direction and ten in the other, with nine inserted strips, giving a 29 by 19 chequerboard (551 elements); this provides some idea of the complexity of such carvings. At Brougham itself, more than 1,000 fragments of 30 different types of bone veneer were recorded. The type represented at Lancaster was that most frequently found, occurring in nearly ten percent of the deposits in which bone veneer was extant; fragments of this particular type of veneer were described as 'very common'. Whilst the possibility that this was a fragment of decoration from a funeral bier must be entertained, it must be emphasised again that the use of this material was not exclusively funerary.

The Westfield War Memorial Village Burials

The interpretation of the six skeletons from the west of the fort (**Site 21**) has long been known to be difficult. The original discovery of a skull, arm and leg bones in 1934 (*Lancaster Guardian*, 12 October 1934) and the subsequent excavations by J. E. Spence in 1935 have not been published, although a copy of Spence's excavation journal and plans (Spence 1935) and three osteological and interpretative reports (Tildesley 1934a, 1934b; Cave

1935?) are held in the City Museum, along with at least some of the material recovered. The original dating of the first discovery as Iron Age from a provisional dating of an iron ring is recognised as unsound, and a Roman date is thought to be more likely (Chandler 1982; Shotter and White 1990, 90).

The site lies low down on the side of Castle Hill, where it has started to flatten out into the Marsh area of Lancaster. There, west and a little south of the fort, a memorial village was constructed in the 1920s to house veterans of the First World War. To the east of the village was a small gravel pit that was presumably used for road and other repairs. Spence (1935) notes that a single contracted male skeleton was discovered under stones 'on the east side of the [gravel] quarry' in 1934. He gives little further detail, but fortunately the osteological report by M. E. Tildesley, Human Osteological Curator of the Royal College of Surgeons, is more forthcoming and includes details of the findspot. The skeleton was associated with an iron ring and is described as having been about four feet (1.2m) down in gravel at the top of a mound of about 25 feet (7.5m) in height. This is supposed to have been 'a round barrow, of unusual height' wherein '... round stones were built up in an arch four to five feet wide across the body'. He further notes that 'The flexed posture eliminates the Roman invaders themselves' (Tildesley 1934a, 2). The iron ring was submitted to the British Museum for identification and was suggested to be of La Tène origin, the whole giving a probable date of the second century BC (Tildesley 1934a, 3). This dating must be taken, however, with much more than a pinch of salt (Andrew White *pers. comm.* 2009), and it would be wise to see this item as indicating only a post-Bronze Age date. Equally, the contention that flexed burials must be pre-Roman has long been discarded. At Cirencester (Viner and Leech 1982, 76–85) the Roman cemeteries do show a preference for supine or prone burials, but there are many that are otherwise arranged and a hard and fast rule can no longer be supported; indeed, subsequent burials found at the same site (below) seem almost certain to be of Roman date.

It is also notable that sixteen large pits in the Roman cemetery at Low Borrowbridge in Cumbria were interpreted as inhumation graves for both crouched and extended burials (Hair and Howard-Davis 1996, 103), despite the fact that ground conditions precluded the survival of unburnt bone on the site. Further, it is noted that two pits had stone packing possibly intended to lie around or above the corpse, and this is compared with the same phenomenon at both Cirencester (Viner and Leech 1982, 92) and Winchester (Clarke 1979, 143); limited evidence from one of these features suggested a date around the end of the second to the mid-third century. Two further pits were also lined with large stones, and one was associated with a fine sandstone tombstone of mid-third century date to Aelia Sentica, the wife of Aurelius Verulus (Hair and Howard-Davis 1996, 103–4). The similarities between these burials and the discoveries in Lancaster in 1934 have been pointed out by Rachel Newman (*pers. comm.* 2009).

Following the discovery of another skull on the Westfield site on 30 July 1935, two phases of excavation were undertaken by Spence, at the request of the then museum curator, G. M. Bland, and with the permission of the Committee and Secretary of the War Memorial Village. The first phase comprised two days of excavation (30 July – 1 August) and recovered the skull and an associated set of remains, which were of a child, and went on to discover another burial, that of an adult female. Both of these burials lay in clay and cobble cists on the southern edge of the gravel quarry. The overburden there contained animal bone and quantities of charcoal, suggesting that a fire had been burnt over the closed cists. The adult had a bronze finger ring and what were taken to be the rusted remains of an iron brooch. The second phase of excavation on 27 September 1935 was to the west of the July/August dig and recovered three further contracted adult male skeletons lying on their left side in a pit covered by large stones. A small samian fragment 'possibly dating to about 100 AD' and a larger 'part of a piece of red ware, coarse in texture, part of the foot of a bowl' (Spence 1935) were recovered from the pit. Spence notes that it is possible that the Samian fragment may have fallen into the pit from above, but considers this unlikely, and notes that the larger sherd could not have entered after the grave was closed.

Tildesley's second report (Tildesley 1934b) is also on human bones from Lancaster. It is, however, undated and has been assigned to 1934 simply because it was attached to the first, dated, report. It describes the sparse skeletal remains of one male and one female adult (the former being the older), with some specimens exhibiting interesting pathology being retained by the College of Surgeons. He concludes that the remains might be of 'a few hundred to a couple of thousand' years of age. The site is not named or described, but it is noted that the burials were placed with the heads to the west, some two feet six inches (0.75m) from the surface, in 'shale probably deposited by the river when its course was not the same as now'. Tellingly, it also states that the person who dug up the skeletons reported no trace of a grave and that he was not a trained archaeologist, and thus it cannot relate to the material from the 1935 excavations and, if it relates to the 1934 discoveries, concerns material that is not otherwise documented by Spence. It seems most probable that it concerns material from an entirely different site. Further examination of the reports, the material in the museum store, and the material at the College of Surgeons is proposed, to try and clarify this matter.

A further osteological report is, however, found attached to Spence's notes. It covers the 1935 discoveries and is by Dr A.J.E. Cave, the Assistant Conservator of the Royal College of Surgeons' Museum. Dr Cave describes the remains and notes that 'The type of burial, and associated finds, date these remains to the Roman period: the available somatological evidence from the remains themselves (so far as it goes) is in agreement with this dating' (Cave 1935).

In the absence of any further investigations on the material in the Museum, it seems appropriate to accept Dr Cave's conclusion as valid. A date of c. AD 100 from the Samian fragment, which Spence notes as only about half a square inch, seems, if it is to be relied upon, rather early for 'Roman' inhumations. Whilst it is tempting to suggest that these may have been some of Lancaster's missing 'natives', the burial of 'Romans' in barrows – indeed in barrow cemeteries – is not unknown, for instance at Colchester (Pooley *et al.* 2006, 67f.). It is worth noting, however, that the Colchester barrow burials were all of cremations, within distinct ring ditches, and have been interpreted as the remains of Romanised Germanic people, either part of or closely associated with the late Roman garrison, continuing their older traditions within their new homeland. In contrast, the Roman barrow cemetery at Petty Knowes, High Rochester, Northumberland, contained both cremations and inhumations (Charlton and Mitcheson 1981) of early second- to early fourth-century date and must, therefore, be taken to represent a normal tradition in at least that part of Roman Britain. Further scientific examination of the Westfield finds, as well as further comparison between this Lancaster site, other Roman barrow burials and earlier traditions of burial in the area (for example, Olivier 1987), is needed.

Burrow Heights

The last of the historical discoveries is the possible mausoleum site at Burrow Heights, Scotforth, some 3.5km south of the fort (**Site 22**). A group of sculpted stones, comprising four large heads, a smaller headless statue and two crouching stone animals, was discovered in 1794 during the excavations for Lancaster Canal south of the city (see photographs – Shotter and White 1990, Plate 3 and Edwards 1971, Plates 3–5; drawings – Watkin 1883, 180–1). The exact point of their discovery is uncertain, but a site on the west side of Burrow Heights is probable (Edwards 1971, 28–30). The items, now exhibited in Lancaster City Museum, are all carved from the same pale sandstone and are all about two feet (0.6m) high. As Edwards (1971, 31) notes, the four heads and the small figure are all intended to be seen from the front only, while the two animals are in the round. He then draws a parallel with items from Towcester, in Northamptonshire, and Colchester, and continues:

'It seems likely, therefore, that the whole group of sculptures represents a fair proportion of the statuary from a mausoleum, and the position of the find, near to the line of the main road leading south from the fort accords well with this suggestion' (Edwards 1971, 32).

A more detailed treatment of the possible mausoleum is given below in Appendix 1, and a location for this tomb on the top of the glacial knoll of Burrow Heights, standing above and to the west of the line of the Roman road (Leather 1972, RR/70D/4; Dames 2000), seems a reasonable supposition. In 1970, G. M. Leather (1972, B65/3) undertook a small excavation on the eastern flank of the hill, focussed on a rectangular cropmark. This revealed a cobbled surface at a depth of 600mm, along with a single sherd of possible Roman pottery. Whilst this may have been part of the Roman road surface, this surface was interpreted at the time as the corner of a structure. A number of Roman coins, mostly of the first and second centuries AD, has also been recovered in this general area (Shotter 2000b, 28), perhaps implying a military connection.

Modern Discoveries

Some of these sites are discussed in more detail in chapters 3 and 4 below, but it is considered appropriate to include them briefly here.

92–94 Penny Street (Formerly 'Squirrels' Wine Bar) – Site 25

The first 'controlled' recovery of a Roman burial in modern times was that of the lower part of a black burnished ware urn with cremated remains during the excavation of a foundation trench behind this site in 1987. The vessel, found by builders at a depth of c. 1.5m on the line of a former boundary wall, was recovered by Marie Ellis of Lancaster Museum (Ellis 1987), and is thought to be of mid-second century date. White (1997) illustrates the profile of the vessel, and compares it with LM92 from the Museum (Site 5 above) and the discovery at 77–79 Penny Street (Site 26 below).

77–79, 81 and 99–101 Penny Street – Site 26

An evaluation, which was carried out on this site in 1995 (Salisbury and Coupe 1995) as part of a development proposal, recovered more than 75% of a black burnished ware vessel with some associated cremated remains. Problems with this work resulted in the Lancaster University Archaeological Unit undertaking a more thorough and extensive excavation on the rear part of the site, including the earlier evaluation trench area (LUAU 1996). This excavation identified what may well have been a small cemetery enclosure with a series of intercutting pits and more than 100 further pottery sherds. This had at least two phases of burial, dated to perhaps the second century and around the fourth century, most cremations being interred without complete vessels. This coincides with the results of later work at the Streamline Garage site, a short distance away (Site 27 below), where burials without urns were the norm.

Due to difficulties, which included the accidental collapse of 81 Penny Street during underpinning operations, a full and final report was never commissioned for this site. The subsequent demolition of no. 81 did, however, allow the opportunity for investigations to the rear of this building prior to the redevelopment of the complete plot, nos 77–81. This work, undertaken in 2003 by Oxford Archaeology North, was disappointing, the area having been badly truncated by the clearance of the collapse and demolition debris, as well as by cellaring in the eighteenth and nineteenth centuries. Nevertheless, two significant features were identified which, although containing only a small amount of cremated bone, were interpreted as a Roman cremation burial and an associated stakehole (OA North 2003a).

A further evaluation, undertaken on the former Gardners Tile Shop and Yard site (99–101 Penny Street) in later 2003 (OA North 2003b), did not reveal any traces of further burials. Whilst one heavily truncated feature of indeterminate date was discovered during the excavation of five trial trenches, the majority of the site appeared to have been terraced into the natural subsoils or disturbed during the insertion of modern foundations and drains.

Streamline Garage Site, King Street (Site 27)

In 2000, in response to a redevelopment proposal and the advice of the Lancashire County Archaeology Service, the Lancaster University Archaeological Unit (LUAU) undertook an archaeological evaluation of the site occupied by the former Streamline Garage on the south-western side of King Street. Positive results from this work (LUAU 2000a), including the identification of Roman cremation burials, led to the full excavation of an area of surviving stratigraphy and monitoring of the development of the other parts of the site. A post-excavation assessment report was produced (LUAU

2001a), but the full publication of the report has been held back for the present volume (chapter 3, below).

Arla Foods Depot, Aldcliffe Road (Site 28)

This site was also the subject of a redevelopment proposal and an archaeological evaluation on the advice of Lancashire County Archaeology Service. This work, undertaken by the University of Manchester Archaeological Unit (UMAU) in May and June 2005, recorded the presence of eighteenth- to nineteenth-century cellars over the northern part of the site, but also found that the southern part had suffered much less disturbance and that the remains of the main Roman road leading into Lancaster survived (UMAU 2003; 2005). As a consequence of this, a formal excavation of the southern part of the site was undertaken late in 2005 and, as at the Streamline garage site, a watching brief held during the other development works. The excavation produced evidence for pre-Roman activity on the site, as well as examining the structure of the road. It also examined a Roman roadside enclosure and, most spectacularly, produced a particularly fine example of a Roman cavalry (Reiter) memorial stone of the rider and barbarian type (UMAU 2007). This site is described in more detail below (chapter 4).

Electricity substation site, Spring Garden Street (Site 29)

The most recent archaeological fieldwork within the putative area of the Lancaster Roman Cemetery was undertaken in 2006. Excavations required during the expansion and refurbishment of an electricity substation were initially monitored by an archaeological watching brief by Oxford Archaeology North. Whilst post-medieval cellaring had disturbed much of the area, some fragments of Roman pottery and small flecks of what might possibly have been cremated bone were found in a sondage into an apparently undisturbed area south of the cellars (OA North 2008). At this point, the decision was taken to change the watching brief to an archaeologist-led excavation of the remaining trenches required on the site. This did not lead to the discovery of any further remains (OA North forthcoming).

CHAPTER 3

Excavations on Penny Street and King Street, Lancaster, 1995–2003

By John Zant, Denise Drury and Vix Hughes

With contributions *by Christine Howard-Davis, Jacqueline McKinley, Stephen Rowland, Andrew Bates and Elizabeth Huckerby*

Introduction

Between 1995 and 2006, archaeological investigations were undertaken in advance of redevelopment at Penny Street, King Street and Spring Garden Street in the centre of the historic city of Lancaster (Fig. 3.1). The excavations at 77–79 Penny Street and Streamline Garage (King Street) were carried out by the former Lancaster University Archaeological Unit (LUAU), which had become Oxford Archaeology North (OA North) by the time 81 Penny Street was investigated in 2003. The most significant result of this work was the discovery of a number of Romano-British burials, although limited evidence for other Romano-British occupation, and for medieval activity, was also recovered in some areas. The burials seemingly formed part of the cemetery south of, and associated with, the civil settlement, and are likely to have been situated alongside a Roman road adjacent to the line of modern Penny Street. The archaeological work discussed in this chapter has all been funded as part of commercial development activity, as referred to above in chapter 2.

It should be noted that, even though several separate excavations are described below, context numbers are simply italicised *321* and do not have the site code appended. The reuse of context numbers for separate excavations should not be taken to imply any identity (or even similarity) of contexts between excavations, unless this is specifically stated.

Results of the Excavations

77–79 Penny Street

Evaluation of the 77–79 Penny Street site in 1995 (Salisbury and Coupe 1995), involving the excavation of two small trenches (Fig. 3.2), demonstrated that the western part had been deeply cellared during the nineteenth century, resulting in the total destruction of earlier archaeological levels. To the east, however, archaeological deposits of Romano-British date had survived. The 1996 excavation comprised a roughly square area of *c.* 60m² situated towards the rear of the property, surrounding the easternmost evaluation trench (Fig. 3.2). Evidence for Romano-British activity was recorded, principally towards the north-east corner of the site, although the remains were generally quite ephemeral and consequently difficult to interpret.

The principal discovery made during the evaluation comprised a disturbed cremation burial interred within a black burnished ware Fabric 1 jar, datable to the period *c.* AD 230–300 (Pottery 1; below on pp.36ff). The urn had been smashed in antiquity, perhaps by subsequent agricultural activity, and the broken sherds had been scattered (Salisbury and Coupe 1995); no trace of a pit or other feature into which the burial might have been placed was noted. With the exception of a fragment of a radius, thought to derive from a mature adult (Salisbury and Coupe 1995, 4), the few small pieces of calcined bone found in association with the urn were too poorly preserved to permit further identification (for further discussion of human bone, see below on pp.40ff).

The remains of the burial were situated towards the base of a thick (up to 1.08m) layer of homogeneous brown silty clay that sealed the natural yellowish-brown or reddish brown stony clay and was itself directly overlain by nineteenth-century levels. The lower 0.1–0.2m of this deposit, which is likely to have been formed by prolonged agricultural or horticultural activity, produced 17 sherds of Roman pottery, in addition to the remains of the burial urn itself. The assemblage included five calcite-gritted sherds of possible late third- to fourth-century date.

During the excavation, the natural subsoil was found at a depth of *c.* 1.3–1.6m below the modern surface (*c.* 18.2–18.5m Ordnance Datum). The earliest anthropogenic deposits comprised spreads of stony, sandy clay, 0.25–0.45m thick. These were similar in character to the underlying subsoil, but were generally more mixed and, in some cases, yielded small quantities of Romano-British pottery and a few small fragments

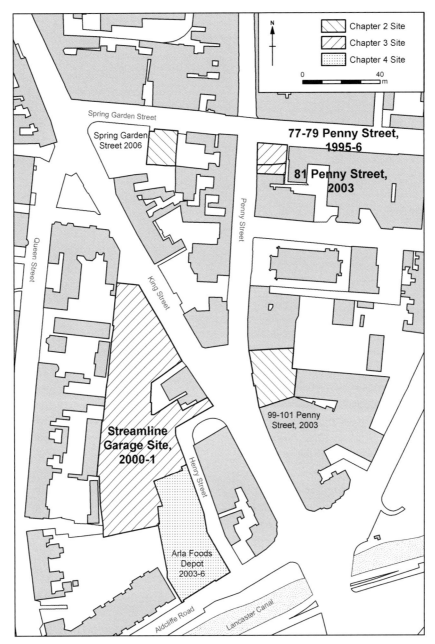

Figure 3.1 Locations of archaeological investigations undertaken by
Lancaster University Archaeological Unit and Oxford Archaeology North

and flecks of burnt bone and charcoal. They were presumably formed as a result of disturbance to, or reworking of, the surface of the natural clay. Two of these deposits, *88* and *90* (not illustrated), produced a small assemblage (22 sherds) of abraded pottery, all oxidised wares that can be only broadly dated to the second to fourth centuries.

Layer *90* was cut by two large, intercutting features, *103* and *115* (Fig. 3.3); the earlier (*115*) had been mostly destroyed, only its western edge having survived, but it may have been sub-rectangular or oval in plan, at least 2.2m north to south, in excess of 1m wide, and up to 0.3m deep. It was filled with a very mixed, orange-brown silty clay (*104*) containing sparse charcoal fragments and flecks, and small, calcined bone fragments. This deposit produced ten sherds of pottery,

including seven calcite-gritted sherds of probable late third- to fourth-century date (below pp.36ff). Traces of a possible discrete cut (*116*) were noted at the base of the feature. This comprised a small, very shallow depression, containing a concentration of poorly-preserved bone fragments (*112*), most of which disintegrated upon excavation and could not be recovered. It was not clear if *116* formed part of *115* or represented the remains of an earlier feature, possibly a small cremation burial, that had been truncated by it. Feature *103*, which had been dug through *115*, was an elongated oval, 2.3m north to south by 1.4m and 0.5m deep. The primary fill of very mixed, dark yellow-brown silty clay (*107*) contained small fragments of charcoal and burnt bone (*c.* 5–10%), together with three sherds of pottery, whilst the upper fill, a dark

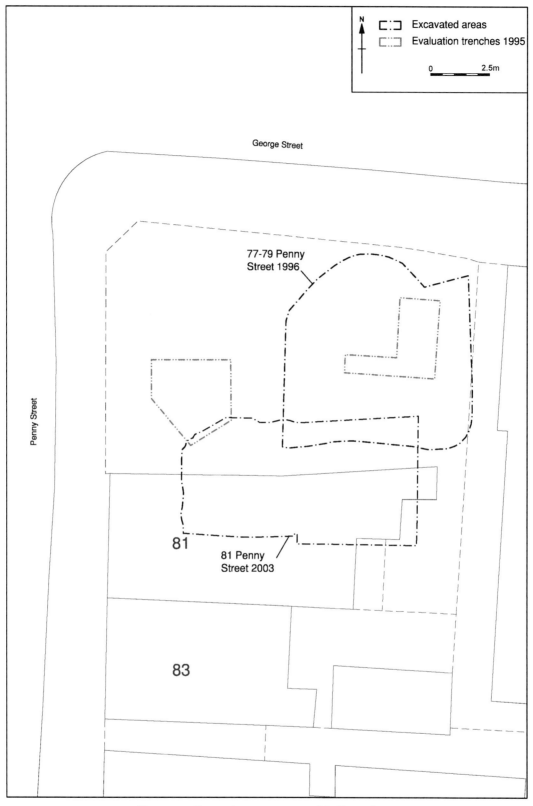

Figure 3.2 Excavations at 77–79 and 81 Penny Street

yellow-brown sandy clay (*102*), yielded 22 sherds and further fragments of calcined bone. The pottery from deposit *107* was all in a calcite-gritted fabric of probable late third- to fourth-century date, and included a rim datable to *c.* AD 300–70. Eleven calcite-gritted sherds also came from fill *102*, together with a small fragment from a third-century Nene Valley colour-coated beaker.

The significance of features *103* and *115* remains unclear; whilst it is conceivable that both were the vestiges of Roman inhumation burials, this could not be proven, since unburnt bone did not survive in the prevailing soil conditions (except for a few fragments in late post-medieval levels) and no trace of grave goods or furniture was found, the potsherds recovered from the fills seemingly representing redeposited material incorporated into the backfilling.

Features *103* and *115*, together with the early spreads of soil elsewhere on the site, were overlain by a further build-up of highly mixed, yellow-brown or orange-brown sandy or silty clays, 0.1–0.3m thick (deposits *72*, *73*, *79*, *80*, *87*, *89*, *100*; not illustrated). Layers *87*, *89* and *100* contained sparse charcoal flecking and a few small fragments and flecks of charcoal and burnt bone. In total, 49 sherds of Romano-British pottery were recovered from these levels; most are undiagnostic oxidised wares of second- to fourth-century date, but five late third- to fourth-century calcite-gritted sherds came from layer *100*, and a single sherd in the same fabric was recovered from deposit *87*.

Deposits *80* and *87* were cut by two small pits, *78* and *98*, possibly the remains of disturbed cremation burials (Fig. 3.3). Feature *78* was oval, 0.5m by 0.39m and 0.2m deep, with sloping sides and a flattish base. It was filled with dark grey/black silty soil (*71*) containing charcoal and some fragments of calcined bone (below on p.40f), together with five sherds of undiagnostic Roman oxidised and grey wares. The eastern half of feature *98* lay outside the excavated area, but it measured 0.44m by at least 0.26m and was 0.22m deep, with steeply sloping sides and a flat base. It was filled with a very mixed yellow-brown sandy clay (*94*), containing some charcoal and a few small fragments of burnt bone. In both burials, the bone was too poorly preserved for the

age and sex of the cremated individuals to be established. Both of these features, together with all other Romano-British remains on the site, were overlain by post-medieval soils up to 0.5m thick, which were in turn overlain by the remains of structures and surfaces of nineteenth-century and later date.

81 Penny Street

The investigated area at 81 Penny Street, excavated in 2003 following demolition of a building that had formerly occupied the site, straddled the line of the former boundary between the property and 77–79 immediately to the north, with the result that the two excavation areas actually overlapped slightly (Fig. 3.3). A sub-rectangular area of *c.* 45m² was excavated to a maximum depth of 0.8m below the modern surface.

In the centre of the northern part of the site, the natural clay was cut by *152*, probably a small oval pit (Fig. 3.3), 1.2m east to west, at least 0.6m north to south (it extended beyond the limit of excavation to the north), and 0.2m deep, with rounded sides and a slightly rounded base. The silty clay fill (*151*) contained a concentration of small cobbles that appeared to have been deliberately packed over a thin deposit of black, charcoal-rich humic material. No fragments of calcined bone were observed as the deposit was excavated, but subsequent analysis of a sample of the material

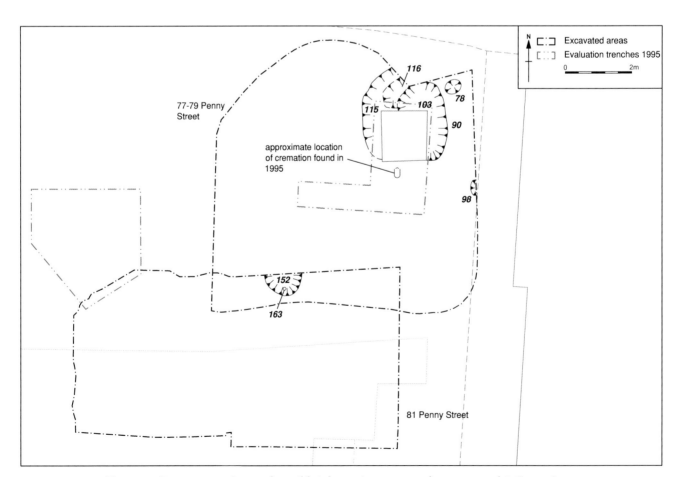

Figure 3.3 Roman cremations and possible inhumations excavated at 77–79 and 81 Penny Street

recovered three small fragments of burnt bone. Two of these were certainly or probably human, whilst the other was a fragment of bird bone. The charcoal was mostly oak, and a few charred weed seeds were also recovered. The feature is not closely dated, since it contained only a single iron hobnail and a sherd of undiagnostic Roman grey ware, but it may have been the truncated remains of an unurned Romano-British cremation burial. At the base of the pit was a stakehole (*163*), 0.1m in diameter and 0.12m deep (Plate 3.1). This did not cut through the fill of feature *152*, and had therefore either been removed before the pit was filled, or was the remains of an earlier feature that had been truncated by *152*.

No further evidence for Romano-British activity was recorded on the site. The putative cremation was directly sealed by modern demolition debris, and there was clear evidence that the entire site had suffered severe truncation in the late post-medieval period.

Streamline Garage, King Street

The Streamline Garage excavation, undertaken in 2001 following an evaluation the previous year, represented by far the largest archaeological investigation conducted in the Penny Street/King Street area. The development site as a whole comprised a roughly triangular plot of *c.* 4336m² (Fig. 3.4), but evaluation demonstrated that the greater part of this area contained nothing of archaeological significance (LUAU 2000a). Important remains were, however, located towards the northern end of the site, and it was there that an open area of *c.* 600m² was subjected to controlled excavation. The natural ground surface within the development area sloped gradually from south to north, from *c.* 23m Ordnance Datum to *c.* 19m Ordnance Datum,

reflecting the general topography of this part of the city. Prior to the commencement of the excavation, the site had been largely occupied by the former Streamline Garage, which was cleared in 2000. The area examined by the watching brief (*c.* 130m²) lay *c.* 25m south of the main area of excavation, adjacent to Henry Street (Fig. 3.4).

The natural subsoil, a yellow-brown silt overlying compacted, pinkish sandy clay, with occasional bands of gravel, was cut by numerous features of certain or probable Romano-British date (Phase 1). These included the remains of a rectilinear ditched enclosure (Phase 1a), and a number of certain and possible burials (Phase 1b), comprising both cremations and putative inhumations. Medieval activity was indicated by a single ditch or gully (Phase 2), possibly a field boundary.

The survival of archaeological remains was somewhat localised, with most of the evidence being confined to the southern part of the excavated area, and largely consisting of truncated negative features cut into the underlying natural geology. It seems likely that this pattern of survival was the result of extensive erosion or truncation of deposits towards the northern end of the site, perhaps caused by post-Roman agricultural activity.

Phase 1a: the Romano-British ditched enclosure (early second century AD?)
The earliest activity on the site was represented principally by *131*, a rectilinear enclosure (Fig. 3.5), defined on the south, east and west by a ditch (*144=165=168=171*) up to 1.65m wide at the lip and 0.4–0.6m deep. The profile of this feature was quite variable, but it was mostly roughly V-shaped, with a flattish base (Plate 3.2). The north side of the enclosure was not located with certainty, although the poorly

Plate 3.1 81 Penny Street: possible cremation *152* after excavation, showing stakehole *163* at base of cut

Figure 3.4 Streamline Garage development site: areas of archaeological investigations

preserved remains of a probable linear feature (*169*), up to 1.1m wide and 0.65m deep, were noted, cutting the north end of the western arm (*168*) of the ditch. It is possible that this may have been a later recutting of the north ditch, and that it had removed all trace of the primary feature. However, *169* was quite different in character from the earlier ditch, being more trench-like in appearance, with vertical or near-vertical sides and a flat base. It was filled with mid-orange-brown sandy clay-silt (*170*).

If feature *169* did indeed represent a recut of the north ditch on the same line, enclosure *131* would have measured 14.1m north-west to south-east and 11.7m north-east to south-west, externally. For most of its excavated length, the perimeter ditch was filled with compacted brown or reddish-brown sandy clay-silt containing varying quantities of small, medium and large cobbles and a few charcoal flecks (*145, 166, 167* and *172*). However, at one point, slightly east of the central axis on the south side of the enclosure, a deposit (*163*) of

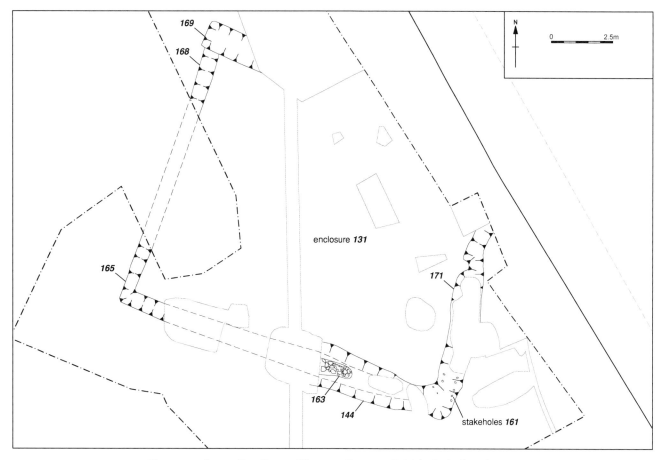

Figure 3.5 Streamline Garage Phase 1a: Romano-British ditched enclosure *131*

Plate 3.2 Streamline Garage Phase 1a: section of ditch *144*, the southern area of the perimeter ditch of enclosure *131*, showing cobble feature *163*

large, water-worn cobbles (Fig. 3.5; Plate 3.2; Plate 3.3), overlain by a compacted layer of redeposited natural subsoil, had been laid within the ditch. This was at least 1.4m wide (its full width could not be determined, as the section of ditch immediately to the west had been destroyed) and filled the lower 0.3m of the ditch cut, which at this point was 0.45m deep. Its precise significance is unclear, but it might have been the remains of a causeway marking the position of an entrance inserted into the perimeter ditch, or a foundation for some other feature of unknown character and function. It was ultimately sealed by a

Plate 3.3 Streamline Garage Phase 1a: south-east corner of enclosure *131*, showing perimeter ditch *144/171*
and cobble feature *163* at the base of *144*

layer of brown clay silt (*143*) that filled the top of the ditch cut; this broadly equated with the soil that filled the rest of the enclosure ditch.

Nothing similar to *163* was found elsewhere within the ditch. However, at the southern end of the eastern arm, at the south-east corner of the enclosure, two rows of stakeholes (*161*) were noted. These were set towards the base of the ditch, parallel with its long axis, and were *c*. 0.55m apart, on either side of the cut, towards its base. The individual stakeholes were circular in plan, 50mm in diameter and 0.1m deep, and were filled with the same material as the ditch in this area. Their function is unclear, although, as they were not recorded elsewhere on the perimeter, a defensive purpose seems unlikely.

No trace of contemporary features or deposits was found inside enclosure *131*, despite the fact that almost the entire internal area was investigated, and its function, therefore, remains unclear. Fill *143* in the south arm of the perimeter ditch produced 15 abraded sherds of Romano-British pottery (no finds came from elsewhere in the ditch, or from feature *169*, the possible recut of the northern arm), together with six iron nails. Most of the ceramic assemblage is undiagnostic, but a few sherds of black burnished ware Fabric 1 were present, suggesting a Hadrianic or later date for its filling.

Phase 1b: the Romano-British cemetery (mid-second century to third century AD)
Twelve certain or possible Romano-British cremations were recorded during the excavation. Some had been cut into the silted-up perimeter ditch of the Phase 1a

enclosure, others were dug directly into the natural subsoil south of the enclosure's south-east corner; two were situated well to the south, within the area of the watching brief. Additionally, six larger rectangular and sub-rectangular features were recorded. Like the cremations, some of these cut the Phase 1a enclosure ditch, whilst others lay to the south; one was situated in the area of the watching brief in the southern part of the site. Very little direct evidence survived to shed light on the significance of these features, most of which had been truncated by post-Roman activity, but in view of the fact that this was clearly, on the evidence of the cremation burials, the site of a Romano-British cemetery during the second century AD (and perhaps into the third century and beyond), the most likely hypothesis is that some of these features at least represent the remains of inhumation burials. Whilst calcined bone survived reasonably well on this site, the local soil conditions were not conducive to the survival of unburnt bone, except that deriving from late post-medieval contexts, which had been in the ground for only a comparatively short period. For this reason, skeletal remains did not survive in any of the features tentatively interpreted as inhumation burials, which were identified largely on the basis of the morphology of the putative grave cuts.

For the most part, it did not prove possible to establish any kind of chronological sequence to the pattern of burial. In only one case, where two cremations were cut by a putative inhumation, could a direct stratigraphic relationship be demonstrated, and even there the precise character of the possible inhumation is open to question, since there is a possibility that it was in fact a cremation interred in an unusually large burial pit (*154*) (see below, p.33). Pottery associated with the cremation burials indicates that this burial rite was practised on the site from around the mid-second century AD to the late second to third century. Virtually no dating evidence was recovered from the putative inhumations, although one (*132*) produced part of a grey ware jar datable to *c*. AD 250–340, which represents the latest Romano-British pottery recovered from the site.

The cremation burials

At the south-east corner of enclosure *131*, the silted-up southern ditch and the south end of the eastern arm were cut by seven certain or possible cremations, four (*103*, *104*, *156* and *162*) in the eastern ditch and three more (*105*, *113* and *150*) in the southern ditch (Fig. 3.6). One probable cremation (*112*) and another feature that might possibly have been the remains of a burial (*120*) were recorded immediately south of the enclosure's south-east corner. An isolated cremation was also excavated during the evaluation phase of the project, within what became the southern part of the main excavated area; this was also located south of the Phase 1a enclosure (*E112*). Another two cremations, *WB3* and *WB9*, were found during the watching brief at the end of the project. All the features outside the enclosure had

been dug directly through the natural subsoil. The spatial positioning of the graves cutting the enclosure ditch suggested that this feature was still visible, perhaps as little more than a linear hollow or depression, when the burials were deposited. Three of the twelve cremations had certainly been interred in ceramic urns set upright in the burial pits, and a further four were probably urned, although the remains of the vessels were too fragmentary for this to be certainly established; five burials appear to have been unurned.

Cremation burial *103*, perhaps the best preserved of the graves in the Phase 1a enclosure ditch, was situated at the western edge of the eastern arm of the enclosure, close to its south-eastern corner (Fig. 3.6). It comprised a steep-sided, sub-circular cut, *c*. 0.5m in diameter and 0.24m deep (Plate 3.4), containing an upright, near-complete Wilderspool rough-cast beaker, of probable mid- to late second-century date (Pottery 9; below on pp.36ff), and the fragmentary remains of two mid-second century black burnished ware Fabric 1 jars (Pottery 2 and 3). Intense burning on the black burnished ware sherds suggested that these vessels may have been placed on the funeral pyre and a few fragments collected afterwards for burial. Slight traces of an unidentified carbonised deposit on the internal surface of the individual sherds further suggested that the jars may have contained food or some other form of offering. The beaker, which held the principal deposit

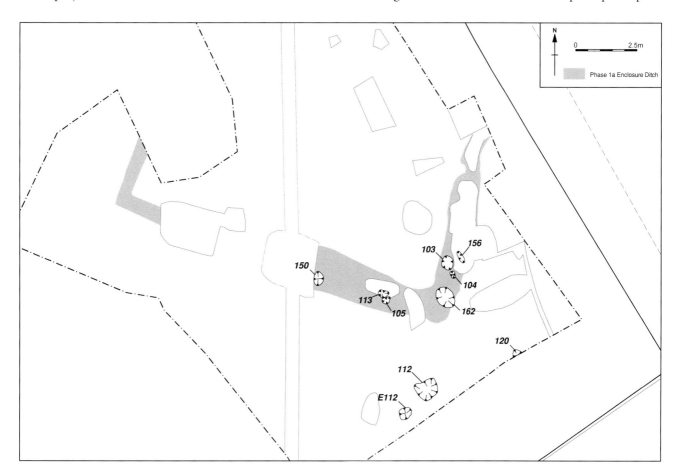

Figure 3.6 Streamline Garage Phase 1b: cremation burials

Plate 3.4 Streamline Garage Phase 1b: cremation *103*

of cremated bone, charcoal and other pyre material, showed no evidence of burning. It contained the remains of a possible female aged *c.* 20–35 years (below on p.43), together with a group of 93 iron hobnails. These presumably derived either from shoes worn by the deceased, or a pair that had been placed on the pyre, since the beaker is too small to have held a pair of unburnt shoes. The fill (*109*) of the grave-pit also contained considerable amounts of charcoal and burnt bone, suggesting that additional pyre material was placed in the grave after deposition of the urn.

Less than 0.3m north-east of *103*, towards the centre of the earlier ditch (Fig. 3.6), was a grave (*156*) comprising a small, vertical-sided, sub-rectangular pit, 0.45m by 0.2m and 0.3m deep. The fill of the pit, *157*, a dark grey-brown sandy clay, contained small amounts of charcoal and some burnt bone, probably derived from two individuals, a sub-adult of *c.* 16–18 years, and a possible immature individual, the latter represented only by a few skull fragments. A few sherds of pottery from two different vessels were recovered, including black burnished ware Fabric 1 dating to the Hadrianic period or later. It is not clear if these represented the remains of a burial urn and/or grave goods, although this seems likely.

Immediately south of grave *103*, and also within the eastern arm of the enclosure ditch (Fig. 3.6), was burial *104*, which comprised a small, steep-sided cut, *c.* 0.3m by 0.2m and 0.2m deep (Plate 3.5). This had contained an upright grey ware jar of probable second-century date, most of which had been truncated or smashed. What remained of the vessel, together with the rest of the grave cut itself, was filled with a deposit of charcoal-rich material (*107*) containing fragments of cremated bone deriving from a possible female over 18 years of age; no other grave goods were present.

Some 0.5m south of *104*, in the extreme south-east corner of the enclosure ditch, was an unurned cremation (*162*), comprising a comparatively large oval cut, 0.85m by 0.6m and 0.2m deep. The fills of the pit, *160* overlain by *124*, contained much charcoal; interestingly, that from the upper fill (*124*) was predominantly oak (*Quercus*), whilst that from the primary fill (*160*) was mainly diffuse porous taxa, principally alder (*Alnus*) (below on p.44). Fill *160*, which yielded almost 90% of the bone assemblage from this burial, contained the remains of an adult, possibly a female; these were identified as pertaining to a person between 18 and 25 years of age and probably less than 23. They were found together with the remains of what was probably a young infant, whilst the bone from deposit *124* derived from an adult or sub-adult, *c.* 16–20 years of age (below on p.43). It is not known if the remains from fill *124* and those of the adult ?female in *160* derived from the same body, although in view of the differences in the charcoal content of these deposits, it is conceivable that two individuals are represented. The presence of a roughly circular, vertical-sided and flat-bottomed void (*125*), 0.3m in diameter and 0.15m deep, within fill *160* suggested that the grave might have held an organic container, perhaps a round wooden box. A collection of 51 iron nails was recovered from the grave fill; these are unlikely to have derived from such a small box and it may be that they came from other objects placed on the pyre, or even from the pyre structure itself. A possible fragment of burnt animal bone found

Plate 3.5 Streamline Garage Phase 1b: cremation *104*

mixed with the cremated human remains might represent an offering of food deposited on the pyre.

In the southern arm of the Phase 1a enclosure ditch (Fig. 3.6), burial *105* comprised a sub-circular, steep-sided pit, 0.3m in diameter and 0.25m deep, containing a truncated black burnished ware Fabric 1 jar of late second- to late third-century date (Pottery 4). Evidence of intense burning on the vessel suggested that it may have been placed on the pyre and reused in the subsequent burial, although this is not certain; no other grave goods were noted. Both the vessel and the grave pit were filled with the same charcoal-rich material (*111*), which contained a very small amount of burnt bone from an unsexed adult over 18 years of age, together with two iron nails. The paucity of bone from this feature suggests that it may have served as a 'cenotaph' or memorial rather than a formal burial (see below on p.41f).

Immediately adjacent to the north-western edge of *105* was a very similar feature (*113*), comprising a roughly circular pit, *c.* 0.25m in diameter and 0.2m deep. This had been very heavily disturbed, but was filled with dark brown silty clay (*115*), containing some charcoal and a very small amount of cremated bone, together with two fragments from a black burnished ware Fabric 1 jar of mid-second- to mid-third-century date (Pottery 5). The bone derived from an unsexed adult at least 18 years of age. As with the adjacent feature (*105*), the absence of all but a few fragments of bone in this deposit suggests that this also may have been a 'cenotaph'.

It was not clear if *113* intercut *105* and, if so, which of the two features was the earlier, or if the two were in fact part of a single grave. The third feature identified as

a possible cremation burial in the southern enclosure ditch (*150*) was located approximately 1.8m west of these. This comprised a steep-sided, oval pit, *c.* 0.5m by 0.45m and 0.25m deep, filled with a mid-brown sandy silt containing many charcoal flecks and mottles (*146*). However, as little or no burnt bone was present in the fill, the identification of this feature as a burial must remain uncertain; it produced no pottery or other artefacts.

Of the two features located outside the south-east corner of the enclosure, only *112* could be identified with certainty as a cremation. This comprised a shallow, sub-square cut, *c.* 1.0m by 0.8m and 0.05–0.1m deep (Fig. 3.6), filled with a mixed, charcoal-rich silty clay (*123=130*) containing numerous fragments of burnt bone, the remains of an adult over 18 years of age, together with two iron nails. Fragments from a black burnished ware Fabric 1 jar, datable to *c.* AD 120–60, were recovered from this feature (Pottery 6); whilst these sherds probably represented the remains of a burial urn, this is not absolutely certain. The second feature in this area (*120*) could not be confidently interpreted as a burial, for its grey-brown sandy loam fill (*121*) contained some charcoal but no burnt bone, and at least half of the feature lay outside the excavated area. It comprised a small, possibly circular cut, 0.25m deep with a U-shaped profile, and may in fact have been a posthole rather than a cremation pit.

The single burial recorded during the evaluation phase of the project comprised a sub-circular pit (*E112*), *c.* 0.5m in diameter and 0.17m deep (Fig. 3.6; Plate 3.6). The primary fill of dark grey-brown clay loam (*E111*) contained numerous small fragments and flecks of oak

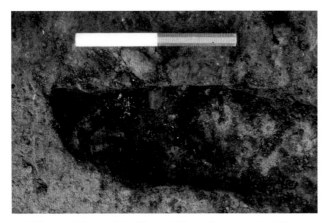

Plate 3.6 Streamline Garage Phase 1b: cremation *E112*

charcoal and numerous small fragments of burnt bone, which were concentrated particularly towards the base of the pit. The secondary fill (*E116*) was similar, but appeared to have been disturbed and contained less charcoal and bone. The cremated remains were those of a probable adult of indeterminate sex, though some fragments of animal bone were also present. It was cut by a large stakehole (*E118*), 0.13m in diameter and 0.25m deep. This feature was not certainly associated with the burial, but it is conceivable that it represented the remains of a wooden grave marker. With the exception of two corroded nails and a very small fragment of a black burnished ware Fabric 1 vessel of

Hadrianic or later date, all of which came from deposit *E111*, no artefacts were recovered from this burial, which appears to have been unurned.

The two cremations, *WB3* and *WB9*, discovered during the watching brief (Fig. 3.7), were located *c.* 30m south of the enclosure. Burial *WB3* (Plate 3.7) comprised a sub-square pit, 0.9m by 0.8m and 0.11m deep, the base of which was filled with a deposit (*WB2*) composed largely of a concentrated mass of calcined bone fragments, mixed with some charcoal. The bones proved to be those of an adult, possibly a female, *c.* 20–40 years of age. The upper fill (*WB1*) of dark grey/black sandy silt contained small amounts of charcoal and calcined bone. A number of nails (six in total) recovered from both fills might have derived either from items placed on the funeral pyre or from the pyre structure itself, whilst a burnt fragment of animal bone (of immature pig/sheep size) mixed with the cremated human remains may represent food placed on the pyre. The second burial (*WB9*) comprised a rectangular pit, 0.45m in diameter and 0.19m deep. The single fill (*WB8*) contained small amounts of charcoal and calcined bone, 11 iron nails, and four fragments from a black burnished ware Fabric 1 jar, probably of second-century date, that may have been the remains of a truncated and badly disturbed burial urn.

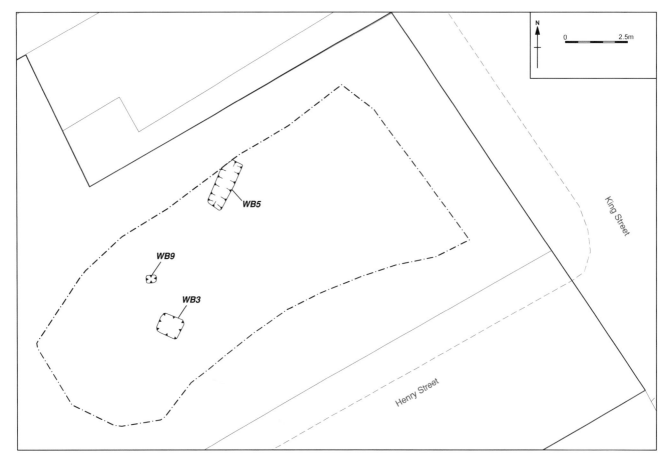

Figure 3.7 Streamline Garage Phase 1b: burials excavated during the watching brief

Plate 3.7 Streamline Garage Phase 1b: cremation *WB3*

The possible inhumation burials

In total, six possible inhumation burials were recorded; two, *142* and *147*, were located in the eastern arm of the Phase 1a enclosure ditch, and two, *152* and *154*, were placed in the southern ditch, in all cases close to the enclosure's south-east corner (Fig. 3.8). One (*132*) was also recorded in the area immediately south of the enclosure, whilst another (*WB5*) was found further south still during the watching brief (Fig. 3.7).

North of cremation burials *103*, *104*, *156* and *162*, the eastern arm of the Phase 1a enclosure ditch was cut by a large, sub-rectangular feature (*142*) aligned north-east to south-west, that seemed to have been deliberately located within what remained of the earlier ditch (Fig. 3.8). This feature had steeply sloping sides and a flat base, measuring at least 1.5m in length, up to 0.66m wide and 0.3m deep. It was filled with a mid-dark brown sandy clay silt (*141*) that did not yield any finds. In common with several of the other putative inhumation burials found on the site, it is not entirely clear whether this feature was a grave or not, as it produced no evidence of a coffin, shroud, grave goods or other funerary material.

Also cutting the eastern arm of the Phase 1a enclosure ditch was feature *147* (Fig. 3.8; Plate 3.8). This was located between possible inhumation burial *142* to the north and cremations *103*, *104*, *156* and *162* to the south, and comprised a rectangular cut, aligned north to south, *c.* 3.7m long, 1.1m wide, and up to 0.89m deep, with vertical sides, a flat base, and an apparent step at its southern end. It was filled with a fairly clean, mid-dark brown sandy clay silt (*148*) that produced 34 iron hobnails and 84 sherds of pottery, by far the largest collection of pottery from any Romano-British feature on the site. The assemblage includes 40 sherds from a small, near-complete Wilderspool flagon, datable to the late first to second century or perhaps later; there were also a fragment of a North Gaulish colour-coated indented beaker (Pottery 11) of late first- to early second-century date, and part of a cornice-rim beaker of *c.* AD 80–130 (Pottery 12). This material is amongst the earliest pottery recovered from the site, but a Hadrianic or later date for the filling of feature *147* is indicated by the presence of a black burnished ware Fabric 1 jar (Pottery 8). The purpose of this feature is not certainly known; superficially it had the appearance of a particularly well-preserved, if rather long, grave cut, and this remains a likely interpretation, especially in view of the concentration of hobnails and the near-complete flagon within its fill. It was not, however, interpreted as such during the course of the excavation, when it was thought to represent a partial recutting of the eastern arm of the Phase 1a enclosure ditch.

In the southern arm of the enclosure, cremations or possibly 'cenotaphs' *105* and *113* were cut by a rectangular feature (*154*), aligned east to west, *c.* 1.4m by 0.6m and 0.53m deep. This was filled with mixed, dark brown silty clay (*155*) containing small amounts of cremated bone and charcoal, two iron nails, and a number of sherds of pottery, including part of a late second-century black burnished ware Fabric 1 jar (Pottery 7). Although the burnt material was thought likely to have derived from the earlier cremations, the identifiable bone was that of an adult or sub-adult over 13 years of age, whereas the very small amounts of bone associated with cremations *105* and *113* represented the remains of adults (or possibly only one adult?) over 18

Plate 3.8 Streamline Garage Phase 1b: possible inhumation *147*

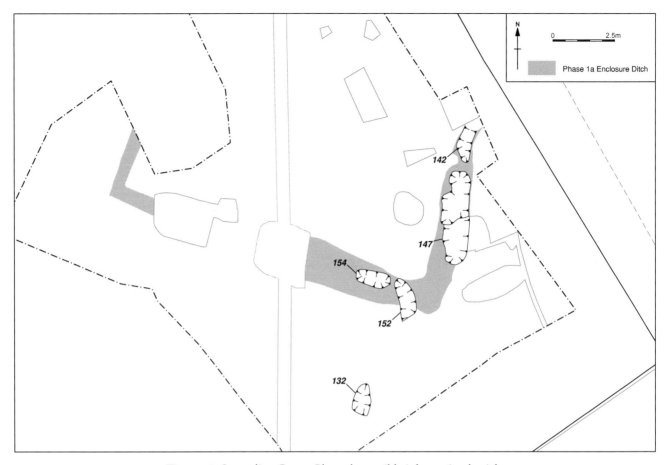

Figure 3.8 Streamline Garage Phase 1b: possible inhumation burials

years of age (see above on p.31). It is therefore unclear whether feature *154* was itself a cremation, albeit placed in a very large pit, or whether the calcined bone found within it derived from *105* or *113*, or even from another burial that had been completely destroyed when *154* was dug. It is also unclear whether the pottery in fill *155* was associated with this putative burial, perhaps the remains of a vessel deposited as grave goods (or even an urn, if *154* was in fact a cremation), or was residual. No evidence for a coffin, shroud, or other grave furniture was noted. Immediately east of *154* was *152*, another sub-rectangular feature of similar size, in this case orientated north to south, *c.* 1.6m by 0.7m and 0.45m deep. The northern end of this cut the southern arm of the Phase 1a enclosure ditch. Its fill (*153*) produced nine iron nails, several abraded sherds of black burnished ware Fabric 1, and a small amount of burnt bone, representing an adult over 18 years of age (below on p.43), although this material was probably residual.

South of enclosure *131*, two possible inhumation burials were recorded, one, *132*, during the main excavation phase and another, *WB5*, during the watching brief. Feature *132* comprised a sub-rectangular cut, aligned approximately north to south, 1.2m by 0.7m, and 0.22m deep (Plate 3.9). The principal fill (*133*), a mixed orange-brown sandy clay, contained three iron nails. Around the south-eastern edge of the cut was a slightly different deposit (*137*) that appeared to

Plate 3.9 Streamline Garage Phase 1b: possible inhumation *132*, prior to excavation

represent backfill between the edge of the grave cut and something, perhaps a coffin, that had once occupied the space subsequently filled by *133*. Deposit *137* yielded fragments of a small grey ware jar datable to *c.* AD 250–340 (Pottery 10), which represents the latest Romano-British ceramic material recovered from the site. Feature *WB5* was located *c.* 27m south of *132*, and was rectangular in plan, *c.* 2m north to south, 0.82m wide and 0.11m deep (Fig. 3.7). It was filled with mid-grey silty clay (*WB4*), containing sub-rounded sandstone fragments, seven iron nails, and small amounts of charcoal.

Phase 2: medieval and later activity

With the exception of three residual sherds of medieval pottery from the evaluation, the only evidence for medieval activity on the site was provided by a gully or narrow ditch (*119/135*), aligned east to west, that extended into the south-east corner of the excavated area from the east for 9m before terminating in a rounded butt-end (Fig. 3.9). This feature, which directly cut the natural subsoil and had no stratigraphic link with any of the earlier features on the site, was 0.6–0.9m wide and 0.25m deep, with steeply sloping sides and a flat base, although it had doubtless been truncated by later activity. It was filled with mid-dark orange-brown or yellow-brown sandy clay (*118*, *134* and *136*), which yielded a range of residual Romano-British

pottery, in addition to six sherds of medieval or early post-medieval date, the latest probably datable to the fifteenth to seventeenth centuries (see below on p.39).

Feature *119/135*, together with all the Romano-British features recorded on the site, was sealed by a homogeneous layer of pale/mid-orange-brown clay silt (*102*), up to 0.35m thick, that covered the southern part of the excavated area, except where it had been removed by later features (not illustrated); to the north it had been removed by late post-medieval truncation. With the exception of residual Roman pottery, this deposit produced no datable artefactual material, but it may represent an agricultural or horticultural soil of medieval origin that continued to accumulate for much of the post-medieval period.

Cut into soil *102* was a large post-medieval sandstone wall (*151*), which ran from the south west in a north-north-easterly direction, where it was truncated by later diesel tanks (*178*). The alignment of this wall, parallel with the former plot boundary and the rear of the adjacent public house site, indicates that it is probably a former property boundary. On the eastern side of the excavation, a small stub of sandstone wall flanking a cobbled area, measuring *c.* 1.5m by 1.0m, represented the remains of a small post-medieval yard (*174*), set at a right angle to the street frontage. Approximately 4.5m to the south of this yard were the remains of a well (*126*), made of roughly-shaped sandstone blocks. These

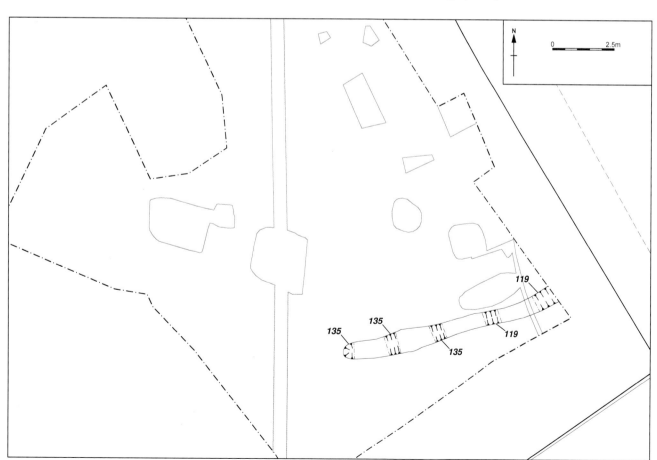

Figure 3.9 Streamline Garage Phase 2: medieval gully *119/135*

features represented the remains of buildings that fronted onto King Street, prior to the construction of the modern garage.

Remnants of the former garage, mainly in the form of concrete stanchion bases, were the most modern features encountered during the excavation. All earlier deposits in the north-eastern corner of the site had been removed by the insertion of a number of large diesel tanks (*178*) and the north-western corner had been heavily disturbed by the insertion of a very large waste-oil tank. A sewage pipe, cut into a deep trench and set in concrete, ran from the north-east corner of the site between the two sets of tanks.

The Roman Pottery
by Christine Howard-Davis

Roman pottery was recovered from the 1995 evaluation and 1996 excavation at 77–79 Penny Street, and from the various phases of archaeological investigation undertaken at the Streamline Garage site in 2000–1.

Only a single sherd of undiagnostic Roman grey ware was found at 81 Penny Street, in fill *151* of the possible cremation *152* (see above on p.24f).

The pottery from 77–79 Penny Street
The assemblage from the 1995 evaluation (Salisbury and Coupe 1995) comprises one near-complete vessel, which had been utilised as a cremation urn, and a few other sherds that are assumed to have come from the fill of the cremation pit. The subsequent excavations (LUAU 1996) yielded 142 sherds from 19 contexts. Many are severely abraded, often less than 10mm in length, and several show signs of secondary burning, although the cause of this is not clear.

The burial urn (Pottery 1; Fig. 3.10; Plate 3.10) had been smashed at some stage, and the sherds scattered (it was reconstructed from 35 separate fragments), but it appears to have been the primary funerary vessel containing the principal deposit of cremated material. It is a black burnished ware Fabric 1 jar, probably Gillam form 145 (Gillam 1970), with a narrow band of

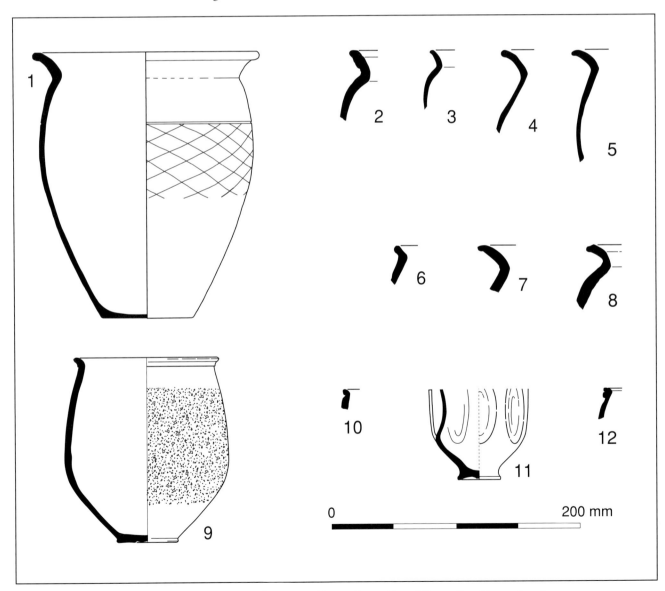

Figure 3.10 Roman pottery from 77-79 Penny Street (1) and Streamline Garage (2-12)

Plate 3.10 77–79 Penny Street: burial urn found during the evaluation of 1995 (photograph: Peter Iles by courtesy of Lancaster City Museum)

obtuse, burnished lattice decoration on the upper part of the body, and can be dated to *c.* AD 230–300. There is considerable abrasion at the maximum girth of the jar and some evidence for secondary burning. Whilst it is possible that the burning resulted from the vessel being placed on the funeral pyre, this seems unlikely in view of the fact that it was clearly intact at the time of burial. More probably, both the burning and the abrasion may indicate that the vessel had been used for other purposes before being selected as a burial urn.

The small number of other Romano-British sherds present in the evaluation archive include five fragments in a very hard, pale grey, calcite-gritted fabric with burnished decoration, similar to the late third- to fourth-century material that was recovered in some quantity from the subsequent excavation (see above on p.24), and a single, very abraded late first- to early second-century jar rim in a fine, sandy grey fabric. The latter, at least, seems likely to be residual.

Of the 19 contexts from the 1996 excavations which produced Romano-British pottery (Table 3.1), only five yielded ten or more fragments. Layer *100* and fill *102* of cut *103* produced 26 and 22 sherds respectively, although in the case of layer *100* it is likely that most, if not all, of the oxidised orange ware fragments are from a single vessel. There were very few sherds diagnostic of form or date, and only two rims were represented. It seems likely, however, that forms were dominated by jars and flagons.

The assemblage can be dated only in general terms, but the quantity of calcite-gritted fabrics seems to suggest a late third- to fourth-century date for many contexts. A tiny fragment of a Nene Valley colour-coated indented beaker with scale decoration from fill *102* points to a third-century date (Tyers 1999, 173),

Table 3.1 *Summary of Roman pottery from 77–79 Penny Street*

Context No.	Samian	BB1	Calcite-gritted	Oxidised white	Colour-coated	Oxidised orange	Grey ware	Total
12*	1		2	3		2	1	9
64*						1		1
66*		2	4			2		8
71				3			2	5
72			3			3	1	7
73	1	1		1				3
79						11		11
80		1						1
82			1					1
86						3		3
87		1	1			4		6
88				7				7
89						2		2
90				14		1		15
100	2		5			16	3	26
101						1		1
102	1	1	11	4	1	2	2	22
104	1		7			2		10
107			3					3
Unstratified						1		1
Total	**6**	**6**	**37**	**32**	**1**	**51**	**9**	**142**

*Note: BB1=black burnished ware Fabric 1; * = post-Roman deposit*

although calcite-gritted fabrics in the same context are probably later. One of the two rims, recovered from fill *107*, also of cut *103*, derives from a calcite-gritted jar, probably Gillam type 161 (Gillam 1970), datable to *c.* AD 300–370. The other, a heavily abraded beaded rim from layer *72*, cannot be dated with precision, but seems most likely to be of second-century date. The presence of calcite-gritted fabrics in the same context, however, would suggest that it was probably residual.

The six fragments of samian ware are in extremely poor condition, the surface finish either being badly damaged or absent. Only one fragment, from a decorated Central Gaulish Dr. 37 bowl, can be attributed to a production centre (Lezoux), and even this sherd was so heavily abraded that it was not attributable to a specific potter. However, the flowing freestyle decoration is suggestive of a date later in the second century (Webster 1996, 48). The fragment also shows clear signs of repair, in the form of two rivet holes, suggesting that it may have been in circulation for some time prior to deposition.

The pottery from Streamline Garage, King Street

In total, 491 fragments of Roman pottery were recovered from the Streamline Garage site, representing approximately 21 vessels, several of which had originally been deposited in their complete form, as burial urns for cremated human remains. The range of fabrics and vessel types present is not extensive, with only nine fabrics recognised, including a small amphora sherd. The majority of the vessels are jars, although some flagons and beakers are also present.

Discussion

Two fragments of samian ware (Fabric 1; Table 3.2) were recovered, a badly degraded body fragment from a

Table 3.2 *Streamline Garage Site: fabric types recovered*

Fabric Series	Description
Fabric 1	Samian; Central Gaulish, probably Lezoux.
Fabric 2	Rusticated ware; fine, slightly sandy, mid-grey fabric, *c.* AD 80–130 (Swan 1975, 12).
Fabric 3	Black burnished ware Fabric 1. Appears on northern sites with military links after *c.* AD 120 (Williams 1977; Tomber and Dore 1998, 127).
Fabric 4	Oxidised ware; sandy, orange fabric with a darker red slip. Possibly a Wilderspool product (Hartley 1981). A single large flagon is represented.
Fabric 5	Oxidised ware; sandy, white fabric. A single large flagon is represented.
Fabric 6	Wilderspool products; sandy oxidised, pinkish-orange fabrics. Forms include a rough-cast beaker and a white-slipped flagon (Hartley and Webster 1973; Tomber and Dore 1998, 122).
Fabric 7	Grey wares; sandy, relatively hard-fired, mid-grey fabric. Probably locally made, from a range of sources.
Fabric 8	Colour-coated ware; grey fabric with pinkish surfaces and patchy brownish colour-coat. Possibly Anderson's North Gaulish fabric 2 (Anderson 1980).
Fabric 9	Amphora.

Table 3.3 *Catalogue of illustrated vessels (see Fig. 3.10)*

Catalogue No.	Context/IRF Nos	Description	Feature
1	–	Fabric 3: black burnished ware Fabric 1 jar, probably Gillam form 145 (Gillam 1970); *c.* AD 230–300.	None recorded
2	109/1005	Fabric 3; black burnished ware Fabric 1 jar; mid-second century AD.	Cremation 103
3	109/1005	Fabric 3; black burnished ware Fabric 1 jar; mid-second century AD.	Cremation 103
4	111/1010	Fabric 3; black burnished ware Fabric 1 jar; *c.* AD 180–280.	Cremation 105
5	115/1045	Fabric 3; black burnished ware Fabric 1 jar, perhaps Gillam 138 or 139 (Gillam 1970); *c.* AD 150–250.	Cremation 113
6	112/1047	Fabric 3; black burnished ware Fabric 1 jar, perhaps Gillam 168 (Gillam 1970); *c.* AD 120–60.	Cremation 112
7	155/1059	Fabric 3; black burnished ware Fabric 1 jar; late second century AD.	Inhumation(?) 154
8	148/1031	Fabric 3; black burnished ware Fabric 1 jar; second century AD.	Inhumation(?) 147
9	109/1003	Fabric 6; Wilderspool rough-cast beaker; mid- to late second century AD.	Cremation 103
10	137/1049	Fabric 7; Grey ware, small jar, possibly Gillam 172 (Gillam 1970); *c.* AD 250–340.	Inhumation(?) 132
11	148/1024	Fabric 8; indented beaker; late first to early second century AD.	Inhumation(?) 147
12	148/1032	Fabric 8; cornice-rim beaker, possibly Gillam 72 (Gillam 1970); *c.* AD 80–130.	Inhumation(?) 147

Dr. 37 bowl from Phase 1b (fill *WB4* of cremation *WB3*), and a plain rim from a late post-medieval context recorded during the evaluation. Both are probably from the Lezoux production centre in Central Gaul, and can be dated to the mid- to late second century AD.

Rusticated ware (Fabric 2; Table 3.2) was represented only by two small sherds, one from Phase 1b (fill *WB4* of cremation burial *WB3*), the other from Phase 2 (late-medieval/post-medieval soil layer *102*). Both sherds were residual, but could conceivably have been associated with the use of the Phase 1a enclosure (*131*), the perimeter ditch for which was silting up during the second century AD.

The bulk of the Romano-British pottery assemblage (215 sherds) comprises black burnished ware Fabric 1 (Fabric 3; Table 3.2); all the identifiable sherds derived from jars. This fabric was present in fill *143* of the perimeter ditch of the Phase 1a enclosure (*131*), and black burnished ware jars had been deposited as certain or possible burial urns and/or grave goods in several of the Phase 1b cremations (Pottery 2, 3, 4, 5, 6; Fig. 3.10). The fabric was also recovered from the fills of putative inhumation burials *152*, *154* (Pottery 7; Fig. 3.10) and *147* (Pottery 8; Fig. 3.10). Many fragments appeared to have been burnt, and were consequently extremely friable and easily abraded. Whilst it is possible that such burning reflects the reuse of old cooking vessels as urns and for other funerary purposes (the vessel from burial *WB9*, for example, has soot on its outer surface but is otherwise not extensively burnt), in many cases the sherds appear to have been subjected to very intense heat, resulting in widespread oxidisation of the surfaces. In these cases, the vessels may well have been placed on the funeral pyre and collected later for incorporation in the burial deposit. Although most of the black burnished ware Fabric 1 from the site appears to be of mid- to late second-century date, rim forms that could extend into the third century (Pottery 4 and 5; Fig. 3.10) are also present (Gillam 1970, Figs 1 and 2).

Only a single large flagon was noted in Fabric 4, from the fill (*148*) of possible inhumation *147* (Phase 1b). This has not been further identified, but seems closely related to the vessels in 'Raetian' red-slipped fabric produced at Wilderspool (Hartley 1981). Likewise, only a single large flagon was noted in Fabric 5, residual in Phase 2 post-Roman ploughsoil *102*. This seems likely to be of second-century date.

Wilderspool products (Fabric 6) are represented by a large rough-cast beaker, utilised as an urn in Phase 1b cremation burial *103* (Pottery 9; Fig. 3.10), and a small flagon (Hartley and Webster 1973, Fig. 2.3) from putative inhumation *147*. Wilderspool products are generally dated to the late first to second century AD, but evidence from excavations at Walton-le-Dale (Evans in prep) seems to point towards production of Wilderspool-type wares continuing there into the third century.

Surprisingly little grey ware (Fabric 7) was present on the site, the 45 fragments recovered probably representing only two vessels. It is likely that these were locally made, as was much of the grey ware from sites elsewhere in the Lancaster settlement (Hird and Howard-Davis in prep). Although fragmentary and truncated, the vessel utilised as an urn in cremation burial *104* was unburnt, and had clearly originally stood upright. The vessel from putative inhumation burial *132* was amongst the latest from the site, dated to c. AD 250–340 (Pottery 10; Fig. 3.10).

Colour-coated ware (Fabric 8) was represented by only four fragments, all from Phase 1b (fill *148* of possible inhumation *147*). These probably represent two vessels, a late first- to early second-century indented beaker (Pottery 11; Fig. 3.10), probably of North Gaulish origin and possibly Anderson's North Gaulish fabric 2 (Anderson 1980, 34), and a cornice-rim beaker (Pottery 12; Fig. 3.10), possibly Gillam type 72 (Gillam 1970), datable to c. AD 80–130.

A small fragment of amphora (Fabric 9) was recovered from cremation burial *WB3*. In view of its size, it seems unlikely that this was deliberately deposited within the grave, although it might possibly have derived from feasting associated with the funeral ceremony. Alternatively, like the two small fragments of pre-Hadrianic rusticated ware (Fabric 2), it might have been associated with occupation prior to the establishment of the cemetery in this area.

With the exception of Pottery 1, which is the black burnished ware Fabric 1 burial urn discovered during the 1995 evaluation at 77–79 Penny Street (see above), all the illustrated vessels are from the Roman cemetery phase (Phase 1b) on the Streamline Garage site.

The Medieval Pottery
by Christine Howard-Davis

Six fragments of medieval pottery were recovered from ditch *119/135* on the Streamline Garage site (Phase 2), representing at least two vessels, one of which was green-glazed. Three more medieval fragments were recovered as residual material from late post-medieval contexts during the evaluation. Three distinct fabrics are represented: a coarse, gritty oxidised fabric with occasional large and distinctive red grits; a medium gritty fabric, incompletely reduced and with a patchy green glaze; and a fine, fully reduced fabric with thick olive to dark green glaze. The latter is probably Silverdale ware, produced in the later part of the medieval period and into the early post-medieval period (White 2000).

The Ironwork
by Christine Howard-Davis

Some 237 small fragments of iron were recovered from the Streamline Garage site, 12 from the evaluation, 201 from the excavation, and 24 from the watching brief. Although none of the material was subject to X-radiography, most fragments could be readily identified as small nails and hobnails. Almost all of the nails were recovered from Phase 1 (Romano-British) contexts (Table 3.4), the great majority being associated with the Phase 1b cemetery.

The correlation between nails and hobnails and the Romano-British burials of Phase 1b is striking; the hobnails clearly indicate the presence of shoes, or more likely the cremated remains of shoes, in several of the grave deposits, either worn by the deceased or placed separately on the funeral pyre. The association of shoes with burial deposits was widespread during the Romano-British period, and was presumably intended to equip the deceased for their journey to the afterlife (Philpott 1991, 173; Howard-Davis 1996, 114). The presence of 34 hobnails in fill *148* of feature *147* lends support to the idea that this was an inhumation burial (see above on p.33).

The Human Bone
Introduction
by Jacqueline I. McKinley and Stephen Rowland

The principal assemblage of cremated human remains was recovered from the Streamline Garage site, where the greatest number of Roman burials was recorded. However, the archaeological investigations at 77–79 and 81 Penny Street also yielded small groups of material, both from discrete cremation burials and, at 77–79 Penny Street, from other Romano-British (and post-Roman) contexts, principally soil spreads. The latter,

although presumably residual, probably derived either from disturbed burials or, more speculatively, from pyre sites situated somewhere in the vicinity.

Osteological analysis followed the standard procedure for the examination of cremated bone (McKinley 1994a, 5–21; 2000a). The material was identified and recorded using standard reference works, including Bass (1995) and Brothwell (1972). Age was assessed from the stage of skeletal and tooth development (van Beek 1983; McMinn and Hutchings 1985) and the general degree of age-related changes to the bone. Sex was ascertained from the sexually dimorphic traits of the skeleton (Buikstra and Ubelaker 1994).

The Human Bone from 77–79 and 81 Penny Street
by Stephen Rowland

Small assemblages of calcined human bone were recovered from the sites at 77–79 and 81 Penny Street. The assemblage recovered from the main phase of excavation at 77–79 Penny Street came from a wide range of Roman and post-Roman contexts. The bulk of the material comprised very small, undiagnostic, fragments scattered through Roman and post-Roman soil deposits, presumably derived either from disturbed Roman cremation burials or (possibly) from a pyre site located outside the excavated area. Only a few fragments were present in any single deposit. Small amounts of calcined bone were also recovered from the fills of probable Roman cremation burials (*78* and *98*), and as residual material from the fills of possible inhumation burials *103* and *115*. A few fragments were also apparently associated with the burial urn found during the 1995 evaluation (Salisbury and Coupe 1995).

Irrespective of the context of origin, the bone was generally in a fair state of preservation, though fully calcined to a uniform white colour and highly

Table 3.4 *Provenance of iron nails and hobnails*

Phase	Context	Feature	No. of nails/hobnails
1a	143	Perimeter ditch 144 of enclosure 131	6
1b	109	Cremation 103	93
1b	111	Cremation 105	2
1b	123	Cremation 112	2
1b	124 and 160	Cremation 162	51
1b	WB1 and WB2	Cremation WB3	6
1b	WB8	Cremation WB9	11
1b	133	Possible inhumation 132	3
1b	153	Possible inhumation 152	9
1b	155	Possible inhumation 154	2
1b	WB4	Possible inhumation WB5	7
1b	148	Possible inhumation 147	34
2	102	Medieval/post-medieval soil	1
-	-	Modern contexts	10
Total			237

fragmented, to the extent that very few pieces exceeded 20mm in length; many were considerably smaller. This fragmentation is likely to relate in part to the friable condition of the bone, but also to the fact that much had been redeposited, disturbed, or had undergone some degree of bioturbation. It is thus unsurprising that the assemblage was composed largely of cortical fragments of the more robust limb bones, whilst those parts of the bone useful for ageing and sexing, together with the more delicate elements, such as the pelvis and vertebrae, were largely absent. As such, whilst many of the bones could be identified as likely to be those of human adults on the basis of their shape and texture, they provided very little additional information.

Of those contexts directly associated with funerary activity, fill *71* of cremation *78* contained almost 50 small fragments of human bone, including parts of the mandible and the major and minor limb bones, whilst the 35 equally small fragments from fill *94* of cremation *98* included pieces of skull and long bone. Neither the age nor sex of either individual could be determined. The few small fragments recovered from putative inhumations *103* and *115* were little different; fill *107* in feature *103* yielded a few fragments of long bone and rib, probably from an adult. This material is, however, of some interest, since its presence demonstrates that cremation was being practised somewhere in the vicinity before features *103* and *115* were dug, although no early cremations were found on the site itself. With the exception of a fragment of a radius, thought to derive from a mature adult (Salisbury and Coupe 1995, 4), the few small pieces of calcined bone found in association with the burial urn recovered during the 1995 evaluation were too poorly preserved to permit further identification.

Elsewhere on the 1996 site, layer *89*, which post-dated features *103* and *115* but pre-dated the deposition of cremations *78* and *98*, yielded a fully formed upper third molar. Although the enamel had flaked off during the process of cremation, there was no obvious wear to the dentine, implying that the owner of the tooth may have died in early adulthood. The only other material of note came from fill *76* of a post-medieval gully. The assemblage comprised approximately 20g of poorly preserved and fragmented bone, including identifiable fragments of the left tibia and ulna. The proximal epiphysis of the tibia was fused, leaving no trace of the line of union, indicating that it derived from an adult individual.

At 81 Penny Street, only three small pieces of calcined bone were recovered from fill *151* of possible cremation pit *152*, although the entire contents of the excavated portion of this feature were sieved. The remains comprise a fragment of human rib, another tiny piece that is probably of human origin, and a probable fragment of bird bone (see below on p.44).

The Human Bone from Streamline Garage, King Street
by Jacqueline I. McKinley with Stephen Rowland

Cremated bone from 13 Romano-British deposits was analysed, including material from nine features interpreted on excavation as the remains of cremation burials. With one exception, the fill of each putative grave cut was recovered as a single whole-earth deposit. These fills were wet-sieved to 2mm fraction, and bone separated from the >4mm fraction residues for specialist analysis. All the material was analysed by Jacqueline McKinley, with the exception of the assemblage from cremation *E112*, recovered during the evaluation phase of the project, which was studied by Stephen Rowland.

Results
The interpretations of deposit type have been based on the primary field records and the evidence derived from the osteological analysis. It has been assumed that the single fills of features containing cremation-related deposits had a relatively even distribution of all the archaeological components (for example, cremated bone and fuel ash). Given the size of the majority of the deposits, and the relatively small quantities of bone and fuel ash recovered in many cases, it is suggested that there had been at least some degree of bioturbation within most deposits. Each fill was excavated and lifted *en masse*, with no sub-division by spits and/or quadrant, although it should be noted that cremated bone was sometimes found to be highly concentrated in one part of the fill.

The presence of three possible types of deposit is implied, all of which have been recognised amongst cremation-related deposits of most periods in Britain and previously defined (McKinley 1996; 1997, 56–7; 2000b; 2000c; 2004). Most correspond to similarly varied types of mortuary deposits recorded across a wide geographic range in the rest of Europe (Todd 1977; Flouest 1993; Witteyer 2000, Figs 13 and 14). These types comprise burials, either urned or unurned but otherwise 'contained', with or without redeposited pyre debris in the grave fills; discrete, formal deposits of pyre debris; and cenotaphs or memorials.

Urned burials are where the bone has been buried within a vessel. Unurned burials comprise a discrete concentration of cremated bone, probably originally contained in some form of organic container which, in Romano-British features, were usually placed at the base of the grave. The burial may have been preceded or succeeded by the deposition of pyre debris within the grave. Where pyre debris is deposited subsequent to burial, particularly in an unurned burial, the fuel ash can filter in between bone fragments over time, and create the impression of a mixed deposit.

Pyre debris represents all the material remaining at the pyre site after the bone and pyre goods intended for formal burial have been removed. If redeposited, pyre debris tends to comprise a mix of fuel ash (charcoal), often including varying quantities of cremated bone and pyre goods, burnt clay/soil, and fuel ash slag. The nature of such a deposit generally implies that there was a formal burial to which it related somewhere in close proximity to the deposition site.

Cenotaphs appear to represent substitutes for formal burials, where the remains of the individual were not available, perhaps because the bulk had been deposited elsewhere. They share many of the characteristics of formal burials (including the deposition of vessels), but may contain only very small quantities of bone. It is misleading to refer to such deposits as 'token burials', since all archaeological cremation burials could be described as such, in that they very rarely, if ever, contain the total quantity of bone which would remain after cremation (McKinley 1997; 2000c). Where it is clear that more than 99% of the expected minimum weight of bone is absent from an undisturbed or relatively intact deposit, it obviously does not represent a burial in the same way as others containing more representative amounts of the available cremated bone.

Two deposits, *107* in burial *104* and *109* in burial *103*, may have comprised a mix of partly urned and partly unurned burials, a deposit type seen, for example, in the cemetery associated with the Roman fort at Brougham, Cumbria (Cool 2004). Although both deposits appeared to comprise a mix of bone and charcoal, it is felt they are most likely to represent the remains of burials with subsequent deposits of pyre debris. Similarly, deposits *157* from burial *156*, *160* from burial *162* and *WB2* from burial *WB3* are also most likely to represent the remains of burials with subsequent debris deposits, although in all cases, the possibility of their representing formal deposits of pyre debris cannot be conclusively excluded. Deposit *123* from burial *112* survived to such a shallow depth (*c.* 50–100mm) that it is not possible to interpret the type of deposit with any security. At least one, and probably two, of the deposits, *111* from burial *105* and *115* from burial *113*, appear to have the characteristics of cenotaphs; perhaps significantly, these burials were located side-by-side, and may even have been part of a single grave.

Disturbance and Condition

All the features and deposits appeared to have been truncated, the surviving depths ranging from 50mm to 300mm, although most were more than 200mm deep. As the bone in Romano-British cremation burials tends to be concentrated towards the base of grave cuts (in urned burials the vessel rarely being filled to capacity), there is unlikely to have been substantial (if any) loss of bone from the deposits examined, other than in the case of deposit *123* from burial *112*.

Visual inspection showed the bone to be in good condition, with no evidence for surface erosion or abrasion. Trabecular bone is also relatively well represented, suggesting the burial microenvironment was not adverse to good preservation of burnt bone. The commonly noted inclusion of fuel ash within the burial matrix is also likely to have assisted in this.

Demographic Data

A minimum of eight, and possibly nine, individuals were identified from the remains, including seven adults (four most likely to be females), one sub-adult, and probably one young infant from a dual cremation (fill *160* of burial *162*). These figures include individuals identified from the possible cenotaph deposits, burials *105* and *113*, as, by their nature, these are likely to be the only remains of these individuals buried within the confines of the cemetery.

Demographic comment is limited both by the small size of the assemblage, and by the likelihood that the burials surviving in the south-eastern part of the excavated area are unlikely to represent the whole cemetery or, indeed, the totality of Lancaster's Roman burials. The apparent lack of males amongst the burials from this site could be misleading, as the remains of several individuals could not be sexed.

Pathology

There was very little evidence for pathological lesions, with minor changes being observed in the remains of only two individuals, both adult females from burials *103* and *104* (Table 3.5). The development of both osteophytes (new bone growth at joint margins) and exostoses (new bone growth at ligament/tendon insertions) are generally considered to reflect age-related stress or degenerative processes, though there might be other predisposing factors (Rogers and Waldron 1995).

Pyre Technology and Cremation Ritual

The surviving bone is almost uniformly white in colour, indicative of full oxidation during the cremation process (Holden *et al* 1995a; 1995b). The surviving weights of bone from individual deposits is generally low (Table 3.5), with the maximum recorded being 437.4g from fills *124* and *160* of burial *162*, representing a maximum of 43.7% (or average 27.3%) of the total weight of bone expected from an adult cremation (McKinley 1993). Some small fraction (<2mm) of bone was not available for quantification/analysis, but this is unlikely to have added substantially to the overall weight of bone. The weight of bone from two cremation burials excavated at the Mitchell's Brewery site on Church Street in 1999 (McKinley in prep; see above on p.15 and below on p.98) was also low, at 270.6g and 434.6g, although both

Table 3.5 *Summary of cremated human bone (Phase 1b)*

Deposit/ burial	Deposit type	Weight (g)	Age/sex	Pathology	Pyre goods
107/104	UB + Rpd	121.3	Adult >18 Female??	Exostoses – femur	
109/103	UB + Rpd	211.6	Adult *c.* 20–35 Female??	Osteophytes – atlas	
111/105	Cenotaph? with urn + Rpd?	9.3	Adult >18		
115/113	Cenotaph? with urn?	8.9	Adult >18		
123/112	UB + Rpd, or Rpd	23.5	Adult >18		
124/162	UN-UB + Rpd, or Rpd?	49.7	Sub-adult/adult *c.* 16–20		
153/152	Redeposited in possible inhumation burial	2.2	Adult >18		
155/154	Redeposited in possible inhumation burial	9.6	Sub-adult/adult >13		
157/156	UB? + Rpd, or Rpd	151.9	Sub-adult *c.* 16–18 (possibly + other immature skull vault)		
160/162	UN-UB + Rpd, or Rpd?	407.7	Adult *c.* 18–25 (<23) Female?? + some infant?		Possible animal bone
WB2/WB3	UN-UB + Rpd	255.4	Adult *c.* 20–40 Female??		Animal bone: immature sheep/pig size
EIII and EII6/ /EII2	UN-UB + Rpd	240.5	Adult > 18		Animal bone; pig, caprovid or roe deer, and large mammal

Key: UB = urned burial; UN-UB = unurned burial; Rpd = redeposited pyre debris

may have lost some bone as a result of disturbance. It has been observed (McKinley 2004, 297) that the average weight of bone from Romano-British urned burials appears to be consistently lower in cemeteries associated with military establishments in the 'frontier zones' of the North and West, for example at Low Borrowbridge (McKinley 1996), Brougham (McKinley 2004), and Caerleon (Wilkinson 1997), than in urned burials from other Romano-British cemeteries (McKinley 2004), and it is possible that this reflects a genuine variation in burial rite between the two types of cemetery (McKinley 2004, 297).

The largest recorded bone fragment from the Streamline Garage site was *c.* 64mm, with the maximum dimension from most deposits being relatively low, at 30–40mm. Most fragments were recovered from the 10mm sieve fraction (50–81% of the total from burials), though the 2mm fraction was not scanned and the figures might thus be slightly misleading. There are several factors which can affect the size of cremated bone fragments, the majority of which are independent of any deliberate human action other than cremation itself (McKinley 1994b). There is no conclusive indication of deliberate fragmentation within the bone from this site.

With the exception of one heavily disturbed fill (*123*, of burial *112*), all the burials included some identifiable elements from all areas of the skeleton and, as is commonly the case, there is no evidence to suggest deliberate selection of specific skeletal elements for burial. There are relatively few small bones, with only one tooth root, few phalanges, and even fewer carpals. A similar observation was made with respect to the burials from the cemetery at Brougham, where it was suggested that the scarcity of small bones might reflect the manner of collection from the pyre site at the end of cremation (McKinley 2004), possibly indicating hand recovery of individual fragments. The two possible cenotaph burials, *105* and *113*, with their very small quantities of bone (<10g), contained identifiable fragments of skull and upper limb alone, although in view of the fact that only 40–50% of the bone was identified to skeletal element, this might present a distorted view.

Pyre goods, in the form of cremated animal bone, were recovered from burials *WB3* – fill *WB2*: 46.9g, *162* – fill *160*: 0.9g and *E112* – fills *E111* and *E116*: 42.5g. The tradition of placing bones, or joints of meat, upon the pyre was common and widespread in the

Romano-British period, with 3.5% to 47% of burials from a range of cemeteries having been found to contain cremated animal remains (McKinley 2004). The difference in the charcoal assemblages recovered from the upper and lower fills of cremation *162*, the former (*124*) dominated by oak (*Quercus*), the latter (*160*) comprising principally alder (*Alnus*; below on p.45), suggests that these deposits may have come either from separate pyres, or from different parts of the same pyre.

Conclusion

The apparent variations between Romano-British cemeteries in the northern frontier zone and those throughout the rest of the country have been the subject of recent discussion (McKinley 2004), and the material from the Streamline Garage site shares some of the traits identified: these include uniformity of oxidation, low bone weights, lack of small bones, and the character of deposit types. The notion of a cenotaph deposit is not as unusual as it may at first appear (McKinley 2000c; 2004), and it has been proposed that, in some cases at least, these features may represent individuals foreign to the area, who were cremated in the vicinity of the site but whose remains were returned to their place of origin for formal burial (McKinley 1996; 2000c; 2004).

The Animal Bone
by Stephen Rowland and Andrew Bates

The small assemblages of animal bones recovered from the excavations were identified using the standards established by Halstead and Collins (1995), Hillson (1992) and Schmid (1972). All the material was calcined and extremely fragmentary, and certainly or probably derived from Roman funerary contexts; unburnt bone did not survive the unfavourable soil conditions, except for a few comparatively recent pieces from late post-medieval contexts, which were not analysed.

At 81 Penny Street, fill *151* of cremation *152* yielded a fragment of a bird long bone shaft, and another fragment from a similar bone came from the fill *76* of a post-medieval feature recorded at 77–79 Penny Street. The latter could have derived from a Roman funerary context, since this late deposit also contained several fragments of calcined human bone (see above on p.41). Both bones could conceivably represent the remains of food consumed during a funerary feast, or a food-offering placed on the funeral pyre. Also at 77–79 Penny Street, some small fragments of bone from medium-sized mammals (pig/sheep/roe deer) came from fill *107* of possible inhumation *103*, and a single piece of bone from a medium-sized mammal was recovered from fill *104* of putative inhumation *115*.

However, the best evidence for the deposition of animal bones with cremated human remains came from the Streamline Garage site. There, cremation burial *E112* yielded several small fragments of pig bones (including skull fragments, a piece of tibia and a metacarpal) and some of caprovid/roe deer (including a tibia which had clearly been broken prior to burning); there was also a fragment of tibia from a large mammal (cow/horse). Additionally, a small assemblage of burnt animal bone, including material consistent in size with an immature sheep or goat, came from the fill of cremation *160*, and a single small fragment was recovered from cremation *WB3*.

Charcoal and Charred Plant Remains
by Elizabeth Huckerby

A brief assessment was made of the charcoal and charred plant remains recovered from probable cremation *152* at 81 Penny Street, and from a number of cremations and other deposits excavated at the Streamline Garage site. No material from 77–79 Penny Street was appropriate for analysis.

Methodology

The sample from 81 Penny Street was hand-floated and the flot was collected on a 250 micron mesh and air dried. The flot was then scanned with a Leica MZ6 stereo microscope and the plant material was recorded and provisionally identified. With one exception, the samples from Streamline Garage were wet sieved to 2mm and air dried. The exception, from deposit *130*, was floated and the flot retained on a 250 micron mesh and air dried. The charcoal was scanned with a Leica MZ6 stereo microscope and 100% of the fragments from the smaller samples were examined; however, only a representative sample of the larger assemblages was assessed (Table 3.6). The charcoal was identified as mostly oak (*Quercus*), with some diffuse porous or other species (*Alnus* and *Prunus* sp., possibly blackthorn), and the relative proportions were noted. Plant remains were scored on a scale of abundance of 1–4 (shown as + to ++++ in Table 3.6), where 1 is rare (up to five items) and 4 is abundant (>100 items). The components of the matrix were also noted. Botanical nomenclature follows Stace (1997).

Results

At 81 Penny Street, the flot recovered from fill *151* of cremation *152* was rich in charcoal fragments (>2mm) and charred stems, the latter possibly of rushes (*Juncus*) and mosses, and included stem bases and rhizomes (Table 3.6). There were also occasional fragments of possible heather (*cf. Calluna*) stems. Most of the charcoal was oak (*Quercus*), but there were also some diffuse porous fragments, *Alnus* and *Prunus* sp., possibly blackthorn, which would have derived from short-lived taxa. Occasional charred weed seeds were identified, including blinks (*Montia* sp.) and sorrels (*Rumex* sp.).

Table 3.6 *Summary of charcoal and charred plant remains from 81 Penny Street and Streamline Garage, King Street Site*

Site	Context	Deposit type	Oak	Diffuse porous	Other
81 Penny Street					
	151	Fill of cremation 152	Mainly	++	Charred stems and rhizomes, possible heather; few charred weed seeds
Streamline Garage					
	107	Fill of cremation 103	+	One fragment	
	109	Fill of cremation 104	+		
	111	Fill of cremation 105	+	Mainly	
	115	Fill of cremation 113	+	Mainly	
	123 **	Fill of cremation 112 (same as 130)	+++		
	130	Fill of cremation 112 (same as 123)	Mainly	+	Roundwood; grass/rush stems; tuber fragment
	153	Fill of ?inhumation 152	50%	50%	
	155	Fill of ?inhumation 154	One fragment		One indeterminate
	157	Fill of cremation 156	+	+	Diffuse roundwood
	124	Upper fill of cremation 162	Mainly	+	One fragment pine
	160 **	Lower fill of cremation 162	+	Mainly	

** *indicates that only a representative sample of the charcoal from these contexts was examined*

The number of charcoal fragments in the Streamline Garage samples was relatively low, except from deposits *123=130* and *160*, the fills of cremations *112* and *162* respectively. Oak charcoal dominated the fills of cremations *103*, *104* and *112* – fills *107*, *109* and *123=130* respectively – whilst diffuse porous charcoal was dominant in fill *115* of burial *113*. The charcoal from the upper fill (*124*) of cremation *162* was mainly oak (*Quercus*), but that from the lower fill (*160*) was principally alder (*Alnus*). The remaining four deposits assessed, fills *111* and *157* of cremations *105* and *156*, and fills *153* and *155* of possible inhumations *152* and *154*, were more mixed.

Discussion

At 81 Penny Street, the presence of *Montia* seeds and possible rush/moss stems in fill *151* of cremation *152* suggests that some of the charred material in this feature may have come from a damp environment, as does the evidence of alder (*Alnus*) charcoal. The assessment of the charcoal from the Streamline Garage site revealed differences in the charcoal assemblages recovered from some of the excavated features. Perhaps the most notable is the apparent difference between the fills (*111* and *115*) of the two cremation burials identified as possible cenotaphs (*105* and *113*), above, which are dominated by diffuse porous taxa, probably alder/hazel (*Alnus/Corylus*), and most of the other cremations, where oak (*Quercus*) charcoal dominates (although

deposit *160*, the lower fill of cremation *162*, also contained mostly alder (*Alnus*) charcoal).

Since the sample from deposit *130*, the fill of cremation *112*, was processed in a different way from the other samples, charred plant materials in addition to charcoal were identified in the flot. These included grass/rush stems (Poaceae/*Juncus*) and a small fragment of plant tuber, identified as *cf.* onion-grass (*Arrhenatherum elatius* ssp. *Bulbosum*) (Denise Druce *pers. comm.* 2009). It is conceivable that these materials had been used as kindling.

The charcoal assemblage from deposits *124* and *160*, the upper and lower fills of cremation *162*, are markedly different from each other, *124* being dominated by oak (*Quercus*) and *160* by alder (*Alnus*) taxa. The precise significance of this remains unclear, but it may be of relevance that the cremated human remains from these deposits also exhibit some differences (above on p.42f). The bone from *124* was identified as that of a sub-adult or adult, *c.* 16–20 years of age, whilst the material from *160* represents the remains of a possible female, *c.* 18–25 years of age, together with some possible infant bones. This, taken together with the charcoal evidence, makes it conceivable that the two deposits derived from different funeral pyres (or different parts of the same pyre?), although the possibility that the sub-adult/adult bones from fill *124* actually derive from the putative adult female represented by the material in deposit *160* cannot be ruled out.

General Site Discussion

The Streamline Garage excavations of 2000–1 recovered evidence for two main phases of Romano-British occupation on the site. The earliest (Phase 1a) was represented by a rectilinear ditched enclosure (*131*) of uncertain purpose, which had gone out of use by the time a cemetery was established (Phase 1b), probably around the mid-second century AD. The 17 certain and possible burials recorded on the site comprised twelve cremations and five putative inhumations. A further six possible graves – four cremations and two features tentatively interpreted as inhumations – were found at 77–79 and 81 Penny Street, bringing the total number of burials for the three sites to 23. Structural evidence for medieval activity was limited to a single ditch or gully at the Streamline Garage site (Phase 2). This was sealed by a probable ploughsoil of late medieval to post-medieval date, which was in turn overlain by modern deposits of the nineteenth and twentieth centuries. At 77–79 Penny Street, post-Roman deposits comprised a post-medieval agricultural or horticultural soil overlain by nineteenth-century and later deposits, whilst the Romano-British cremation at 81 Penny Street was directly overlain by modern debris.

The Romano-British enclosure (*131*)

Enclosure *131* was probably rectangular in plan, 14.1m by at least 11.7m, and was defined by a reasonably substantial ditch, up to 1.65m wide and 0.6m deep. It was located a little over 20m west of modern Penny Street, which is thought to follow the line of a Roman road leading north to the River Lune (Shotter 2001a, 8; 20), and appears to have broadly shared the road alignment. The presence of black burnished ware Fabric 1 in one of the fills of the perimeter ditch indicates that this feature was silting-up in the second quarter of the second century AD, or later, but the date at which the ditch was dug, and when the enclosure was in use, is not known. A date in the early Romano-British period (late first to early second century AD) is presumed, but a late pre-Roman Iron Age origin cannot be completely discounted, since the ditch could, in theory, have been kept clean for many years before being allowed to silt up when the enclosure finally went out of use.

In view of the subsequent use of the site as a Romano-British cemetery, when cremation burials and other features were dug into the fills of its perimeter ditch, it is tempting to suggest that enclosure *131* may itself have been associated with funerary activity. Rectilinear funerary enclosures defined by ditches are known from the cemetery outside the fort at Low Borrowbridge in Cumbria (Hair and Howard-Davis 1996), although these were far smaller (only *c.* 1.5–4.5m wide, externally) than the Lancaster example, and most enclosed one or more burials. In the case of enclosure *131*, there is no evidence to support such an hypothesis,

and it seems more likely, in view of the lack of associated features, that it had some other purpose. One possibility is that it was associated with occupation within the settlement; excavations and (particularly) geophysical surveys undertaken at a number of military *vici* in the North, including those at Maryport on the Cumbrian coast (Biggins and Taylor 2004), and at Haltonchesters and Birdoswald on Hadrian's Wall (Breeze 2006, 182–3; 306–7), have demonstrated the existence of ditched enclosures on the periphery of the settled area, normally adjacent to the main roads. However, in view of its position, over 800m south of the centre of the settlement on Church Street, and well beyond its likely southern extent, together with the lack of evidence for internal features (despite the fact that most of the interior lay within the excavated area), and the paucity of associated artefactual material (only 15 sherds of pottery and six iron nails were recovered from the perimeter ditch fills), a domestic association seems unlikely. In the absence of any other evidence, it seems more probable that *131* had some kind of agricultural function, possibly as a pen for livestock.

The burials at Streamline Garage, 77–79 Penny Street and 81 Penny Street

On the evidence recovered from the recent excavations, and from the very limited data available from earlier discoveries in the Penny Street/King Street area, it would appear that the cemetery south of the Roman settlement at Lancaster was established during the second century AD. The seemingly widespread use of black burnished ware Fabric 1 jars as burial urns or grave goods in many of the recorded cremations, including up to six of those at the Streamline Garage site and the burial found in 1987 to the rear of 90 Penny Street (Ellis 1987; see above p.19), indicates that these graves must date to the Hadrianic period or later. In fact, the ceramic evidence from the Streamline Garage site suggests that the *floruit* of the cremation cemetery, in this area at least, was during the mid- to late second century.

It is possible, although unlikely (see above p.15), that the two cremation burials found on the Mitchell's Brewery site at the east end of Church Street (Howard-Davis *et al.* in prep) represent part of an early cemetery that was abandoned following the putative eastwards extension of the settlement in the second half of the second century (White 1975a), and this could conceivably provide a context for the establishment of the southern cemetery. However, the memorial stone of Insus from Aldcliffe Road (Bull 2007; see below pp.58f; 68ff) demonstrates that burials were already taking place well to the south of the settlement, adjacent to the main road south, by the late first to early second century, so it may be that the second half of the second century saw the intensified use and/or expansion of an existing burial ground.

The latest vessel associated with a cremation at the Streamline Garage site dates from the period *c.* AD 180–280, whilst the urned cremation found during the 1995 evaluation at 77–79 Penny Street, *c.* 60m to the north-east, was interred in a black burnished ware Fabric 1 jar datable to *c.* AD 230–300 (above on pp.36ff). That burial in the southern cemetery continued into the fourth century is, however, indicated by the 1996 excavation at 77–79 Penny Street. There, both of the possible inhumation burials, features *103* and *115*, produced calcite-gritted pottery of probable late third- to fourth-century date; furthermore, the uppermost fill (*107*) of the stratigraphically latest putative grave (*103*) yielded a calcite-gritted rim datable to *c.* AD 300–370. These features were overlain by a build-up of soils, some of which also yielded fragments of calcite-gritted pottery of the late third to fourth century, which were in turn cut by two probable unurned cremations (*78* and *98*) placed in small pits.

The presence of seemingly fourth-century cremation and inhumation burials at Lancaster is consistent with the evidence from elsewhere in the region. Across the Roman Empire as a whole, inhumation replaced cremation as the principal burial rite between the late second and late third century AD (Simmonds *et al.* 2008, 130), but in northern England, cremation appears to have been practised throughout the Roman period, being attested during the fourth century (and in some cases into the second half of the century) at several cemeteries in the North West, including those associated with the forts at Birdoswald (Wilmott 1993), Beckfoot (Caruana 2004, 154–5), Brough-under-Stainmore (Jones 1977), and Low Borrowbridge (Hair and Howard-Davis 1996, 99–101), and a probable rural settlement located *c.* 0.75km north of the fort at Old Carlisle (Grahame 1999, 3–4; Giecco 2000, 3).

The seven possible inhumation burials recorded during the investigations of 1995–2003 could be identified only tentatively as graves, since local soil conditions were not conducive to the preservation of unburnt bone, no grave goods were present, and little or no evidence for coffins, shrouds, or other grave furniture was recovered. The interpretation was, therefore, based principally on the fact that these were 'grave-like' features situated in what was clearly, on the evidence of the cremation burials, a Romano-British cemetery.

Of the seven putative burials, one – Streamline Garage burial *152* – produced only a few abraded sherds of black burnished ware Fabric 1, indicating a Hadrianic or later date, whilst another – Streamline Garage burial *154* – yielded pottery of the same fabric of the late second century. Streamline Garage burial *132* produced part of a grey ware vessel datable to the period *c.* AD 250–340; this was the latest Roman pottery recovered from that site. Burial at 77–79 Penny Street

also continued into the late third to fourth century, with both cremation and inhumation rites seemingly being practised at this time. In the case of the burials at 77–79 Penny Street, it was possible to demonstrate stratigraphically that the two cremations were later in date than the two putative inhumations. At the Streamline Garage site, however, one of the possible inhumation burials (*154*) cut two cremations (*105* and *113*), although it was not entirely clear whether feature *154* was indeed an inhumation, or was in fact a cremation placed in an unusually large pit. It has been suggested (above on p.41) that the two earlier cremations may have been cenotaphs rather than proper graves, since both contained extremely small quantities of bone.

The 16 certain or possible cremation burials from the three sites were all of broadly similar type, comprising quite small, sub-circular or oval pits containing small fragments of calcined human bone and pyre debris, either deposited in a container (normally a ceramic urn) or placed directly into the burial pit. The majority of the urned burials contained only one pottery vessel, namely the burial urn itself. In cases where fragments of other vessels were present, they appeared to have been smashed and/or heavily burnt. It seems likely that the burnt sherds represent the remains of vessels that had been placed on the funeral pyre, presumably to hold food or other material intended to accompany the deceased to the afterlife. Nails found in some of the graves hinted at the possible use of wooden boxes as containers, although it is possible that some or all of the nails derived from other funerary goods that had been placed on the pyre, or even from the pyre structure itself. Some of the unurned burials could also have been provided with containers fashioned from other forms of organic materials, such as leather or cloth, which would have left no trace in the archaeological record. Perhaps the best evidence for the use of a wooden container came from burial *162*, where a roughly circular, vertical-sided and flat-bottomed void, 0.3m in diameter, was visible within the fill of the burial pit. It seems quite likely that this marked the position of a round box similar to an oak example, 0.4m in diameter, found in association with a cremation in the Roman cemetery at Brough-under-Stainmore (Jones 1977, 19).

It was a consistent feature of all the excavated cremations that only a small proportion of the bone generated by the cremation process was actually deposited in the grave. This is a common feature of Romano-British cremations (Simmonds *et al* 2008, 128–9), and may reflect a belief that the ritual of interment was of greater significance than ensuring that all the remains of the deceased were collected and placed in the grave. It has been suggested (Barber and Bowsher 2000, 80) that it was the pyre site, and not the grave itself, which was the main focus for the funerary rite. This possible lack of concern for the physical remains of the dead, provided that the appropriate rituals were performed, is also reflected in instances of urned burials where some of the collected bone was not placed within the container, but was deposited in the grave pit, mixed with other pyre debris. This phenomenon was noted on the Streamline Garage site and is known from many other Romano-Britsh cemeteries, including Brougham (Cool 2004), Low Borrowbridge (Hair and Howard-Davis 1996), Trentholme Drive in York (RCHME 1962), Derby racecourse (Wheeler 1985) and in London (Barber and Bowsher 2000).

Other possible grave/pyre goods recorded on the site were confined to collections of hobnails, probably representing the remains of shoes that had been placed either on the funeral pyre (perhaps being worn by the deceased) or in the grave, and, in two cases only, fragments of animal bone. There is a considerable amount of evidence from Roman Britain that the provision of footwear was a symbolic gesture, presumably intended to facilitate the deceased's journey to the afterlife (Barber and Bowsher 2000, 137; Philpott 1991, 173). Animal bones, presumably derived from joints of meat provided for consumption in the afterlife, are also frequently found in Romano-British burials (Worley 2008, 121). The three examples from the Streamline Garage site were burnt, suggesting that they derived from offerings placed on the funeral pyre, although it is possible they were the remains of a meal consumed by the mourners at the graveside.

The vessels found within the graves were restricted to jars, flagons and beakers. Most of the jars had been utilised as burial urns, although in some cases heavily burnt; broken sherds may have derived from vessels placed on the funeral pyre, which had perhaps held food for consumption by the deceased. The inclusion of flagons and beakers, both forms associated with drinking, within the grave assemblages might also have been of significance (Wheeler 1985, 266–7), perhaps being associated with ritual meals or the provision of drink for the deceased.

The post-Roman period

It seems clear that the area in which the Streamline Garage and Penny Street sites lay was peripheral to the medieval and early post-medieval town. At 81 Penny Street, Roman levels lay directly beneath modern debris, a consequence of late post-medieval truncation, but at the other two sites extensive deposits of probable ploughsoil were recorded, sealing Roman levels and in turn overlain by nineteenth- to twentieth-century remains. The only medieval feature recorded, a gully or narrow ditch at the south-east corner of the Streamline Garage site, was aligned roughly perpendicular to modern King Street, and was most probably the remains of a field boundary. The soil which this cut, containing both Roman and medieval finds, is interpreted as a plough soil representing the medieval and later agricultural occupation of the site (LUAU 1997, 8f; LUAU 2001a, 13).

At all three sites, intensive occupation does not appear to have commenced before the nineteenth century, although the evidence of maps points to occupation alongside Penny Street from at least the early seventeenth century (Penney 1981a, 22 and Fig. 4). Housing development along King Street and Henry Street appears in 1807, and there is further development shown on Binns' map of 1821 (LUAU 1997, 9f). The OS 1:500 mapping of 1892 shows considerable detail, and two yards, 'Railway Inn Yard' and 'Queen's Place', are named. By this date, most of the formerly empty land within the Streamline Garage site had been occupied, principally by a steam-powered saw mill and timber yard complex. Changes occurred in the detailed layout of these structures, but they seem to have persisted until the development of the modern garage site in the mid-twentieth century. Re-grading associated with that development, as well as the insertion of concrete stanchion bases and underground tankage, resulted in major disturbance and presumably led to the loss of earlier deposits, particularly on the northern part of the site.

CHAPTER 4

Excavations on the Site of the Arla Foods Depot, Aldcliffe Road, 2005

by Peter Iles and Peter Noble

With contributions *by Charlotte O'Brien, Christine Howard-Davis, David Shotter, Paul Holder, Ben Edwards, †Fred Broadhurst and Andrew White*

Introduction

Between October 2003 and February 2006, the University of Manchester Archaeological Unit (UMAU) undertook several phases of archaeological work at the former Arla Foods Depot site, on land off Aldcliffe Road, Lancaster, as part of a redevelopment scheme. These works consisted of a desk-based assessment and evaluation trenching, followed by open-area excavation of a portion of the site and then a watching brief during the redevelopment. The site lies at the southern edge of Lancaster's town centre, *c.* 20m north of the Lancaster Canal (SD 47696129), and consists of a sub-rectangular area of land, 63m north-north-west to south-south-east and a maximum of 30m west-south-west to east-north-east (Fig. 4.1). The northern, and part of the western, boundaries abut the former Streamline Garage site (chapter 3 above).

Trial excavation (UMAU 2005) had revealed that the majority of the site was underlain by a series of cellars and walls, of late eighteenth- to nineteenth-century date. The southern portion of the site, which originally served as the depot's car park, was not, however, so heavily disturbed and included the remains of the Roman road that entered Lancaster from the south. As a result, formal excavation of this area was required prior to development commencing, with the remainder of the site being subject to a watching brief. The excavation area measured *c.* 12m north west to south east by *c.* 25m north east to south west (Fig. 4.1; Plate 4.1), and was excavated following the demolition of the depot's portal-framed building to ground level.

This work revealed cut features, deposits and structures of prehistoric to nineteenth-century date, but the most significant archaeology was of Romano-British date, and included the discovery of a substantial Roman (Reiter) cavalry memorial stone, of the 'rider and barbarian' type. This is a unique discovery for Lancaster, and the object is of international significance.

Several soil layers on the site effectively sealed earlier activity and thus facilitated phasing. A general lack of diagnostic artefacts from key features, however, meant that these phases were generally based only on their stratigraphic relationships and only approximate date ranges are suggested (UMAU 2007).

Not all fills and layers encountered on the site are described in detail here; those details are available in the site report (UMAU 2007). This chapter will again use the convention of setting the context numbers in italics *321*.

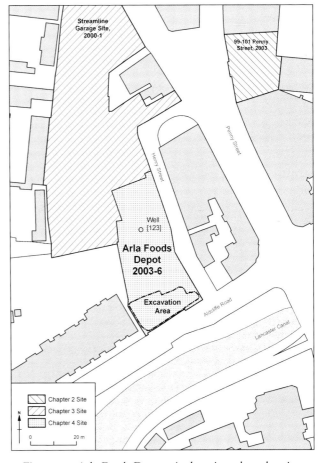

Figure 4.1 Arla Foods Depot: site location plan, showing excavation area

Plate 4.1 Arla Foods Depot: general view of excavation area

The whole site was underlain by a micaceous mid- to dark-purple-red sandstone (Millstone Grit). The drift sealing this comprised a friable light to mid-yellow-brown silt clay, with a maximum depth of 0.3m.

Results of the Excavation

Phase 1a: Neolithic

The earliest activity on the site was represented by shallow sub-circular pit *35* (Fig. 4.2; Plate 4.2), 1.08m north to south by 1.04m east to west, with irregular sides and a flat base and a maximum depth of 0.22m (Fig. 4.3). It was cut into the natural drift geology and contained three fills (earliest to latest: *36, 34, 37*), of which the uppermost (*37*) included an abundance of charred hazelnut fragments (see Palaeoenvironmental Report on p.83f).

These hazelnut fragments suggest that the pit may have been used for food-storage or the disposal of domestic waste. A sample of the hazelnuts provided a date of 3240 calBC – 3100 calBC (4550 +/- 30 BP; SUERC-22506, GU-18140), in the Neolithic period. It may be notable that the only other significant find of this period within the City consisted of fragments of a Mortlake bowl from Church Street (Penney 1978; 1981a, 9), and that discoveries of the Bronze Age are far more common in Lancaster (see chapter 2).

Phase 1b: Prehistoric to Romano-British

Two buried soil horizons, *54* overlain by *53*, were uncovered during the excavations. The earlier of these (*54*; Figs 4.4, 4.5, 4.6 and 4.7; Plate 4.3), comprised a friable dark-brown clay silt, which extended across the entire excavation area, although it varied in depth, thinning to only 20mm in several places. It was sampled for environmental data (see below on p.83f), but the

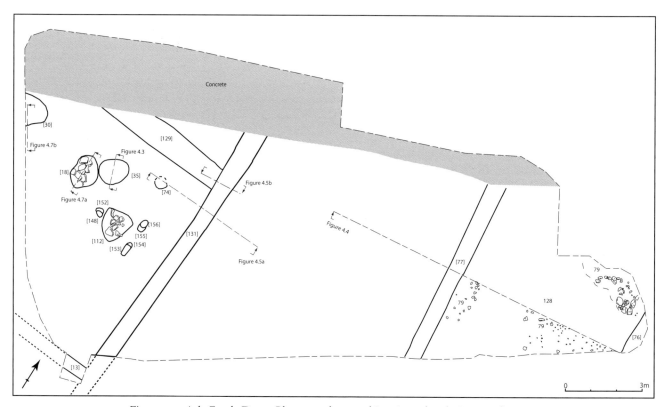

Figure 4.2 Arla Foods Depot Phase 1 and 2a: prehistoric and early Roman features

Plate 4.2 Arla Foods Depot: west-facing section of pit *35*

results were disappointing. The few grains of pollen suggest that hazel and oak probably grew in the vicinity, with the few local herbs suggesting open ground nearby with some damp areas. This soil clearly post-dates Neolithic pit *35*.

Deposit *30* (Figs 4.2 and 4.7b; Plate 4.3) lay in the extreme north-western corner of the excavation area and clearly extended to the west. The visible portion measured 1.95m east to west by 1.44m north to south, and had a height of 0.9m. It was a mid- to dark-grey sand silt clay deposit with regular small sub-rounded stones and occasional charcoal inclusions, forming an irregular convex mound, perhaps originally of turf. It lay above the earlier buried soil layer (*54*) but the buried soil (*53*) appeared to have built up against it. This feature seems to represent a bank or mound, which was constructed on top of (thus post-dating) soil *54*, before soil *53* began to form.

Soil *53* was also seen across the entire site, sealing *54*. This was a mid-brown sand clay silt with regular small to medium sub-rounded stones and a maximum depth of 0.46m. In several areas this layer appeared mottled and disturbed, most noticeably on the western part of the site, but the reason for this is unclear.

Environmental sampling recovered an uncharred fat-hen seed that may have grown either as an arable weed or as a ruderal on areas of waste or disturbed ground, and a few hazelnut fragments were also recovered. A very small number of alder and pine pollen grains were also present; given the low number of these, no real conclusions can be drawn, except to suggest that tree cover in this vicinity appears to have been very sparse. Microscopic charcoal fragments may also suggest some localised fires, perhaps related to clearance, although the later use of the adjacent Streamline Garage site (chapter 3) as a cremation cemetery may suggest another source. The top of soil *53* is taken to represent the ground surface at the beginning of the Romano-British period.

Phase 2a: Road *128* and Enclosure 1 (*c.* late first to early second century AD)

The construction of road *128* and its associated ditches (*76* and *77*; Figs 4.2 and 4.4; Plate 4.4) was evidently the primary Roman act on the site, and all other features within this period were to a large extent dictated by their presence. This road is part of the main route from Lancaster to the south, branching at Galgate to both Ribchester and Wigan (Route 70a: Margary 1957, 90–1), which although undated is undoubtedly early.

The road crossed the site in a north-north-east to south-south-west direction, with an excavated length of 6.8m, the remains continuing to both the north and south of the excavated area. It had a width of 6.95m in the excavation area, which is *c.* 0.5m wider than the average width recorded of Roman roads in Britain and compares to that found at Watling Street West and Devil's Highway (Davies 2002, 57).

The surviving structure of the road was composed of two deposits, a wearing or metalling layer (*79*), over a foundation layer (*80*), the two forming a raised linear mound or *agger* (Fig. 4.4; Margary 1955, 13–16). The basal layer was composed of large water-rolled cobbles and boulders in a matrix of very compact mixed mid-brown silt sand clay and coarse gravel, with a depth of 0.25m. Only some 0.32–0.39m survived of the upper

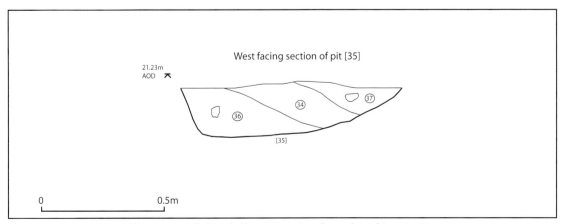

Figure 4.3 Arla Foods Depot: section through prehistoric pit *35*

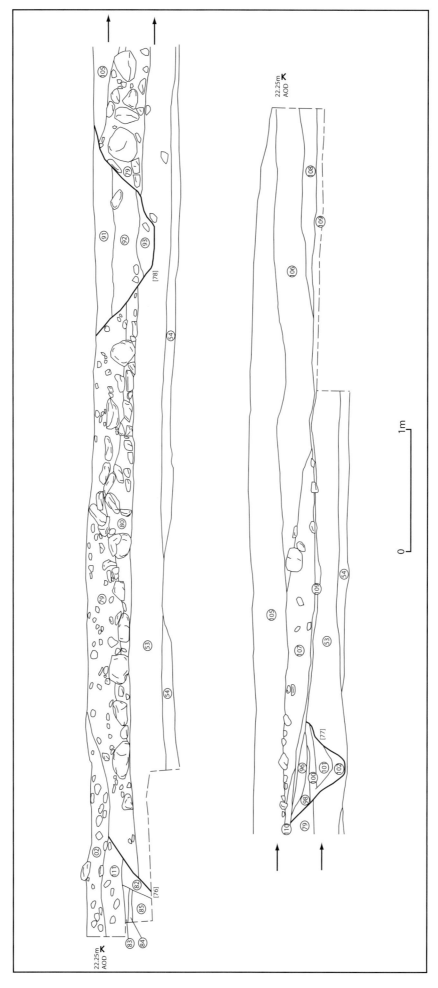

Figure 4.4 Arla Foods Depot: section through the Roman road

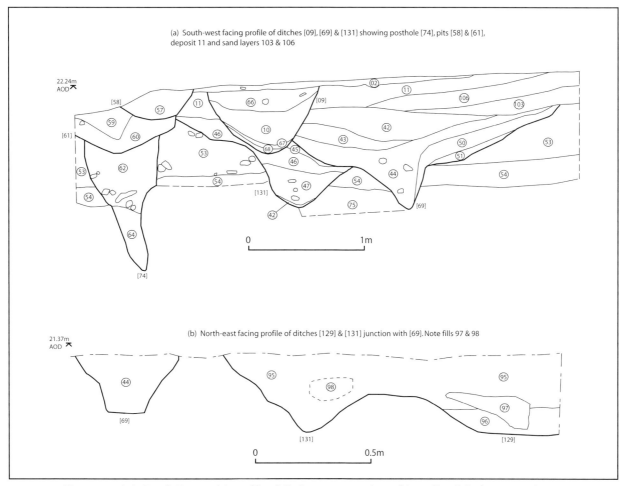

Figure 4.5 Arla Foods Depot: (a) profile of ditches 09, 69 and 131; (b) profile of ditches 129 and 131

layer; it comprised a compact coarse mid-brown sand gravel with pockets of clay and frequent small to medium pebbles. No evidence of repair or wheel rutting were observed, but it is possible that any evidence for such, along with an unknown depth of the upper surface, has been removed by later agriculture (Phase 3; below on p.61f).

As is usual (Bagshawe 1979, Fig. 3; 15), the road was closely flanked by drainage ditches on the east (*76*) and west (*77*), although only the latter was fully exposed in the excavation area (Figs 4.2 and 4.4). The eastern ditch (*76*) was seen projecting from the eastern section and was >0.5m wide and >0.23m deep. Western ditch *77* (Plate 4.5) was 0.65m wide and 0.32m deep and was cut into the upper of the two buried soils (*53*). It had a sub-U-shaped profile with a rounded base, that lay 0.5m below the top of the surviving road metalling. If both ditches had a similar width, it can be assumed that the total width of the road and ditches was 8.25m.

The roadside ditches subsequently filled with a series of soils (Fig. 4.4), which presumably derived from material washed off the road and surrounding area (earliest to latest: *102, 101, 100, 98* in ditch *77*; *82, 85, 84, 83, 111* in ditch *76*). Ditch *77* was subsequently sealed by thin deposits of sand and clay (earliest to latest: *96, 109, 110*) with a combined thickness of 50–80mm (Fig. 4.4), which accumulated against the camber of the road.

Plate 4.3 Arla Foods Depot: buried soils *54* and *53*, with pit *35* (foreground), feature *18* (centre) and feature *30* (rear)

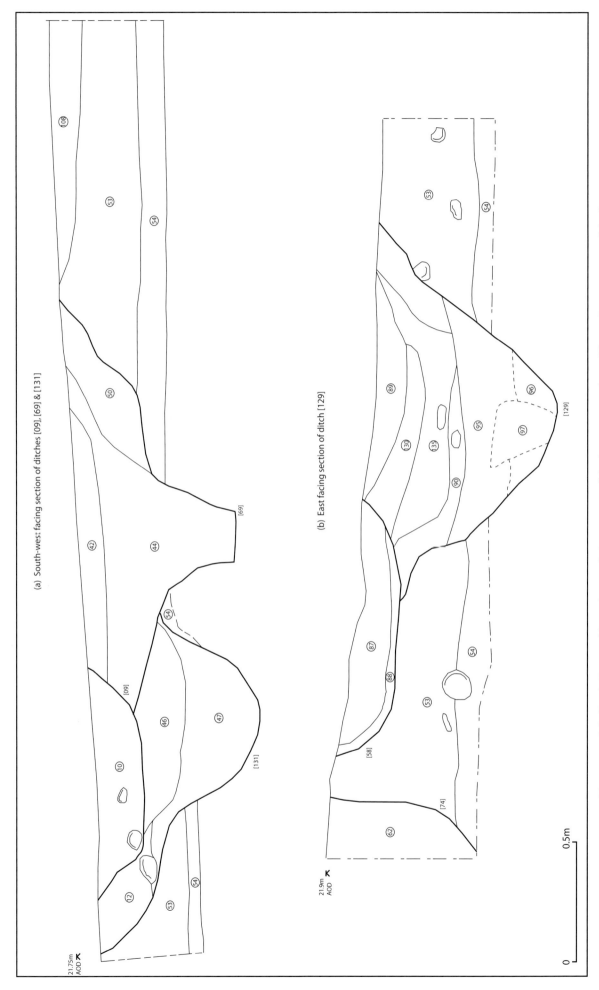

(a) South-west facing section of ditches [09], [69] & [131]

(b) East facing section of ditch [129]

Figure 4.6 Arla Foods Depot: (a) south-west facing section of ditches 09, 69 and 131; (b) east facing section of ditch 129

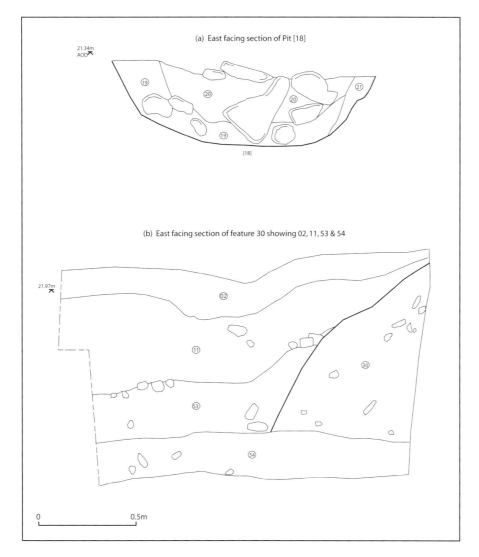

Figure 4.7 Arla Foods Depot: (a) east facing section of pit 18; (b) east facing section of feature 30

Plate 4.4 Arla Foods Depot: road *128* viewed from the west

Enclosure 1

The enclosure ditches

A large ditch (*131*) lay approximately 6.5m to the west of road *128* (Figs 4.2, 4.5a,b and 4.6a), and was aligned approximately parallel to it. It extended to the north east and south west of the excavation but was traced for 9.7m and was up to 0.82m deep. The original width is uncertain, as its eastern edge had been truncated by a later recut (Phase 2b; below on p.57) leaving only the rounded base and western edge, which was stepped in profile. These parts had a width of 1.5m, which would suggest – if the eastern edge had similar dimensions to the western – that the original ditch measured *c.* 2.2m in width. A thin lens (1mm) of indurated iron pan (*42*) denoted the basal edge, and the ditch also contained a lens of basal silt (*72*) and fill *47*, sealed by fill *46* and then *45*. Fill *47* was a particularly distinctive plastic mid-brown-red clay, which notably contained a pocket of plastic very dark-blue-grey organic clay (*98*), 0.3m long by 0.2m wide and 0.1m deep, at the junction with ditch *129* (below).

It has been noted that ditch *131* lies nearly 30 Roman feet (or one-quarter of an *actus*) from the edge of the road, and it seems probable that its original function was to mark out the 'road-zone' (Margary 1955, 16) and thus to define the edge of any roadside activities.

Subsequently, a large east-south-east to west-north-west aligned ditch (*129*) (Figs 4.2 and 4.5b) was cut adjoining, and at a right angle to, ditch *131*, with the junction 1.4m south west of the northern limit of excavation (Fig. 4.2; Plates 4.6 and 4.7). This feature, like *131*, had a stepped profile with a rounded base (Figs 4.5b and 4.6b), and measured in excess of 5.2m long (it extended north west of the excavated area) by 1.6m wide and 0.82m deep. The ditch was filled with a series of deposits (earliest to latest: *96*, *95*, *90*, *132*, *133*, *130* and *89*). A single fragment of late second- to mid-third-century samian ware was recovered from fill *132*. At the junction of ditches *131* and *129* fill *95* was shown to be identical with fill *47* of ditch *131* and it is notable that, as *47* contained a lens of organic clay (*98*) at this point,

Plate 4.5 Arla Foods Depot: roadside western ditch *77*; note sand layers *105*, *106*, *107* and *108* sealing ditch fills

Plate 4.6 Arla Foods Depot: junction of ditches *131* and *129*; ditch *69* is in the foreground

Plate 4.7 Arla Foods Depot: north-east facing section of ditches *69*, *129* and *131*; note junction between *129* and *131*

fill *95* also contained a pocket of a very similar clay (*97*), measuring 0.37m long by 0.26m wide and 0.26m deep (Fig. 4.6b). The basal profiles of the two ditches, as shown in Fig. 4.5b, indicate that *129* was cut subsequently to (perhaps immediately after) *131*, and their common fills indicate that they were open at the same time.

A small (4m east to west by 1.4m north to south) machine-excavated sondage was placed in the extreme south-western corner of the site. No hand excavation was undertaken for health and safety reasons, and results were limited. However, a 1.8m long section of a ditch (*13*; Fig. 4.2) was discovered, aligned east-south-east to west-north-west. It had a width of 0.65m, was filled with a compact light to mid-brown-red clay (*14*), and had a depth of >0.5m. It is unfortunate that no clear and established relationship exists between this and any other Romano-British ditches, making its interpretation uncertain. However, like feature *129*, which was situated *c.* 8.2m to the north, it was aligned perpendicular to ditch *131*, and there was a clear similarity between fills *47*=*95* and *14*. It is possible, although less likely, that ditch *13* could be associated with either ditch *69* (Phase 2b below) or *09* (Phase 2d below), but on balance it seems most likely that it was broadly contemporary to and associated with ditches *131* and *129* and that together they define three sides of a rectilinear enclosure – termed Enclosure 1 for convenience, although no other such enclosures were encountered – measuring 8.2m north-north-east to south-south-west by >5.2m east-south-east to west-north-west (Fig. 4.2). It has also been noted that the distance between the external edges of ditches *13* and *129* is 30 Roman feet, which tends to suggest a deliberate relationship between the two features.

Internal features

Within the excavated area of Enclosure 1, a possible contemporary feature (*18*) was located (Figs 4.2 and 4.7a; Plate 4.3). This was a sub-oval pit measuring 1.38m north to south by 1.0m east to west, with very steep sides, a flat base, and a maximum depth of 0.62m. It shared many similarities in form and its fill matrix with a later pit *112* (below on p.58f); no other features within the site were found to contain such large water-rolled stones. In pit *112* these stones were used to pack the memorial stone's base and it is probable, therefore, that pit *18* was another setting for a memorial stone.

Phase 2b: enclosure 1; recutting of the eastern ditch (?second century AD?)

Following the filling of ditch *131*, the eastern boundary of Enclosure 1 was redefined on much the same line by a new ditch *69*, which had been dug alongside but still within the upper fills of the earlier feature (Figs 4.5a, 4.6a and 4.8; Plates 4.6 and 4.7). Ditch *69* was traced south-south-west to north-north-east across the whole of

the excavated area and was 0.84m deep. The full width of the ditch was unclear, as a later ditch on the same alignment (*09*) truncated its western edge (below on p.60), although a near-complete profile was recorded. It had a surviving width of 2.37m and was estimated to have had an original width of *c.* 2.75m, with a stepped profile, and gently sloping sides. There was, however, a noticeable difference in the profile of the base between the two sections excavated. In the section to the south it had a steep V-shaped base (Fig. 4.5a), whereas, in the northern section, the base was distinctly square in profile (Fig. 4.6a). One of the fills within the ditch (*44*) was a compact and plastic light to mid-brown-red clay, with similarities to fills *47*=*95*=?*14* in ditches *13*, *129* and *131* of Phase 2a discussed above. The precise date and purpose of ditch *69* is unclear, although it appears to represent the redefinition of the roadside area.

Phase 2c: accumulation of sand and soil deposits (?second century AD)

Remodelling of the land surface immediately adjacent to road *128* then occurred. This was characterised by a series of sand deposits (earliest to latest: *105*, *106*, *107* and *108*; Figs 4.4, 4.5a, 4.6a and 4.9; Plates 4.4 and 4.5), which possibly served to facilitate roadside drainage. These extended over the western edge of the road surface for *c.* 0.8m (Fig. 4.4), but did not encroach further onto the road. They completely sealed the western roadside ditch (*77*), although both of the roadside ditches were already redundant by this point. They extended west from the road for 6–8m, sealing ditch *69* of Phase 2b and at least partially overlying Phase 2a ditch *129*, which marked the northern

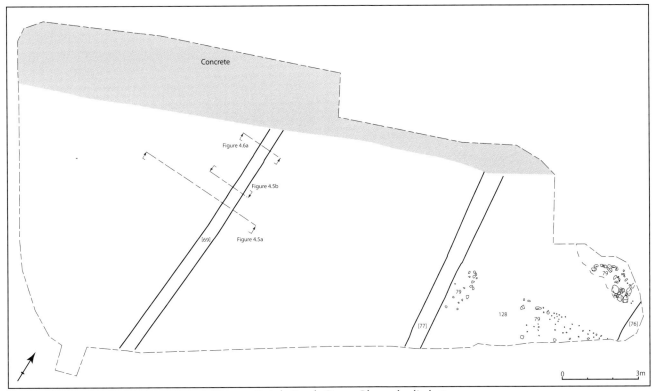

Figure 4.8 Arla Foods Depot Phase 2b: ditch 69

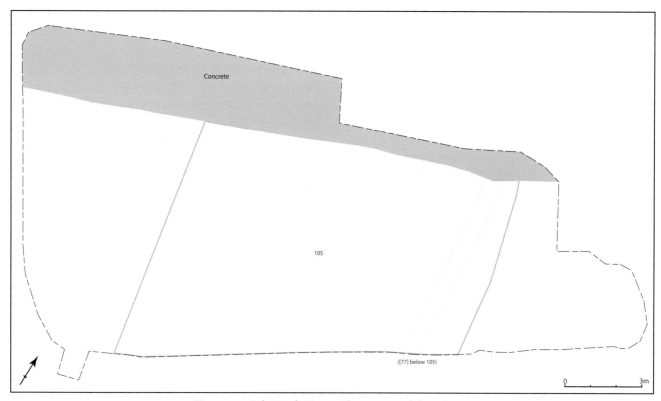

Figure 4.9 Arla Foods Depot Phase 2c: sand deposit 105

boundary of Enclosure 1. It seems clear, therefore, that the enclosure boundaries had wholly or largely disappeared by this date. To the east of the road another sand deposit (*111*) was identified in the limited area available for excavation, where it sealed the eastern roadside ditch (*76*); this layer continued to the east of the excavated area. Due to root disturbance and chemical reaction, it cannot be determined whether these layers reflect a single phase or a series of events.

These deposits appear to have been an attempt to rectify the problem of the silted up roadside ditches, by creating a wide and free-draining berm to either side. This interpretation was also applied to similar deposits recorded on the principal Manchester to Ribchester Roman road at Starling, Lancashire, by the Bury Archaeological Group (GMAG, 1980).

Further to the west, broadly within the area of Enclosure 1, the sand deposits were overlain by soil layer *11* (Fig. 4.5a; Plate 4.5). This was a friable light to mid-grey-brown clay sand silt with occasional small to medium stones and a maximum depth of 0.46m. This deposit had been affected by root and plough action, and the interface between this layer and those above and below was often indistinct. It is unclear whether it represented a natural build-up of soil or a deliberate deposition event. Stratigraphically it appears after the remodelling of the roadside drainage system, and it is possible that the material was imported in order to raise the ground level to reflect the changes alongside the road. It is notable that soil *11* sealed feature *18*, which has been proposed as a memorial stone setting; if a

stone had been present when this deposit was laid down, its bottom portion would have been obscured.

Phase 2d: recutting of the eastern boundary ditch and erection of the memorial stone (?late second to early third century AD)

A pit (*112*) was located approximately 2m south east of feature *18* of Phase 2a, its front edge being some 2.5m closer to the line of road *128*. It lay within the area of Enclosure 1 but was stratigraphically later than it (Fig. 4.10; Plates 4.8 and 4.9). It was sub-circular, being 1.2m north to south by 1.1m east to west, with an irregular base (Fig. 4.11a), having a flat south-eastern half (depth 0.4m) and a sub-rounded north-western half (depth 0.47m); this contrast was mirrored in the edges of the cut, since it had a vertical/undercut south-eastern edge and a stepped north-western edge. It was packed with large water-rolled stones, like pit *18*. The major feature of the pit was the *in situ* basal section of the Roman memorial stone (*03*), that was secured vertically within it by stone packing, and protruded 0.32m above the pit. This roughly triangular stone segment measured a maximum of 0.55m high by 0.91m wide and 0.16m thick; it was orientated with its long axis pointing north east to south west, approximately parallel with the Roman road.

The upper sculpted portion of the memorial stone had broken off in antiquity from the base-section and lay flat, with its carved face down, immediately to the east-south-east; this was presumably the direction in which it was originally facing. The force of the impact

Plate 4.8 Arla Foods Depot: showing memorial stone *03* just after discovery; note basal section *in situ* within pit *112*; viewed from the west

had created two further major fractures towards the top of the stone, which parted fully during excavation and removal. The whole of the upper section measured 1.83m long by 0.91m wide by 0.16m thick and, together with the basal fragment, the minimum overall length of the memorial stone was 2.14m. It should be noted that the upper, fractured, edge of the basal portion does not match the basal fracture of the main body of the stone (although it is clearly part of the same item, see specialist reports below) indicating that a portion of unknown size has been lost between the two sections.

As the memorial stone had fallen face down, and was apparently associated with an adjacent stone wall (*04*, Phase 4, below), it was initially assumed to be a stray fragment of flagged floor and was turned over without being recorded *in situ* (Plate 4.8). It is fortuitous that the builders of that wall did not attempt to remove the stone, as it might well have been lost like other Roman memorials from Lancaster (see above, chapter 2).

Some fragments of burnt oak were recovered from fill *114* of pit *112* (see Palaeoenvironmental Report below), but no cremated bone was found within the fill of this feature nor was there any evidence of a burial having taken place. Indeed, only one very small and unidentified fragment of burnt bone was recovered from the entire site (see feature *09*, p.60 below). Whilst it is possible that heavy ploughing during the medieval period could account for the removal or disturbance of any surface or shallow deposits and could potentially have removed evidence relating to late burial practices, this could not account for any truncation or loss at a deeper level, such as within the fills of this socket or the loss of complete burial pits at the same level. It would also seem unlikely that any burials were

Plate 4.9 Arla Foods Depot: south-west facing section of pit *112*

deliberately removed, as opposed to being disturbed by later burials as at 79–81 Penny Street (above) during the Romano-British period, due to the strict laws protecting them against later disturbance (though see Esmonde Cleary 1987, 192–3 for an apparent example of Romano-British disturbance of a burial). It also appears that the soil conditions were such that cremated bone would survive, given their recovery from the adjacent Streamline Garage site and the conclusion there that the burial micro-environment was not adverse to good preservation of burnt bone (see chapter 3 above, p.40).

A fragment of another stone inscribed in Latin (*15*) was encountered within socket *112* (Plate 4.10), where it was being used as packing for the basal stub of the memorial stone (*03*). Its association with this socket is secure, though it is from an unrelated stone (below, pp.76; 82) that presumably had been broken prior to this fragment being used as packing. The uppermost fill for the stone setting also contained three sherds of Severn Valley ware pottery.

Two postholes, subsequently both recut, 0.65m apart, (*153/154* and *155/156*, Figs 4.10 and 4.11b; Plate 4.11) were uncovered, lying *c.* 0.4m to the east of stone setting *112*. These postholes appear to share a north-east to south-west alignment parallel with Roman road *128*. A third posthole, also subsequently recut (*148/152*; Figs 4.10 and 4.11c), lay 50mm to the west of the stone setting pit, which, together with those mentioned above, formed a triangular grouping around the stone setting pit. It is not, however, easy to find a convincing functional relationship between these postholes.

Plate 4.10 Arla Foods Depot: fragment of inscribed stone *15* from pit *112*

Stratigraphically contemporary with *112* and its associated features was ditch *09* (Figs 4.5a, 4.6a and 4.10). This was orientated north-north-east to south-south-west and crossed the whole of the excavated area. It was 1m wide with a U-shaped profile with a maximum depth of 0.55m, and was closely aligned with the earlier ditch *131* of Phase 2a, the eastern boundary of Enclosure 1. It may therefore represent an attempt to re-define the edge of the enclosure or roadside zone. The ditch contained a series of four fills (earliest to latest: *68*, *67*, *10* and *66*) of which *68* was a light red/brown clay

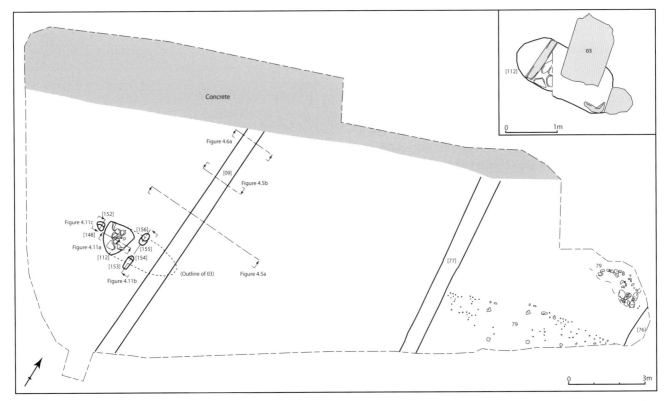

Figure 4.10 Arla Foods Depot Phase 2d: Reiter memorial stone pit 112 and ditch 09; insert shows memorial stone lifted out of place

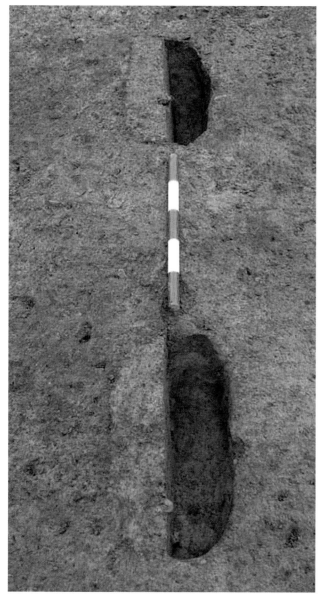

Plate 4.11 Arla Foods Depot: postholes *153/154* and *155/156*

with similarities to deposits *47=95=?14* in ditches *131*, *129* and *13* of Phase 2a, and fill *44* from ditch *69* of Phase 2b.

Some 85 sherds, representing most of a Severn Valley ware vessel, and a single very small fragment of unidentified burnt bone were recovered from the upper fill (*66*) of ditch *09*; a further pottery sherd, presumed to belong to the same jar was found within lower fill *10*. There was no evidence of internal or external sooting upon the jar as would have been expected in the case of a vessel that had been placed upon a pyre. The discovery of this jar in the uppermost fill of the enclosure ditch, and in particular the observation that it was originally placed in the ground upside-down, would strongly suggest that this was a deliberate placement, perhaps as part of a funerary or other rite.

Phase 2: not closely dated

Feature *74* (Figs 4.2 and 4.5a) was a sub-circular cut for a posthole, measuring 0.7m by 0.65m and having a V-shaped profile. The posthole was off-vertical, lying

westwards, with its base offset by 0.12m at a depth of 1.15m. It was located within Enclosure 1 (Phase 2a), *c.* 1.5m north of the memorial stone setting *112* but almost directly beneath the cut for a late eighteenth- to early nineteenth-century wall (Phase 4, *07*; below on pp.62ff). Because of this later interference, posthole *74* could be seen cutting only the later of the two Phase 1 buried soils (*53*), and had no relationships with other Romano-British deposits. Any interpretation must therefore be limited and its inclusion within this grouping is based solely on the morphology of its fills. It would seem to represent the setting for a large wooden upright, with a characteristic V-shaped profile and undercut base. Whether this feature is associated with the cemetery and/or ritualistic practice is unknown, but it is possible that it may have acted as the socket for a wooden marker post. Parallels of a sort for this practice are known, with several of the burials at Petty Knowes, Northumberland, having associated postholes that were interpreted as such markers (Charlton and Mitcheson 1984, 21 and Fig. 5 on p. 16).

Phase 3: medieval to early post-medieval activity (*c.* twelfth to seventeenth centuries)

The latest Romano-British deposits on the site were sealed by layer *02* (Figs 4.5a and 4.7b), a 0.4m thick deposit of mottled and friable mid-grey to light-brown clay silt sand with very frequent small to medium water-rolled pebbles. These stones lay mainly at the base of the layer and formed a regular horizon over the underlying deposits. Layer *02* was found across the entire excavation area (thinning to the north), though the density of stones lessened noticeably to the west of the site, with the highest concentration lying adjacent to the line of the Roman road. These stones were similar in size and shape to those contained within the make-up of the upper part of the road and would appear to denote a disturbed spread of this material. This spread may thus represent the displaced remains of the upper levels of the road make-up (*79*), though perhaps it denotes a truncated layer above this that formed the surface metalling of the road (above on pp.51ff).

Sherds of pottery of the thirteenth to fourteenth centuries and a silver cut halfpenny, probably of Edward I or II (below on p.68), were recovered from layer *02*. It is probable that this layer represents medieval (and possibly early post-medieval) agricultural activity, with the pottery redeposited either as a rubbish spread or through manuring.

Towards the north-west corner of the site was a concave cut, *33*, possibly for a pit or ditch (Fig. 4.12), measuring 1.08m east to west by *c.* 0.3m north to south with a depth of 0.31m. This had no surviving stratigraphic relationship with layer *02*, but both of its fills contained sherds of thirteenth- to fourteenth-century pottery (below, p.67f). It may have been a pit

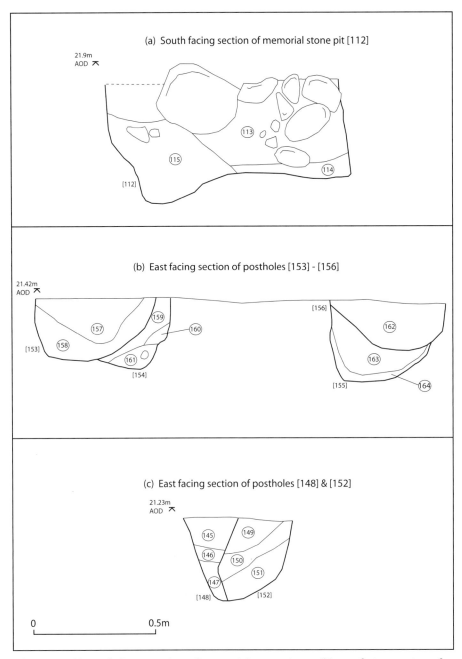

Figure 4.11 Arla Foods Depot: (a) south facing section of memorial stone pit 112; (b) east facing section of postholes 153, 154, 155 and 156; (c) east facing section of postholes 148 and 152

or possibly a ditch, though no evidence for its continuation was seen in other sections. It is equally possible that it represents a plough-furrow associated with, or later than, soil *02.*

Cutting this soil layer (*02*) towards the south-eastern corner of the site was a substantial ditch, *78*, which was traced for 3.4m (Fig. 4.12; Plate 4.12). This was aligned north-north-east to south-south-west, broadly parallel with the earlier Roman features on the site, including road *128*, through the surface of which it had been cut. It had stepped sides and a sub-flat base (Figs 4.4 and 4.13b), with a width of 1.9m and a maximum depth of 0.83m. To the north it had been destroyed by late post-medieval walls and cellars (Phase 4), whilst to the south it extended beyond the limits of excavation. Towards its southern end it was also pierced by a modern

geotechnical pit (*117*), excavated immediately prior to the demolition of the Depot itself. As no artefacts were recovered from the fills of ditch *78*, its precise date is uncertain.

Phase 4: later post-medieval activity (*c.* eighteenth to twentieth centuries)

Layer *127* was a friable mid grey/brown sand clay with regular small sub-rounded stones with a depth of 0.25m. It covered the entire site sealing ditch *78* and soil *02* of Phase 3, but was itself cut and overlain by walls, cellars and other features and deposits of late post-medieval date. It yielded a number of small finds dating from the fifteenth to the twentieth centuries (below, p.67f). It is possible that the sixteenth- to seventeenth-century sherd recovered from *02*, together with two

Plate 4.12 Arla Foods Depot: relationship between ditch *78* and road *128*; viewed from the south

sherds from *127* of similar date, reflect the immediate post-medieval impact upon the site and denote a redeposition of artefacts within cultivated land similar to those within *02* noted above.

Two parallel walls (*04* and *05*) had been constructed in cuts (*07* and *08* respectively) through layer *127*, parallel to the modern Aldcliffe Road (Figs 4.12 and 4.13 a; Plate 4.13), both having been themselves cut into two parts by modern services. The walls ran across the entire site and continued in both directions outside the excavated area, maintaining a 2.6m north to south spacing between them.

Wall *04* (0.5–0.55m wide by 22m long), with a surviving height of between 0.85–1.04m, had up to six surviving regular courses and was built of sub-square and sub-rectangular sandstone. The lowest two courses included large sub-rectangular sandstone blocks and occasional large water-rolled boulders, its base being at the same level as that at which the memorial stone had

come to rest, and the lowest course lay directly over the corner of the fallen part of the memorial stone. Wall *05* (0.45–0.55m wide by 22.3m long), with a surviving height of between 0.6m to 1.0m, also had up to six surviving courses and was of similar construction to *04*. The lowest two courses also included large sub-rectangular sandstone blocks.

In the north-east corner of the excavated area, feature *119* (Fig. 4.12; Plate 4.14) was the cut for a large, potentially sub-rectangular, flagged cellar measuring 2.66m east to west by 2.7m north to south and extending beyond the excavation. The cellar floor consisted of closely laid, unmortared, large square and rectangular limestone flags, and had been laid on a 0.12m deep levelling layer of dark grey ash and clinker, with regular grey roofing slate and hand-made red brick. The three cellar walls *121*, *122* and *165* were composed of between one and six courses of roughly-cut sub-square and rectangular sandstone blocks,

Plate 4.13 Arla Foods Depot: upper courses of walls *04* and *05*, showing modern drain-cut and concrete foundation

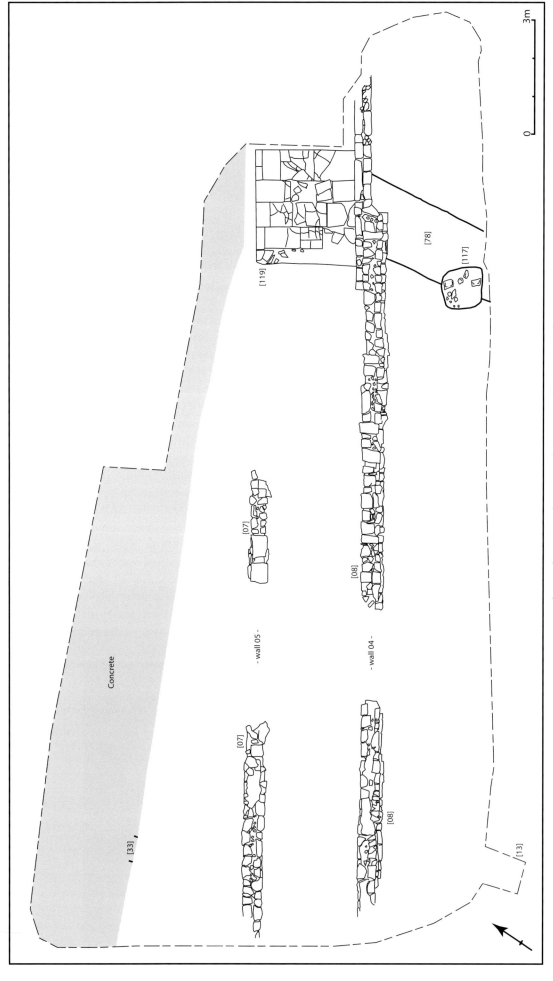

Figure 4.12 Arla Foods Depot Phases 3 and 4: medieval to modern features

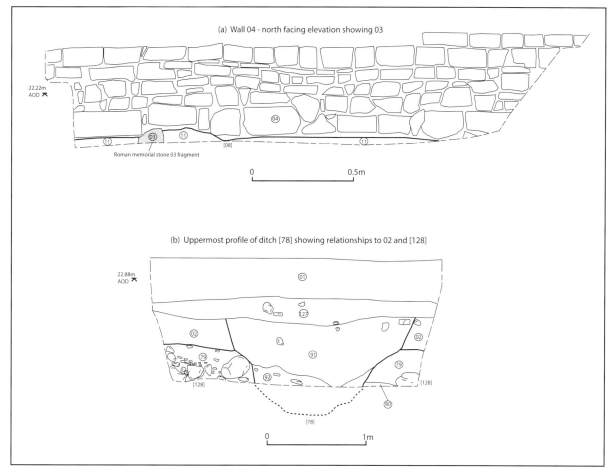

Figure 4.13 Arla Foods Depot: (a) north facing elevation of wall *04*; (b) uppermost profile of ditch *78*

bonded by a very hard, light-grey, lime mortar mix. Several large water-rolled cobbles were visible in the south-facing edge of the excavation, and appeared to have been incorporated within the build of wall *165*.

Walls *04* and *05* would appear to have been related to the five medium-sized terraced houses which are first shown, with outshuts and small yards, on Binns' map of 1821. These houses linked onto a larger building at the corner of Henry Street and Aldcliffe Road; it seems likely that the large cellar (*119*) is associated with this structure and that it was somewhat earlier than the adjacent terrace, perhaps being shown on Mackreth's 1778 map.

To the north of the excavation, a later watching brief also identified substantial remains of cellars and foundation walls associated with nineteenth-century housing. The plan of these structures conforms to that seen on the 1892 1:500 map of the area (Fig. 4.14), with buildings surrounding four courtyards, which were accessed via five passageways running from Henry Street. No evidence of the courtyards was discovered and only below-ground remains were observed. All of the walls had been constructed with roughly-hewn sub-squared and sub-rectangular sandstone blocks and bonded by a very light brown/grey mortar. The height of these features varied across the site, though typically up to twelve courses of wall survived to a height/depth of between 1m and 1.5m. These cellars were all sub-

square in plan with no evidence of flooring, and had been infilled with demolition rubble.

A stone-lined well (*123*) (Fig. 4.1; Plate 4.15) was also encountered during the watching brief. It was circular in plan, 1.2m in diameter, had a depth greater than 5m, and was lined with unmortared sub-rectangular and sub-square sandstone. Its positioning appears to have correlated with a small square structure within Lambs Court, shown on the OS 1:500 map of 1892 (Fig. 4.14), and presumably formed the water supply for the inhabitants.

Plate 4.14 Arla Foods Depot: cellar *119*; viewed from the south

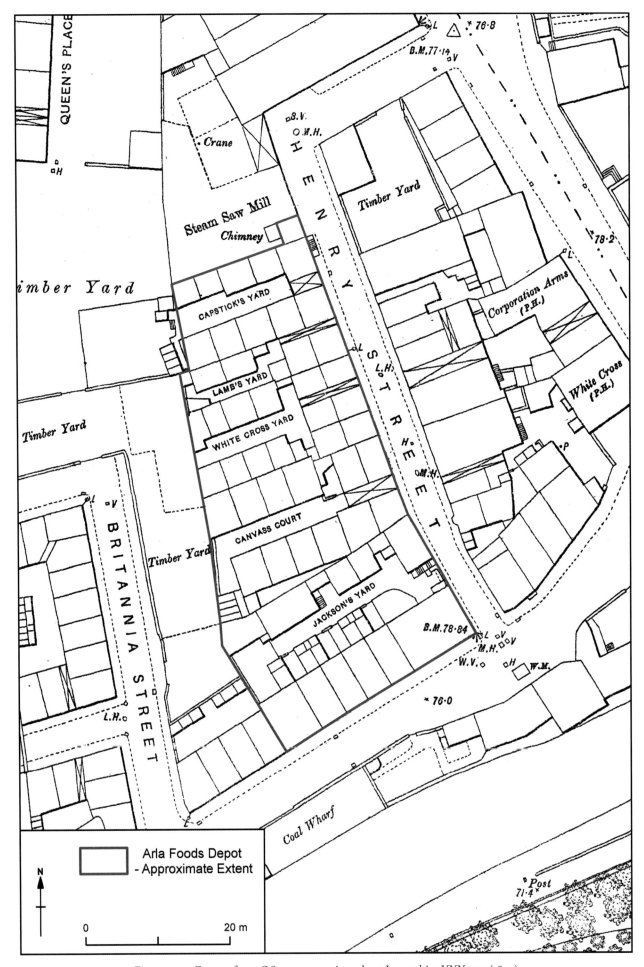

Figure 4.14 Extract from OS 1:500 mapping; sheet Lancashire XXX.15.3 (1892)

Plate 4.15 Arla Foods Depot: stone-lined well *123*

The Roman Pottery
by Christine Howard-Davis

In total, 91 sherds of Romano-British pottery were recovered during the excavation. All but one of the fragments were from securely-stratified Roman contexts, with the majority (86 fragments) coming from enclosure ditch *09*, a single fragment from enclosure ditch *129*, and three from the fill of the memorial stone socket (*112*). The pottery was examined in context groups and catalogued according to the *Guidelines for the Archiving of Roman Pottery* (Darling 2004). The fabrics were recorded in broad groups, and the source suggested where appropriate. The fabric of the pottery was examined by eye, and sorted into ware-groups on the basis of colour, hardness, feel, fracture, inclusions and manufacturing technique. *National Fabric Collection* codes have been assigned where possible (Tomber and Dore 1998).

Only three fabrics were identified: Spanish amphora (BAT SM 1), East Gaulish samian (HGB SA), and Severn Valley ware (SVW OX2). Both the samian (from fill *132* in enclosure *129*) and the amphora (ploughsoil *02*) consisted of small, very badly abraded fragments. Whilst the samian is clearly from a decorated vessel (probably form Dr. 37), all surface detail is lost, although it may have derived from the Heilingenberg production centre (Tomber and Dore 1998), and is thus likely to date from the late second to the mid-third century AD. The group is too small for any discussion of its nature, except to note that all three fabrics might be expected on a site tied into the military supply network in the later second or early third century AD. However, as it can be assumed that much of the supply to the extramural settlement at Lancaster arrived through the same network, this is unsurprising.

The Severn Valley material comprised 86 fragments of a single vessel from enclosure *09* (fills *66* and *101*), and a further three fragments (probably from the same vessel) from fill *113* of feature *112*. All were softened and very badly eroded (a frequently-noted feature of Severn

Valley ware), but the characteristic grey core was obvious on many of the sherds; on the better-preserved fragments, the outer surface could be seen to have been burnished. The vessel represented is a large narrow-necked jar with a flattened everted rim, closely resembling Webster's form A4 (1976). There were no signs of internal deposits or external sooting. The vessel is too badly abraded for a consideration of wear patterns, or evidence of repair.

It is interesting, in view of the circumstances of deposition, that probably only the base and some of the lower body are missing, suggesting that it might have been placed in the ground upside-down, perhaps as part of a funerary deposit. In this case, it can be assumed that the base was lost to later ploughing rather than representing a deliberate removal.

Severn Valley ware is well known at other Roman sites in Lancaster (Hird and Howard-Davis in prep), with dating concentrated in the later second and third centuries. It must be noted that a late product (ware E), said to be from the kilns at Quernmore, to the east of Lancaster, closely resembles Severn Valley ware (Webster 1988, 139). E ware has not, however, been found in Lancaster in any quantity and none has been recorded from the kiln-site, raising some doubt about its attribution (Webster 1988, 143), and leaving open the possibility that it is, in fact, a Severn Valley import.

Medieval and Post-Medieval Artefacts
by Andrew White

Medieval Pottery
The pottery consists of fourteen sherds, many of them abraded, all of small size, from medieval ploughsoil *02*. The origin of the jug fabrics found in Lancaster has not yet been established, although the Mitchells Brewery site of 1988 and 1992 in the city centre produced more medieval pottery than has previously been found on any site within the city (White in prep). The cooking-pot fabrics, however, seem, where identifiable, to be from two sources working within the Northern Gritty ware tradition at Docker Moor in Whittington parish to the north and at Ellel to the south (White 1975b, 121; White 1993b, 5ff). It should be noted, however, that a third source of this type of pottery has been described from Potter Lane, Samlesbury (Wood, Bradley and Miller 2008), where a production site and kiln base were excavated, which seem to have been in operation between the thirteenth and fifteenth centuries (Miller 2004, 69).

One sherd, although still in a medieval tradition, is in Reduced Greenware, and belongs to a type common in the late sixteenth and early seventeenth centuries in northern Lancashire and much of southern Cumbria. It comes from at least two known sources at Silverdale and at Arnside on the Cumbria border (White 2000, 285ff), and may have been made more widely. All the medieval pottery suffers from being made from Boulder clays, which makes exact identification of origin difficult or impossible.

Post-Medieval Pottery

This material is greater in quantity (63 sherds) than that of medieval date, and of much greater variety; it was all recovered from nineteenth-century soil *127*. The earliest item is a single sherd of Cistercian-type ware of a type originating in West Yorkshire, which is uncommon in Lancaster (Brears 1971, 18ff). Two or three other sherds of seventeenth-century date, including some Midlands Yellow ware, equally uncommon in Lancaster, and a handful of eighteenth-century date, are the only exceptions to the overwhelmingly nineteenth-century composition of this deposit. The nineteenth-century finds are not uniform in character, and probably result from rubbish disposal and garden activity.

Clay Tobacco Pipes

The very small sample, again from soil *127*, allows no statistical conclusions to be drawn; however, several of the stem fragments, on the evidence of their very large stembores, are clearly very early (seventeenth century), while the only bowl is a classic south Lancashire type, perhaps from Rainford and perhaps a product of the Birchall family, with its 'IB' stamp on the back of the bowl. It should be noted, however, that there are many pipe-makers with these initials and it is not possible to make a positive identification (Oswald 1967; Davey 1978).

Post-Medieval Glass

A small amount of glass was recovered from soil *127*, all dating to the nineteenth or early twentieth century. Two complete or near-complete clear glass bottles appear to be for patent medicines, and there is also a 'Hamilton'-type carbonated drink bottle of this period. A rather unusual thin glass vessel with a scroll pattern might on its own have been interpreted as a lamp glass, but it seems to have a closed red fluted base and so is perhaps some sort of flask.

Other Finds

There is nothing of note among the other ceramic and metal finds from the medieval ploughsoil *02* and nineteenth-century soil *127*, apart from a cut halfpenny of long-cross type (Henry III or later). Whilst worn, it may read EDWARAN[]/CIVI[TAS.LON]DON for Edward I or II, London mint (Brooke 1950 pl. XXIII).

The Sculpted and Inscribed Stones
by David Shotter (with contributions by Ben Edwards and Paul Holder)

Two inscriptions were recovered during the excavation. One of these was virtually complete and an integral part of a *Reiter* (cavalryman's) memorial stone of good quality; the other consisted of only four letters surviving on a small fragment of sandstone.

The Reiter Memorial Stone

(see also Tomlin and Hassall 2006, 468–73; Bull 2007)
In the quality of its relief-sculpture, this must, in the matter of its detail, rank as one of the most striking of surviving Roman stones of its type to have been found in Britain – indeed, in the Roman Empire as a whole (Fig. 4.15; Plate 4.16). However, its accompanying inscription, although generally well-preserved, is, by comparison, less assured in quality: seven 'guide-lines'

Plate 4.16 Arla Foods Depot: the Reiter memorial stone before conservation, and separated basal section (photograph of basal section: Peter Iles by courtesy of Lancashire Museums)

Figure 4.15   The Reiter memorial stone for Insus (drawing: Adam Parsons of Oxford Archaeology North)

remain visible, and there is at least one error (**CIVE** in line 3). Further, the difference in quality of workmanship between the sculpture and the inscription prompts the suggestion that different masons may have executed them.

It has been suggested (MacKintosh 1986, 2) that such work may have been carried out by masons operating from 'fixed workshops', who did not move with the troops. However, the majority of the inscriptions recorded from Lancaster (*RIB* 600–607) are cut on coarse-grained sandstones, formerly termed 'grits'. The present monument, too, has been cut on sandstone of coarse to medium grain, which has been identified as having derived from the Lancaster area (see below on p.82). It is worth noting that a number of old quarry-sites remain visible adjacent to the road leading south-eastwards from the Roman fort across Lancaster Moor.

The extremely sharp definition of both the sculpture and the inscription suggests that the memorial stone may not have been exposed to the elements for long: three postholes, adjacent to the findspot, raised the possibility that the memorial stone may have been partly covered by a wooden superstructure (see below p.86); it is evident, at any rate, from the rough condition of its reverse side that it was not intended that it should be viewed from the rear. Indeed, it may have stood upright for only a short time before falling or (less likely) being pushed on to its front face and broken. It should be noted that, at the bottom of the rear of the principal block, there are two small, crudely-executed, slots (Plate 4.17); one of these carried slight traces of iron-rust, whilst the other contains a whitish deposit which appears to consist of lead oxide, suggesting that at some stage a repair had been attempted. The slots are approximately 25mm wide, and the longest extends for 150mm. It is clear, however, that these slots are too low down on the memorial stone to represent an attempt to stabilise it in the ground by securing it to another object.

Plate 4.17 Reiter memorial stone: slots cut into the rear with remains of fastenings (photograph: Emily Somerville)

The presence of a large broken piece of sandstone, measuring at its maximum 0.55m by 0.91m by 0.16m, suggests that this may have broken from the principal block (presumably in antiquity) and should be added to the original height of the memorial stone; the 'break', however, is not clean, and the two elements cannot now be joined (Plate 4.16). Even so, despite the fact that there were in the vicinity a number of smaller blocks which could have been part of the complete stone or used to support it, there still does not seem to have been a sufficient length of memorial stone below the inscription for its stable and permanent 'sinking' into the ground in an upright position. It is noted that a number of these smaller pieces appear to have derived from different strata of the sandstone, though probably from the same quarry (see below on p.82).

A prominent position, easily visible from the nearby road, was evidently chosen for this memorial stone, although it remains unclear whether this was its original placement; the fact that the nearly-contemporary tombstone of another Treveran, Lucius Julius Apollinaris (*RIB* 606), was found in 1772 further to the north, and evidently adjacent to the eastern exit road from the Flavian auxiliary fort (see above, on p.82), suggests that, unlike Brougham (Cool 2004, 463ff), Lancaster does not appear, on present evidence at least, to have had a cemetery area dedicated for use by a specific garrison-unit.

The memorial stone is basically of the frequently found 'niche' type, conforming approximately to Vd, with suggestions of Vb, in Schleiermacher's typology (1984, 31f and 272). As it survives, the memorial stone measures (at maximum) 1.83m by 0.91m by 0.16m. If we add the basal fragment mentioned above, the minimum overall height of the memorial stone will have been 2.14m. Although large, however, this stone would still not have been as tall as that of Flavinus, the *signifer* of the *Ala Petriana* from Hexham/Corbridge (*RIB* 1172; Schleiermacher 1984, no. 77), which measures nearly nine feet (2.64m) in height.

Uniquely amongst *Reiter* stones, there is, in the centre of the arcuated niche, a depiction of what appears to be a serpent-haired Gorgon's head (Plate 4.18), recalling the legend that it was from the spilt blood of the Gorgon, Medusa, that the winged horse, Pegasus, was born (Harrison 1922, 187). It is further worth noting that a sculpted pediment-stone, probably from a tomb, was found in 1891 re-used in Chester's north wall. This, too, has a Gorgon's head (male) and a supporting decoration of stylised serpents (Wright and Richmond 1955, 54 and no.163; note also a possible Gorgon head from Bath – Cunliffe and Fulford 1982, 11 and no. 32). This motif may, however, have been regarded as suitable also for another, entirely different, reason, beyond the obvious equine connection: legend had it that the gaze of the Medusa turned to stone all

Plate 4.18 Reiter memorial stone: detail of gable top with Gorgon's head

upon which it fell – in this case, the rider, his mount and his decapitated foe.

The niche is decorated with a double border, both elements of which spring from an oak-leaf at either side; the oak was regarded as sacred to Jupiter, whilst the emblem of the oak-leaf itself is reminiscent of its use in the *corona civica* (see *RIC* I². (Augustus), 278 and Plate 5; Webster 1986, 145) as an award for bravery shown specifically in the saving of a citizen's life. The outer border carries on each side of the Gorgon's head devices that may echo the serpents that provided her hair; the inner border consists of a 'zig-zag' motif that may derive from that of vines trained around columns (Anderson

1984, 28f). This feature is seen also on a number of tombstones – for example, those of Annauso and Romanius Capito from Mainz (Schleiermacher 1984, nos. 21 and 27) and of Facilis from Colchester (*RIB* 200). Alternatively, it could have been intended to symbolise a wooden partition-door of the type still preserved at the House of the Wooden Partition at Herculaneum. The vertical borders of the sculpture function as undecorated pillars, capped by Tuscan capitals in two stepped segments.

At the base of the sculpture is a panel measuring 0.31m by 0.91m by 0.16m, which contains the dedicatory inscription in four lines of text in capital letters of moderate quality (Plate 4.19); as noted above, the horizontal 'guide-lines' for the letters survive – one for the top line, and two each for lines 2–4. The spaces between these 'guide-lines' are as follows: 55mm apart for line 2, 45mm for line 3, and 50mm for line 4. Although there is an attempt at stylistic embellishment – for example, the use of serifs on some of the letters – the general impression of the inscription (as distinct from the sculpture) is of letters rather crudely formed and poorly spaced. There were, however, traces of vermilion paint surviving in some of the letter-beds when the stone was found. It should be noted that some letters have been lost, through fracturing of the stone, on the left-hand side of lines 2–4 and at the bottom right-hand corner of line 4; proposed restorations to 'repair' these gaps are included below in square brackets. There was no sign of the missing letters amongst the adjacent stone-debris.

The Inscription – Text, Translation and Commentary
D I S
[M] ANIBVS INSVS VODVLLI
[FIL] IVS CIVE(S) TREVER EQVES ALAE AVG
[T] VICTORIS CVRATOR DOMITIA [H F C]

Plate 4.19 Reiter memorial stone: the Latin inscription (photograph by courtesy of the *Lancaster Guardian*)

'To the Gods of the Underworld: Insus, son of Vodullius, a Treveran citizen, a trooper in the *Ala Augusta*, *Curator* of the squadron of Victor. Domitia, his heir, saw to the erection of this monument.'

Line 1: Although this consists of a single word, **DIS**, placed towards the left-hand end of the line, some oblique striations to its right suggest that an attempt may have been made to complete line 1 with **MANIBVS**. Normally, the two words would be expected together to form the first line of a tombstone-inscription. The mason evidently started the second word but, perhaps finding himself short of the necessary space, elected to place it instead at the beginning of line 2. The spelling out in full of **DIS MANIBVS** and the absence from the inscription of ligatured letters argue for a date around the turn of the first and second centuries; a similar date has been canvassed for *RIB* 606.

Line 2: After **MANIBVS**, the remainder of the line is devoted to the dead man's name which runs into the beginning of line 3. Edith Wightman (1970, 50f) notes the variability of styles of nomenclature amongst the Treveri in the first century AD. Some – whether Roman citizens or not – used the *tria nomina* (*praenomen*, *nomen* and *cognomen*; Wightman 1985, 57 and 169); this is demonstrated on the other tombstone from Lancaster (*RIB* 606, found in 1772; see above in chapter 2). The name on that tombstone had the *tria nomina* (Lucius Julius Apollinaris), who was also a Treveran and a trooper in an *Ala Augusta* (Edwards 1971). This man *may* have been a Roman citizen, his family's enfranchisement perhaps granted in the name of Lucius Julius Caesar, the grandson and adopted son of the emperor, Augustus. However, the absence from the stone of any mention of a Roman voting tribe leaves the legal status of Apollinaris in some doubt.

Wightman also (1970, 50; citing *CIL* 13. 11736) notes a group of socially less distinguished Treverans who were known, as was the man on the present stone, by a single name, followed by an expression of his paternity – Insus, Son of Vodullius. Such men were definitely *peregrini*, and not Roman citizens. There is no certain parallel for the name *Insus*, although it has been suggested (Anthony Birley and Paul Holder *pers. comm.* 2009) that the name in a graffito on a sherd from St Albans (*RIB* 2 2503, 277), which has been restored as *IASUS*, may in fact be *Insus*. Names beginning with *Indu-* were common enough amongst the Treveri; further, *Insius* is found on an inscription from *Germania Inferior* (*CIL* 13. 12053). The name in the present case, therefore, may have been *Insus* or, less likely, a mistaken rendering of *Ins(i)us*; the restored formulation, *Insus, Son of Vodullius*, is, therefore, almost certainly correct. Vodullius (or possibly Vodullus) is not

a known name, although names commencing with *Vod-* are not uncommon in western Europe (*CIL* 13. 1083; 13. 10034). Nor, in the search for parallels, should we overlook *Bodvoc*, whose name appears on coins of the Dobunni in Britain (Mack 1964, 135f; Van Arsdell 1994, 14–16).

Line 3: If the above interpretation of the name is correct, then] **IVS** at the beginning of the damaged line 3 should be restored as [**FIL**] **IVS** ('son'); three letters missing at the beginning of line 3 would, in terms of space, match the evident length of text at the right-hand end of the line. **CIVE** is an error for *cives*, itself an acceptable alternative to the more usual nominative, *civis*; the form, *cives*, is relatively common on tombstones (for example, *RIB* 108 and 159). Wightman has shown (1970, 42) that the *Civitas Treverorum* may have been administered as one with the *Colonia*, known as *Augusta Treverorum* (Trier). This man may, therefore, have originated either in the town or in its rural hinterland.

ALAE AVG had been suggested as a plausible restoration of an unintelligible portion of the surviving drawing of *RIB* 606 (Edwards 1971, 23ff; see above, Plate 2.3); that is now effectively confirmed by the present inscription. There were a number of auxiliary *alae* which bore the honorific title *Augusta* (*ob virtutem appellata*: Cheeseman 1914, 146f; Holder 1982, 107ff); the most likely candidate in this case is the *ala Augusta Gallorum Proculeiana* (Birley 1939, 213–4 and 224; Shotter 1988a, 214f; Holder 1982, 107 and 109), which was raised in or before the reign of Tiberius (AD 14–37), and which is known to have been at Chesters under Hadrian (Hassall and Tomlin 1979, 346; Holder 1982, 107). Holder has argued that the unit was awarded the title *Flavia* by Domitian (AD 81–96), but that this was changed to *Augusta* after the death of that emperor and following his *Damnatio Memoriae*. The title could have been awarded for service in Britain, or just possibly on the Danube, to where some auxiliary units from Britain were evidently temporarily transferred in the late 80s (Holder 1982, 22); based on the evidence of Trajan's Column (Coarelli 1999, 217), decapitation of enemy soldiers certainly took place during the Dacian Wars. From AD 185 until 242, the *ala* was at Old Carlisle (*RIB* 897; 903). (For the appearance of the unit in military diplomas, see *RIB* 2401. 7, 8, 10; also below on pp.80ff).

The apparent coincidence of two men – the only two whose names we know from the *ala Augusta* during its time at Lancaster – coming from the same tribe may relate to the turmoil which had afflicted Rome's relations with the Treveri during the period of the Gallo-German uprising of AD 69–70. Romanisation was evidently well advanced among members of the tribe by the end of the Julio-Claudian period; the

Treveri neither joined nor took advantage of the rebellion mounted against Nero in the spring of 68 by Gaius Julius Vindex, the governor of *Gallia Lugdunensis*, and the future emperor, Servius Galba; indeed, they were subsequently punished by Galba with land-confiscations for their failure to support him (Tacitus *Histories* I. 53, 3; Wellesley 1988, 36). As a result, the tribe readily joined the revolt against Galba initiated in the Germanies late in AD 68 by Aulus Vitellius (*Histories* I. 63, 1). Vitellius' rebellion, whilst initially meeting with success, was put to a much more severe test when Vespasian was hailed as Emperor in the east. Not only this, but one of Vespasian's agents, Marcus Antonius Primus (Shotter 1977), persuaded a group of the tribe of the Batavi under their leader, Gaius Julius Civilis, to tie down Vitellius' support in the Germanies – a diversionary tactic which very quickly turned sour, as the Batavian revolt soon transformed itself into an open rebellion against Rome, evidently determined to establish an *Imperium Galliarum* ('Independent Empire of the Gauls'). This turn of events caused chaos on the Rhine amongst the Gallo-German tribes, some of whom – nominally, at least – had sided with Vespasian, whilst others, including the Treveri, maintained their earlier allegiance to Vitellius up to the time of his death in Rome in December 69.

Unsurprisingly, conditions along the Rhine became increasingly confused (Tacitus *Histories* 4. 54ff and 69ff; Wellesley 1988, 178ff), especially when the tribes rallied behind a now-openly anti-Roman movement. As Wightman has shown (1970, 45), the Treveri were too deeply involved in this movement to back down, even though the Roman commander, the future governor of Britain, Quintus Petillius Cerialis, is said by Tacitus (*Histories* 4. 73–4) to have addressed them in a down-to-earth oration offering them a reasoned way out; despite this, we are told (*Histories* 5. 19), 113 'Treveran senators' preferred to cross into 'free Germany', rather than remain on the 'Roman side' of the Rhine.

The revolt was now subsiding, but the Romans had learned salutary lessons – that it was unwise to allow tribesmen to serve in Roman auxiliary units in their own provinces and, further, that it was equally unwise to allow them to serve under their own 'Romanised' commanders. Given Cerialis' particular concern with the Treveri, it is not impossible that when, in AD 71, he took over as governor of Britain, he brought Treveran horsemen with him to serve in auxiliary units in Britain – not just because of their equestrian skills, which had been noted a century earlier by Caesar (*On the Gallic War* 5. 3, 1; Wightman 1970, 13), but also to give them a fresh start away from the Rhine and the scene of the earlier troubles.

Line 4: There is clearly a word (or, at least, an abbreviation) missing at the opening of the line, which is required to govern the genitive case of **VICTORIS**; the neatest and most obvious solution is to supply [T](urmae), although **TVR**, for which there is insufficient room in the present inscription, is a more usual abbreviation (*RIB* 1172; Paul Holder *pers. comm.* 2009). Insus is described as **CVRATOR** of this 'squadron of Victor'; although a junior rank which appears on some tablets from *Vindolanda* – (for example, *Tab. Vindol.* 1418) – the precise role of a *curator* is not known for certain, but it seems likely that he had charge of the provisions and/or weaponry of the *turma* (Cheeseman 1914, 41; Birley 2002, 80). Tomlin has pointed out (1998, 42–4 (*Tab. Luguval.* 1.49) and 58–9 (*Tab. Luguval.* 16.38–9)) that the *Ala Sebosiana*, at Carlisle in the Flavian period, also contained a *turma Victoris*.

DOMITIA: The appearance of this name towards the end of the inscription must point to its having belonged to a female relative or household-member who, as Insus' heir, saw to the setting up of his memorial stone. It is then probable that the broken bottom right-hand corner contained the abbreviation [H F C] – *heres faciendum curavit* ('as heir, saw to the setting up of this stone'). Domitia was not an uncommon name amongst the Treveri; indeed, a Domitia, who was a *civis Trever*, is commemorated on *CIL* 13. 633 of AD 258 from Bordeaux.

Finally, it should be said that it is unusual that this inscription omits two normal components of such a dedication – the age of the deceased and the number of campaigns (*stipendia*) in which he had served. However, it seems unlikely that the inscribed fragment found near the memorial stone was intended to rectify this omission. It has also been noted (Stephen Bull, *pers. comm.* 2008) that the inscription for Insus does not carry either of the formulae which would indicate a present burial – that is, **H S E** ('Here lies') or **S T T L** ('May the earth lie lightly on thee'). This omission probably indicates that the stone was intended as a memorial, which stood over a cenotaph, the body or ashes of Insus having been buried elsewhere (see further below on p.86).

The Sculpted Relief

The sculpted relief is a particularly striking example of a type of memorial that appears to have been popular in the first and second centuries AD, deriving from Greek and Etruscan antecedents (MacKintosh 1986). Indeed, the theme is occasionally to be found on the imperial coinage (for example, on an *aureus* of Caracalla: see *RIC* IV (Caracalla), 155 of AD 206–10). In the examples that are known from Britain and the western Empire, the rider is generally shown advancing from left to right; Schleiermacher (1984) has only eight (out of 134 listed in her catalogue) on which the rider proceeds from right to left, and most of these are from eastern Europe (nos. 56,

107, 109, 111, 120, 128, 129); it should be pointed out, however, that she omits from her catalogue *RIB* 595 from Ribchester (Lancashire), on which the rider is depicted as proceeding from right to left. There are basically two types of 'horseman-reliefs': one shows the rider, his mount and a servant, whilst the other – as in the present example – depicts the rider and his mount in triumph at the death of a barbarian foe. The latter type predominates amongst such stones in Britain.

25 cavalry or Reiter memorials of the 'rider-and-barbarian' type are now known from Britain (see below on p.78); indeed, they are found most frequently in Britain and in the German military districts – 71 of the 134 examples listed by Schleiermacher; strong similarities between tombstones from these areas are presumably to be explained partly by the proximity of Britain to the Rhine, and partly by the fact that many of the soldiers serving in Britain were drawn from Gaul and from the German military districts. It may also be the case that some of the masons received 'training' in this art whilst in western Europe.

Clearly, the most arresting feature of the present stone is the depiction of the immediate aftermath of the decapitation of the fallen enemy and the triumphalism with which the rider displays the severed head, which he carries by its hair in his right hand, along with his sword (*gladius* or *spatha*; Plate 4.20); it would be hazardous, however, to categorise the sword in the present case, as 'artistic convention' may have made it shorter than the long sword normally used by cavalrymen. Whilst it is true that decapitated enemies are depicted on Roman sculpture in Britain and elsewhere – as, for example, on the Bridgeness Distance Slab from the Antonine Wall (*RIB* 2139), on which an auxiliary cavalryman is also involved, and on Trajan's Column in Rome (Coarelli 1999, 217) – the present stone is unique in laying such heavy emphasis on the act of decapitation itself. Indeed, it is worth noting that the severed head on the Bridgeness Distance Slab appears to be left simply lying on the ground where it fell. Moreover, the fact that the rider is shown holding his unsheathed sword, rather than the almost-universal lance, indicates that this was a deliberate and premeditated – and perhaps, for him, a ritualistic – action.

The explanation of this lies presumably in the rider's Celtic connections. Although a number of riders on other such stones are shown carrying sheathed swords, only a small number – Valerius Durio from Amiens (Schleiermacher 1984, no. 88), Tiberius Claudius Maximus (Schleiermacher, no. 98) and the rider on a fragment from Britain (Schleiermacher, no. 83) – display the sword so prominently. The nature of the depiction on the stone from Lancaster of the aftermath of the act of decapitation carries two implications: first, the very uniqueness of it makes it unlikely that the

Plate 4.20 Reiter memorial stone: detail showing the severed head and the cavalryman's sword

design derived from a sculptor's 'pattern-book'; it remains unclear, however, whether it was intended as a reference to a Treveran tradition, or whether it might relate to a specific incident in the career of Insus – either in Britain or elsewhere. Secondly, the erection of such a stone in a prominent position in the cemetery (see below on p.100) raises serious questions as to what impression it was intended to convey.

The Treveri were strongly proud of their traditions and were known as ferocious warriors (Caesar *On the Gallic War* 8. 25; Tacitus *Germania* 28, 4); to the Celts, the cult of the human head was of great significance (Ross 1974, 94ff), especially the severed head (Diodorus Siculus 5.29; Strabo *Geographia* 4, 4, 5; Ross 1974, 164; Webster 1986, 39f). This was not, however, a sign of savagery so much as a demonstration of their belief that the person who performed the act of decapitation acquired the physical and military prowess of his defeated foe. Whilst the Roman authorities seem to have regarded this practice as barbaric, they do not appear to have outlawed it amongst their auxiliary units. This stone, therefore, serves as a reminder that, although over the years many of the Treveri had become Romanised, their traditions remained strongly ingrained in them; indeed, the third-century historian, Dio Cassius, notes that, despite the progress of Romanisation amongst the German tribes from the time of Augustus, this in no way precluded continuing respect for their ancient traditions (*Roman History* 56.18,2–3). In another way, that is illustrated by the fact that the rider on the present stone is depicted as wearing a torque on his right wrist. Such manifestations of an ancient cultural identity may have been particularly important to individual Treverans after the traumatic events of AD 69–70; hence the emphasis laid on this stone on the act of decapitation itself. The decapitated enemy is prominently portrayed still on the ground on his knees alone rather than on knees and elbows (MacKintosh 1986, 2), holding his sword in his right hand and his shield, evidently oval in shape, in his left (Plate 4.21).

A further view of the Treveri – and one that is of particular interest in the light of the present sculpture – is provided by Caesar's contemporary, the orator and politician Marcus Tullius Cicero (Shotter 2007): writing in 53 BC to his young friend, the lawyer, Gaius Trebatius Testa, who was serving with Caesar's army in Gaul (*Letters to His Friends* 7. 13, 2), Cicero warned Trebatius to avoid the Treveri, employing a Latin word-play between *Treveri capitales* and *Tresviri Capitales*; the latter were a group of three minor officials in Rome who had charge of prisons and executions. Most of Cicero's commentators have pointed out (rightly) that whilst, in the spoken language, the difference between these two expressions would have been almost indiscernible, the word-play is itself almost impossible to reproduce in English, and have contented themselves with rendering *Treveri capitales* as 'deadly Treveri'. Of course, the word, *capitalis*, can mean 'deadly', but it is as well to remember that it is derived from *caput* ('head'); in other words, with the present stone in mind, it seems that Cicero may have been warning Trebatius Testa (whose *cognomen,* of course, meant 'head') about the Treveran custom of decapitation on the battlefield. Thus, he tells the young man to 'beware of Treveran headhunters', and urges

him to use his time in Gaul 'to make his fortune rather than to lose his head'.

The horseman is not shown wearing distinctive body-armour, but has a sword-belt (baldric) over his left shoulder which hangs across his body down to his right hip. In his left hand, he carries a large oval shield. His attire appears to consist of a jerkin, leggings and boots, perhaps of leather, although the most distinctive item of his dress is a triumphantly-flowing cloak, fastened across his chest by a sun-ray or rosette brooch. His helmet is crowned by three sets of plumes of feathers (Plate 4.18), which is reminiscent of that worn by Flavinus, the *signifer* of the *Ala Petriana* (*RIB* 1172 from Corbridge/Hexham; Schleiermacher 1984, no. 77). It also resembles that worn by the figure on the so-called 'Altar to Mars', an uninscribed stone that can be seen in the Church of St Mary and All Saints at Whalley (Lancashire; Edwards 1969, 103–5), which may derive from the nearby cavalry-fort at Ribchester. The helmet is also equipped with large cheek-pieces which became characteristic in the second century, and which left little of the wearer exposed except for the eyes, the nose and the mouth (Dixon and Southern 1992, 35). In all, the helmet contributes emphatically to the triumphalist context of the sculptured scene.

The mount is also strongly depicted (Plate 4.22) – the excited gape of the mouth, the baring of the teeth, clenched on the bit, and the flared nostrils, whilst the plaiting of the mane and tail recalls a similar decorative feature on the uninscribed cavalryman's tombstone from Ribchester (Edwards 2000, 49 and 73). Indeed, the Lancaster sculpture has similarities with its near-contemporary from Ribchester, prompting the suggestion that the same sculptor may have been involved (Paul Holder *pers. comm.* 2009). The features of the harness are somewhat obscured by the rider: however, clearly visible is a hackamore (muzzle), cheekpiece and browband, although the arrangements

Plate 4.21 Reiter memorial stone: detail showing the kneeling barbarian's decapitated body

Plate 4.22 Reiter memorial stone: detail of the horse's head

for the bit are less clearly depicted. There is a prominent fringed peytral to protect the chest. The horse has a fringed saddlecloth and a fringed crupper-strap to steady the saddle, although there is nothing to be seen of the saddle itself. It is noticeable that there are no decorative medallions (*phalerae*) masking the strap-junctions, although it has been suggested that, in some cases, these may have been painted on to the stone rather than carved into it (Anderson 1984, 32).

Small Inscribed Fragment

A small fragment of a second, separate, inscription was recovered on a piece of sandstone, with maximum dimensions of 210mm by 200mm by 75mm (Plate 4.10); it had been re-used as one of the supporting stones for the cavalryman's memorial stone (see above on p.60). Three capital letters and part of a fourth survive, and are 50mm in height. The reading is:

I] O X V

Whilst the final three letters are unambiguous, the first could be either **I** or **N**, making [**STIPENDI**]**O** in the former case, or [**AN**] **NO** in the latter – 'On his fifteenth campaign' or 'in his fifteenth year'. The former, because of the reference to a campaign, would obviously relate to a serving soldier, whilst the latter, equally clearly on grounds of age, would be too young for military service.

This stone, too, which is of a finer sandstone than that of the cavalry memorial stone, has been identified as having derived from the Lancaster area, although

from a different rock-bed (see below on p.82). It is also notable that the letters are of significantly better execution than the inscribed portion of the other stone.

Chronological and Topographical Distribution of Reiter Memorial Stones
Some of the following information is derived from Schleiermacher (1984)
Although such tombstones can date to any point in the Roman period and derive from most parts of the Roman Empire, the majority appear to belong to the first and second centuries AD and to derive from the western provinces.

22 of those from Britain (Table 4.4) are of the 'rider-and-barbarian' type; the exceptions are: *RIB* 538 from Chester, which is of the 'rider-and-attendant' type, *RIB* 1481 from Chesters, which has rider and horse alone, and the sculpture from Whitcombe Farm (Dorset) which may not be a tombstone. On all 22 examples the rider proceeds from left to right, with the single exception of *RIB* 595 (from Ribchester). We should also note the unusual 'Rider-Relief' found in 1977 at Stragglethorpe (Lincolnshire; see Goodburn 1978, 434); in this case, a mounted god (Mars?) is portrayed, after the manner of a triumphant cavalryman, spearing a serpent; it recalls a coin of Constantine I, issued in Constantinople in AD 327, showing a serpent pierced by a *labarum* (*RIC* VII (Constantinople), no. 19). The imagery in this case may signify the defeat of Licinius in 324, and it may not be insignificant that the Stragglethorpe relief was evidently found in association with a coin of Licinius I (Ambrose and Henig 1980, 135ff; I am grateful to Dr Andrew White for bringing this piece of sculpture to my attention).

Statistical Analysis Relating to Reiter Memorial Stones Listed by Schleiermacher
by Ben Edwards

The figures given in this section are derived from the 134 examples of such memorials catalogued by Schleiermacher, (see Table 4.3).

With regard to rank, there are six legionaries (not including Tiberius Claudius Maximus, the captor of Decebalus, whose entire career appears, uniquely, on his stone) and four standard-bearers (although only one is described as *signifer*). Other ranks/positions given are: *B F COS* (1), *Centenarius* (1), *Curator* (1), *Duplicarius* (4), *Miles* (3), *Missicius* (1), *Princeps* (1), *Tribunus* (1). There is also one stone which commemorates two *equites*.

There are three examples of multiple victims (two of two victims, one of which is accompanied by a fallen horse, and one of three victims); there are two examples with two attendants, and eight attendants (30.8% of those stones depicting attendants) carry spears.

Table 4.1 *The Incidence of Cavalry Memorial Stones in the Western Provinces*

Location	First Century	Second/Third Century	Third/Fourth Century
The Germanies	44	5	3
Gaul	2	-	7
Raetia	-	3	-
Britain	7	7	3
Italy	-	2	-
Spain	1	1	1
Mauretania	4	9	-
Totals	58	27	14

Table 4.2 *The Incidence of Cavalry Memorial Stones in the Eastern Provinces*

Location	First Century	Second/Third Century	Third/Fourth Century
Asia	1	5	1
Dacia	-	3	-
Illyricum	6	-	-
Noricum	-	2	1
Macedonia	3	1	-
Palestine	-	1	-
Pannonia	5	2	1
Thrace	1	2	-
Totals	16	16	3

Table 4.3 *Statistical Analysis relating to Reiter Tombstones*

1. Direction of movement of rider:
To left 8 (6.0%) To right 119 (88.8%) Uncertain 7 (5.2%)

2. Gait of Horse:
Gallop 86 (64.2%) Standing 23 (17.2%) Walking/trotting 4 (3.0%) Uncertain 21 (15.6%)

3. Victim:
Present 43 (32.1%) Absent 62 (46.3%) Uncertain 29 (21.6%)

4. Sword:
Present 39 (29.1%) Absent 38 (28.4%) Uncertain 57 (42.5%) Three swords (7.7% of swords) are unsheathed

5. Spear:
Present 71 (53.0%) Absent 16 (11.9%) Uncertain 47 (35.1%) Five spears (7.0% of spears) are held point upwards

6. Shield:
Present 44 (32.8%) Absent 25 (18.7%) Uncertain 65 (48.5%)

7. Bow:
Present 3 (2.2%) Absent 64 (47.8%) Uncertain 67 (50.0%)

8. Attendant (*calo*):
Present 26 (19.4%) Absent 80 (59.7%) Uncertain 28 (20.9%)

9. Rank:
Eques 46 (34.3%) Others 15 (11.2%) Uncertain 73 (54.5%) See comments above

Reiter Memorial Stones: The Findspots
by David Shotter

The physical distribution of findspots of the Reiter memorial stones of Roman Britain is striking, although a degree of caution is advisable in the interpretation of distribution maps; as the late Professor Anne Robertson (1988, 13) wrote of coin-hoards, they may simply indicate the distribution of the activities that have led to discovery.

Of the 24 provenanced stones of this type from Roman Britain, four derive from sites in eastern Britain and 20 from western locations. Most of these were

Table 4.4 *British Examples of Cavalry Memorial Stones*

Place	*RIB*	Schleiermacher No.	Notes
Bath	159	69	
Bath	-	-	Uninscribed
			It was at one time thought that the above two stones might be portions of the same tombstone; however, they clearly do not fit together: see *CSIR* I. 2, nos 44–5.
Chester	499	70	
Chester	538	-	'Horseman and attendant' type.
Chester	541	-	Fragmentary.
Chester	550	73	
Chester	551	72	
Chesters	1481	68	No evident prostrate enemy or attendant.
Cirencester	108	74	
Cirencester	109	75	
Colchester	201	76	
Corbridge (Hexham)	1172	77	
Dorchester (Whitcombe Farm)	-	78	*CSIR* I. 2, no.114; it is uncertain whether this is, in fact, a tombstone; Wilson 1964, 172.
Gloucester	121	79	
Inveresk (Carberry)	-	-	See Tomlin 2008, 372–4.
Kirkby Thore	-	83	MacKintosh 1986, 16; Bruce 1875, no. 754.
Kirkby Thore	-	-	MacKintosh 1986, 16; Bruce 1875, no. 755.
Kirkby Thore	-	82	MacKintosh 1986, 16; Bruce 1875, no. 756.
			These three stones are illustrated in Bruce 1875, and are currently in the British Museum. Schleiermacher acknowledges that the provenances of these tombstones are not certain.
Kirkham	-	-	Baines 1893, 5. 360.
			A local tradition has it that this stone was found in the Church tower in 1844, but was broken up and used as hardcore for a path at the Church – Ben Edwards *pers. comm.* 2008.
Lancaster	-	-	Above; Tomlin and Hassall 2006, 468–73; Bull 2007.
Ribchester	595	-	This stone is now lost.
			The rider proceeds from right to left; Thomas Braithwaite's description of its discovery in 1604 is preserved in BL MS *Cotton Julius F.*VI, f.302. It appears that this was a funerary monument dedicated to a soldier of the *Ala Sarmatarum* – Ben Edwards *pers. comm.* 2008.
Ribchester	-	-	In Ribchester Museum, uninscribed.
Stanwix	2030	80	
Wroxeter	291	81	
Unprovenanced	-	84	

found many years ago, and details of their archaeological contexts are generally poor or absent. Although, of course, we know of cavalry forts which have not (yet) produced such tombstones, the distribution of the known stones presumably provides an indication of dispositions of legionary and auxiliary units containing cavalry, and represents a 'snapshot' of where cavalry was thought to be necessary and suitable.

The tombstones from Hexham and Chesters, of course, relate to the northern frontier, as does that from Stanwix, whilst the most recent discovery – the inscription from the base of such a tombstone, found in 2007 at Carberry (Inveresk; Tomlin 2008, 372–4) – has been taken to relate to the Antonine reoccupation of lowland Scotland in the second century. There is no recorded discovery of such a tombstone in eastern Britain between the northern frontier and Colchester.

Many factors may have contributed to this: in the first place, garrisons at many of the forts in eastern England were presumably short-lived, and the area appears to have settled relatively early in the occupation into the organisation of Romanised *civitates*. Prior to this, much of the area, before the invasion of AD 43, was in contact with the Roman world through political and commercial links; after the occupation, temporarily at least, a number of tribal leaders, who were favoured by the Roman authorities, were left as 'client-rulers' – for example, Prasutagus of the Iceni and Cartimandua of the Brigantes. Colchester itself, initially a legionary fortress, became the early 'capital' of Roman Britain and a veteran *colonia* (Crummy 1997, 51ff).

By contrast, western England presented a rather different picture both physically and strategically: in the South West, deposits of lead and silver will have made the area sensitive, whilst the west Midlands were adjacent to Wales, an area that was physically challenging and whose people – principally the Silures and the Ordovices – had proved hostile to Rome, evidently supporting the cause of Caratacus. The nearby presence of cavalry is totally intelligible in this 'border-territory', and no fewer than 11 of the known Reiter tombstones from Roman Britain have been found between Bath and Chester. We should also bear in mind that the political sensitivity of this area was undoubtedly heightened both by the presence of Druids and by the mineral resources to be found in Wales. The point is illustrated by the fact that we are told by Tacitus (*Life of Agricola* 18, 1) that a cavalry-formation had been wiped out by the Ordovices immediately prior to Agricola's arrival as governor in AD 77.

In the North West, the nature of the terrain will again have favoured the deployment of cavalry, and it may have taken a little time before the 'writ of Rome' in this area could be regarded as secure. Besides this, the North West, too, had mineral resources, and security may have been served by placing cavalry at Kirkham and Ribchester (on the Ribble) and at Lancaster (on the Lune). In short, then, the distribution of Reiter tombstones by definition reflects the deployment of cavalry-units, which in its turn will have been a measure of a range of uncertainties and necessities – military, economic and political.

Roman Cavalry Garrisons at Lancaster

The present memorial stone enhances our knowledge of the garrison-pattern at Lancaster in an important respect: whilst the lost tombstone of Lucius Julius Apollinaris (*RIB* 606) left it possible that an *ala Augusta* had been in garrison at Lancaster, there remained a chance that a single tombstone might have been transported from elsewhere, or that there was a special reason for

Apollinaris to have been buried at Lancaster. The discovery of this second stone to a Treveran trooper in an *ala Augusta* at Lancaster makes it far more likely that the unit at one time formed the garrison at the fort (Tomlin and Hassall 2006, 472 and note 3; Shotter 2001a, 11–15).

It would, indeed, be reasonable to suppose that the unit had formed the garrison at Lancaster since the conquest of the North West during the governorship of Petillius Cerialis (AD 71–74); as we have seen (above on pp.1ff), a case can be made on numismatic grounds (Shotter 2000b, 191; 2001, 7) that the establishment of a permanent fort at Lancaster should be dated to the early 70s. In its turn, this may imply that, like the *ala Gallorum Sebosiana* which appears to have come to Britain in the early 70s (*ILS* 2533; Tomlin 1998, *Tab Luguval.* 44), the *ala Gallorum Proculeiana* (later *ala Augusta*) may have arrived in Britain in AD 71, alongside Petillius Cerialis himself and the newly-formed *legio* II *Adiutrix*. New documentary evidence from Carlisle (Tomlin 1998) has shown that the *ala Sebosiana* was garrisoned at that site for at least a part of the Flavian period – evidently during the governorship of Gnaeus Julius Agricola (AD 77–83).

How long the *ala Augusta* remained at Lancaster is uncertain, although it is recorded at Chesters in Hadrian's reign and features on a diploma from there, dated to AD 146 (*RIB* 2401. 10). It would appear, therefore, most likely that it was moved from Lancaster in garrison-revisions that accompanied the development of the northern frontier in the first quarter of the second century.

There is, of course, a considerable body of evidence that links the *ala Sebosiana* with Lancaster, although, of this, only the bath-house inscription (*RIB* 605; Shotter 1988c) is datable; the late Professor Eric Birley (1936, 5) placed the consuls named in this inscription, Censor and Lepidus, in the period AD 262–66. Most of the remaining evidence consists of stamps on bricks and tiles found at Lancaster, together with others from the associated industrial site at Quernmore, some three miles to the south-east (*RIB* 2465. 1–2). None of these, however, can be dated; the known sites at Quernmore are generally regarded as having been in production between *c.* AD 80 and 130/140, although there are hints of later production in the area at locations which have so far not been pinpointed in modern times (Leather and Webster 1988, 85–93). As we have seen, the *ala Sebosiana* was still at Lancaster in the mid-third century, loyal – as is shown by its contemporary name, *Postumiana* (*RIB* 605) – to the emperors of the *Imperium Galliarum*.

There is, however, no present indication of the date of arrival of this unit at Lancaster and it is unclear whether it took over directly from the *ala Augusta* or after an interval. Various dates have been canvassed over the years, including the Hadrianic period, the end of the Antonine occupation of Scotland in the reign of

Marcus Aurelius, and the reorganisation of units in Britain by Septimius Severus at the end of the second century. Of these, the Hadrianic period perhaps seems to be most persuasive in view of the currently-accepted dating of the Quernmore kilns. Further, the inscription on the recently-discovered *Reiter*-tombstone from Inveresk (Carberry; see Tomlin 2008, 372–4) suggests that the unit may, in fact, have been in Scotland during the Antonine reoccupation. Further, it should be noted that the numismatic evidence from Lancaster (Shotter, 1990, 18) carries a hint that the garrison may have been absent or reduced during the Antonine period.

The only other unit of the Roman army for which there is any evidence in the Lancaster-area is a unit of Bargemen (*numerus Barcariorum*; *RIB* 601; Shotter 1973). Although these soldiers are often associated with the construction at Lancaster in the fourth century of a new fort of the 'Saxon-Shore' type, the quality of the inscription itself may hint at an earlier date, when the *numerus Barcariorum* was either at Lancaster on its own, or perhaps sharing the auxiliary fort with a cavalry-unit. On a note of caution, however, it is worth remembering that this altar was, in fact, found a short distance upstream of Lancaster, at Halton-on-Lune.

Alae Augustae in Britain
by Paul Holder

Insus' memorial stone and the lost tombstone of Lucius Julius Apollinaris (*RIB* 606) leave no doubt that an *ala Augusta* was garrisoned at Lancaster – and most probably in the late first to early second century AD. However, four cavalry-units bearing the honorific title, *Augusta*, are known to have been stationed in Britain at various times; it is, therefore, important to attempt to determine which of them was at Lancaster.

First, the *ala Gallorum Petriana milliaria civium Romanorum* is recorded only once as *Augusta* – on a monument for a prefect of the unit at Carlisle (*RIB* 957). Otherwise, it is called *ala Petriana milliaria c R* (cives Romani) or *ala Gallorum Petriana milliaria c R*. Prior to the early second century, it was not called *milliaria* (*Tab. Vindol.* 2. 258).

Secondly, the *ala Augusta Vocontiorum c R* is generally recorded with both *Augusta* and *Vocontiorum* on inscriptions and diplomas. Prior to its arrival in Britain, it is not recorded with the epithet, *Augusta*.

Thirdly, *ala Augusta* first appears on diplomas in the reign of Trajan (AD 98–117; *RMD* 3. 151); however, in 122, it has the additional title, *Gallorum*. On inscriptions, it appears as *ala Augusta ob virtutem appellata* from some time in the reign of Hadrian until *c.* AD 242.

Fourthly, *ala Augusta Gallorum Proculeiana* first definitely appears on diplomas with all three name-elements in AD 145/146 (*CIL* 16. 93), and again (although after restoration) in AD 158 (*RMD* 5. 420). In AD 125(?), the unit of the recipient of a diploma is given as [*alae …*] *r(um) Proculeian(ae)* (*CIL* 16. 88); the restoration, [*alae Aug(ustae) Gallo*]*r(um) Proculeian(ae)* seems likely. It should also be noted that the name of the *ala Aug* is not complete on the diploma of AD 127, and not necessarily complete on that of AD 135.

Table 4.5 *Alae Augustae Recorded in Britain*
ALA AVGVSTA

Title as given	Date	Location	Source
ala Aug[usta]	AD 98/105	Vindolanda	*Tab. Vindol.* 2. 263
[Aug]usta (ext)	AD 98/114		*RMD* 3. 151
eques alae Au[g]		Lancaster	*RIB* 606
eques alae Aug		Lancaster	*Britannia* 37 (2006), 468–73
Augusta Galoru (int.)	AD 122		*CIL* 16. 69
Aug Gallor (ext.)	AD 122		*CIL* 16. 69
[Augusta Gallo]r? (int.)	AD 124		*CIL* 16. 70
Aug [—] (int)	AD 127		*RMD* 4. 240
Aug Gal[... (int.)	AD 135		*CIL* 16. 82
ala Aug [o]b virt appel	AD 117/138	Chesters	*AE* 1978, 7
ala Aug ob virtut appel	AD 188	Old Carlisle	*RIB* 893
ala Aug ob virtutem appellata	AD 191	Old Carlisle	*RIB* 894
ala Augusta ob virtutem appellata	AD 180/192	Old Carlisle	*RIB* 946
ala Aug	AD 197	Old Carlisle	*RIB* 895
praef alae Aug	AD 213	Old Carlisle	*RIB* 905
ala Aug Gordia ob virtutem appellat	AD 242	Old Carlisle	*RIB* 897
ala Aug		Old Carlisle	*RIB* 890

Table 4.5 *Continued*
ALA AVGVSTA GALLORVM PETRIANA

Title as given	Date	Location	Source
ala Ga[ll]o[r] Pet[r]iana	AD 56	Mainz	*CIL* 13. 6820
ala Petri		Strasburg	*CIL* 13. 11605
[Gallorum Petria]na cR	AD 98		*CIL* 16. 43
ala Petriana	AD 98/105	Vindolanda	*Tab. Vindol.* 2. 258
eq alae Petr		Corbridge	*RIB* 1172
ala Petriana cR tor		Latschach	*AE* 1990, 775
praef alae Augustae Petrianae torq ∞ cR		Carlisle	*RIB* 957
praef alae Petrianae milliar cR bis torquatae			*PME* C 72
Gallor Petriana ∞ cR (ext)	AD 122		*CIL* 16. 69
Petrian ∞ cR (int)	AD 122		*CIL* 16. 69
Petrian [∞ cR] (ext)	AD 124		*CIL* 16. 70
Gall Petr ∞ cR (int)	AD 127		*RMD* 4. 240
G[allor Petrian ∞ cR] (int)	AD 130/131		*ZPE* 156 (2006), 245
Gall Petr ∞ [cR] (ext)	AD 130/131		*ZPE* 156 (2006), 245
Petr ∞ (int)	AD 135		*CIL* 16. 82
[praef. al]ae Gallor[um Petrianae ci]vium R miliariae			*PME* II, IV Inc.188

ALA AVGVSTA VOCONTIORVM

Title as given	Date	Location	Source
eques ala Vontiorum		Soissons	*CIL* 13. 3463
eq ala Vocont		Vetera	*CIL* 13. 8655
missicius ala Voconit		Kalkar	*CIL* 13. 8671
eq [alae Vocon]it		Kalkar	*CIL* 13. 8672
ala Vocont		Köln	*CIL* 13. 8655
praefect e[quitum alae Aug(ustae)] Vocon[tiorum]		Mersch	*PME* II, IV Inc.236
Augus Vocontioru cR (int)	AD 122		*CIL* 16. 69
Aug Vocontior cR (ext)	AD 122		*CIL* 16. 69
[A]ug Voc cR (int)	AD 127		*RMD* 4. 240
dec alae Vocontior exerci[t]uus Britannici		Hemmem	*CIL* 13. 8805
dec alae Aug Vocontio[r]		Newstead	*RIB* 2121
Aug Vo[cont cR]	AD146/154		*RMD* 3. 168
Aug Vocontior (ext)	AD 178		*RMD* 3. 184
Aug Vocontio (int)	AD 178		*RMD* 4. 293
Aug Vocontior (ext)	AD 178		*RMD* 4. 293
Aug Vocontior (int)	AD 178		*RMD* 4. 294
Aug Vocontio (ext)	AD 178		*RMD* 4. 294

ALA AVGVSTA GALLORVM PROCVLEIANA

Title as given	Date	Location	Source
[alae Aug Gallo]r Proculeian (recipient)	?AD125		*CIL* 16. 88
[Aug] Gal Proc (int)	AD 145/146		*CIL* 16. 93
Aug Gall Procul (ext)	AD 145/146		*CIL* 16. 93
[Aug Gall Pro]cul (ext)	AD 158		*RMD* 5. 420

As can be seen, there is no proven overlap between the evidence for *ala Augusta ob virtutem appellata* and *ala Augusta Gallorum Proculeiana*. The solution appears to be that they are one and the same unit. How, then, did the use of different names on different types of document come about? This can be demonstrated by looking at a close parallel – the *ala I Augusta Gallorum c R*. This unit was based for most of its existence in the province of Mauretania Tingitana (in north Africa), and also has different names on different types of document at different times. On diplomas, it is called *ala I Augusta* in AD 88 (*CIL* 16. 159), *ala I Augusta c R* in AD 109 (*RMD* 2. 84), *ala Aug c R* in AD 114/117 (*CIL* 16. 165), *ala [I Aug] Gallor [...* in AD 117/129 (*RMD* 1. 33), *ala I Aug Gallor* in AD 153, but *ala I Aug Gallor c R* as recipient (*RMD* 5. 410–11). However, on inscriptions of various types it is consistently called *ala Aug(usta)* (Spaul 1994, 52–4).

The solution to this discrepancy appears to be that auxiliary units possessed a formal title to be used on official documents, especially diplomas; in the case of the *ala I Augusta*, the fullest version seems to originate in the reign of Hadrian – that is, *ala I Augusta Gallorum c R*. On the other hand, there were non-official inscriptions with the 'common' or 'colloquial' name of the unit – *ala Augusta*. This example helps to explain the various names of the *ala Augusta Gallorum Proculeiana*: it was originally an *ala* of Gauls, named after its commander – *ala Gallorum Proculeiana*. At some stage, before the reign of Trajan, it was granted the honorific epithet, *Augusta*, for bravery. As with the *ala I Augusta Gallorum c R*, the honorific epithet became the dominant name, because there were so many *alae* of Gauls. Thus, on the two Lancaster tombstones, the Vindolanda address and the Trajanic diploma it was called *ala Augusta*. From the reign of Hadrian, it became *ala Augusta Gallorum Proculeiana* on official documents and *ala Augusta ob virtutem appellata* on non-officials ones.

The Lithology of the Roman Memorial Stone
by Fred Broadhurst†

At the time of examination by hand lens, the monument was dirty and much of its surface obscured by dried mud. This report is based on the stone available for close study.

The stone is composed of a medium- to coarse-grained sandstone, the dominant constituents being sub-angular grains of quartz, accompanied by conspicuous flakes of mica, and variable amounts of pink to buff-coloured feldspar. The binding material of the sandstone is a silica cement.

The stone is weathered and thereby coloured brown by the oxidation of iron-rich minerals, which would form only a small proportion of the original rock. In its original unweathered state, this rock would have been white. The weathering may have occurred before, or after, the date of quarrying. On some of the associated broken sandstone blocks there are striking red and brown rings or bands, making distinctive patterns on the rock surfaces. These, too, are the result of weathering, which may have developed in the rock prior to, or later than, quarrying.

The stone appears to be relatively porous in many places. A likely explanation is that a proportion of the constituent feldspar grains have been broken down by the action of rain (acidic on account of dissolved carbon dioxide) or acid ground water (from peat or another organic source). The ultimate breakdown product of feldspars are clay minerals, which can be flushed from the rock. The rock is weakened but still kept intact by the presence of the silica cement.

Dark brown patches between 1mm and several millimetres in diameter, mainly seen on the surface of the stone, are developed where there has been precipitation of iron oxides/hydroxides, again due to the weathering process but in this case probably by the introduction of the iron from outside and not from the stone of the monument itself.

A separate piece of sandstone, with the lettering I] O X V, is composed of a finer-grained rock than the stone of the monument. It also appears to be richer in feldspar grains. This indicates that the specimen was not derived from the same rock bed as the stone of the monument; however, it may have come from the same quarry site, although from a different rock level.

The assemblage of sandstone pieces associated with the monument is similar in type to the stone of the monument itself, but there is variation in grain size and feldspar content. Nevertheless, they could all have come from the same site but from different strata.

The stone is characteristic of the coarser-grained sandstones (often termed 'grits') of the 'Millstone Grit Series' (old term) or Namurian (modern term) of the Carboniferous System. These rocks are to be found outcropping in the Lancaster district. Knowledge of the routes of the Roman road system together with a geological map would present the possibility of locating a likely quarry site (see below on p.100).

(*Editors' note*: it has recently been demonstrated (Hayward, 2006, 359ff) that the stone for such monuments did not necessarily come from British quarries; the memorial to Marcus Favonius Facilis from Colchester (*RIB* 200), for example, now appears to have been carved on stone that has been identified as originating in Norroy-les-Pont-à-Mousson in eastern France.)

Palaeoenvironmental Assessment
by Charlotte O'Brien

Plant macrofossils

Samples from fill *37* of prehistoric refuse or storage pit *35*, buried soils *53* and *54*, and fill *114* from the memorial stone setting *112*, were assessed for plant macrofossils. In each case, the entire sample was manually floated and sieved through a 500 μm mesh. The residues were retained, described and scanned using a magnet for ferrous fragments. The flots were dried slowly and scanned for waterlogged and charred botanical remains. Identification of these was undertaken by comparison with modern reference material held in the Environmental Laboratory at Archaeological Services, Durham University. Plant taxonomic nomenclature follows Stace (1997).

Results

Charcoal was present in all of the samples, with the largest amount from fill *37*. This sample also contained an abundance of charred hazelnut fragments and a wheat grain. The only other charred plant remains were a ribwort plantain seed and a wheat grain in soil *54*, and a few hazelnut fragments in soil *53*. An uncharred fat-hen seed was present in soil *53*. The results are presented in Table 4. 6

Discussion

The abundance of charred hazelnut fragments in fill *37* suggests that the pit may have been used as a stored food resource, although it could also have been used for the disposal of domestic waste. A wheat grain was also present, but this could not be identified to species, as wheat chaff was absent. The six largest pieces of charcoal from this context were all identified as hazel.

A sample of the hazelnuts was submitted for radiocarbon dating, and has provided a result of 4550 BP ± 30 (3240 calBC – 3100 calBC at 95.4% probability, SUERC-22506, GU-18140), thus placing the fill in the Neolithic period. It is notable that Neolithic/Bronze Age food storage pits at Caythorpe, Yorkshire, were found to contain thousands of hazelnut fragments, in addition to smaller amounts of wheat grains and apple or pear pips (Huntley 1993; Druce 2007, 361).

Few plant macrofossils were present in the buried soil horizons (*53* and *54*), and the few fragments of charcoal were all too small to be identified to species. Wheat and hazelnuts occurred in very small numbers. A charred seed of ribwort plantain suggests the proximity of grassland, and fat-hen may either have grown as an arable weed or as a ruderal on areas of waste or disturbed ground.

Seeds were absent from pit fill *114*. It is possible that the charcoal in the flot was from a funeral pyre, as a Roman memorial stone was found in the pit, although cremated bone was absent from the flot and residue. Alternatively, it may have come from domestic or industrial fires. Five pieces of charcoal from this context were large enough to identify, and all were oak.

Pollen

Pollen assessments were undertaken on buried soils *53* and *54*. A sample was processed using sodium hydroxide digestion, followed by sieving and heavy liquid separation. A *Lycopodium* spore tablet was added to each of the samples in order to facilitate calculation of the total pollen/spore concentration. Pollen identification

Table 4.6 *Plant macrofossils*

	Context			
	37	*53*	*54*	*114*
Volume processed (ml)	6000	13000	12000	1200
Volume of flot (ml)	60	10	5	10
Volume of flot assessed (ml)	60	10	5	10
Residue contents (relative abundance)				
Cracked stones	-	1	1	1
Flot matrix (relative abundance)				
Charcoal (undifferentiated)	3	1	1	2
Charcoal (hazel)	6 pieces	-	-	-
Charcoal (oak)	-	-	-	5 pieces
Charred remains (total counts)				
Triticum sp. (Wheat)	1	-	1	-
Plantago lanceolata (Ribwort plantain)	-	-	1	-
Corylus avellana (Hazelnut shell)	71	2	-	-
Waterlogged remains (relative abundance)				
Chenopodium album (Fat-hen)	-	1	-	-

Relative abundance is based on a scale from 1 (lowest) to 5 (highest)

was undertaken using a modern reference collection and an identification key (Moore *et al.* 1991).

The concentration of pollen and moss spores in both samples was extremely low, at 391 and 779 grains/ml in the samples from buried soils *53* and *54* respectively. Microscopic charcoal was common throughout. The extremely low concentration and degraded nature of the pollen suggests that neither of the contexts was waterlogged, and most of the grains that may have accumulated have been subject to oxidation. The results provide insufficient data to enable reconstruction of the palaeoenvironment of the site. The few grains that have been preserved suggest that alder, hazel and oak probably grew in the area, with the few local herbs suggesting open ground with some damp areas. The microscopic charcoal suggests some localised fires.

General Site Discussion

The earliest deposit excavated was a pit (*35*), which had been used either to store food or for the disposal of domestic waste, and dates to the Neolithic period. The pit was sealed by a buried soil (*54*), which was in turn sealed by a later buried soil (*53*), which formed the ground surface at the beginning of the Romano-British period and lay beneath the Roman road. It is only the second reliably-dated feature of this period reported so far from Lancaster (see above on p.50).

Placed on top of the post-Neolithic soil, but predating the immediately pre-Roman soil, was a mound (*30*), possibly of turf. The feature's stratigraphic relationships indicate a later prehistoric origin, although no definitive date was obtained. Whilst evidence from other sites, notably Petty Knowes (Charlton and Mitcheson 1984), does demonstrate the use of small mounds as grave sites, no evidence for a burial beneath this example was found in the limited portion excavated and its purpose here was not determined.

The majority of the archaeological deposits recorded came from the Romano-British period, with four sub-phases of activity. During this time the site was effectively divided in two, with a road and associated drainage ditches in the eastern portion and, to the west outside the 'road zone', an enclosure and other ritual features. These included an early stone setting and a second stone setting, the latter having been used to support the memorial stone to the Treveran cavalryman Insus, probably from the *Ala Augusta Gallorum Proculeiana*. As no cremation or inhumation was found with the memorial stone, the feature appears to have functioned as a cenotaph.

No dating evidence was discovered associated with road *128*, and its precise date is, therefore, uncertain. It would appear likely, however, that the construction of a road system leading to Lancaster from the south would have quickly followed the establishment of a military presence. As the fort at Lancaster would appear to date to

the early AD 70s (see above, chapter 1), it seems likely that the road would also date to this period. It has long been suggested (e.g. Shotter 2001a, 3) that the present-day Penny Street lies on the line of this Roman road. The line of the road discovered on this site would suggest that the Roman route was quite close to the projected line of the modern Penny Street, but would not exactly correspond, unless there was a small change of alignment a little to the north of the excavation, perhaps at the Penny Street/King Street junction. It should be noted, however, that only a short section of the road was excavated and that its apparent alignment may therefore be unreliable. Contemporary roadside ditches (*76* and *77*) were recorded immediately flanking the road.

Thirty Roman feet to the west of the Roman road was a parallel ditch (*131*), probably marking out the road zone. On the west side of and at right angles to ditch *131* was a second ditch (*129*). This was excavated whilst ditch *131* was still open and, with a third ditch (*13*) that ran parallel to *129*, seem to mark out an enclosure (Enclosure 1), some thirty Roman feet long. Whilst it is tempting to interpret Enclosure 1 as a plot within a roadside cemetery, it must be remembered that no burials were recovered from within it and that the similar enclosure seen on the adjacent Streamline Garage site (chapter 3 above) was not directly associated with the burials found on that site. There, the burials were dug into the wholly or largely silted-up ditches, although they may have still been visible as hollows. Although there was no evidence that either enclosure had a mortuary purpose, it is not possible to rule it out completely.

Within Enclosure 1, and perhaps contemporary with it, was pit *18*. This had strong parallels to pit *112*, which contained the stub of the memorial stone, and is interpreted as another, earlier, stone setting. As no stone was found here, and later changes to the ground levels (deposits *105*, *106*, *107*, *108* and *11*, Phase 2c; Plate 4.23) would have partly buried and obscured a stone set within pit *18*, it is a short step to suggesting that this may have been the original location of the memorial stone (*03*). It is notable that, stylistically, the cavalry memorial stone would appear to date from the late first to early second century AD; this would conflict strongly with the stratigraphic sequence of pit *112* and indicates that originally the stone must have been erected elsewhere.

Stratigraphically, feature *18* post-dates the early Romano-British ground surface and certainly pre-dates the early third century. If, however, it was the original setting for the memorial stone, it would be of a similar age and thus of late first- to early second-century date. This gives a not unreasonable time-span of up to 50 years from the establishment of the fort at Lancaster and the construction of the road (*128*) to the excavation of this pit.

Plate 4.23 Arla Foods Depot: relationship between pit *18* (stone packing in trench, centre) and pit *112* (stone packing, top right), viewed from the west

Although feature *18* is suggested as the original setting for the memorial stone, it is also possible that this was an unrelated feature or the site of another, now lost, stone. This would imply that the memorial stone was brought to setting *112* from another part of the site, perhaps as part of a phase of expansion or redevelopment of a cemetery area. That such changes occurred elsewhere has been demonstrated recently at Carlisle (Botchergate; Zant *et al.* in prep). Whilst it is notable that it is located some distance south of the Roman burials on the Streamline Garage site (currently the furthest away from the settlement area), those remains were dated as being of the second to fourth centuries (see chapter 3 above) and thus could not have been part of the primary phase of cemetery development. This would indicate that there is not a simple correspondence between distance from the settlement and the date of burial, and that plots were positioned with regard to some other order of precedence or requirement. Work at Brougham (Cool 2004) has suggested a similar phenomenon, where there appear to have been areas 'dedicated' for use by specific garrison-units, and at Colchester (Pooley *et al.* 2006, 67ff.) where distinct clusters of burials are recorded; a parallel could also be drawn with the dedication of separate areas for different faith groups in modern municipal cemeteries.

At a later point the ditches *131*, *129* and *13* of Enclosure 1 became filled; one of these fills was a red clay (*47=95=?14*), which seemed unusual to the excavators. It has been speculated that it was deliberately placed as part of a ritual purification or sterilisation ritual, intended to cleanse the area (Robert Philpott, *pers. comm.* 2006). This would imply that the ditches themselves, as well as the area that they defined, had significance. The presence of organic clay deposits

97 and *98* at the junction of ditches *131* and *129* has also been suggested as possible evidence of ritual activity.

Subsequent to this a new ditch *69* was cut on almost the same alignment as the earlier road zone ditch *131*. Whilst it appears to represent a redefinition of the roadside area, it also apparently destroyed Enclosure 1. Its purpose may be linked with the gradual silting up of the roadside ditches (*76* and *77*), and it could indicate an attempt to re-establish the boundary between the road and the area to its west, following a possible period of stagnation or neglect. This was followed (although at what interval is unknown) by the laying down of deep deposits of sand, (*105*, *106*, *107*, *108* and *111*), which may have served to facilitate drainage immediately adjacent to the road. This may also have been an attempt to rectify neglect. Evidently as a response to this, the ground level within the roadside area was also raised by deposit *11* and a new boundary ditch *09* was cut through it, to retain the definition of the zone. Stone setting *112* and the associated post holes (*148*, *152*, *153*, *154*, *155* and *156*) were also cut through layer *11*.

The uppermost fill (*66*) of ditch *09* contained some 85 sherds of a Severn Valley ware vessel. Though other ceramic forms were used, pottery jars provided the majority of cinerary containers in Roman Britain (Philpott 1991), and the deposition of such an object within this ditch has parallels with the cremation deposits discovered at the Streamline Garage site to the north (chapter 3, above). Later medieval ploughing appears to have caught the base of the vessel and spread it, and it is possible that this had distributed any associated cremated remains from within the jar throughout the surrounding soils, where, with a single exception, they have been lost from the archaeological record. As noted, however, soil conditions do not appear hostile to the survival of cremated bone, and if the bone were simply scattered, then the pottery sherds would also have been dispersed, and this seems unlikely. It seems more probable that this vessel was not a cremation container at all and was instead associated with a ritual, which may have been related to an act of burial or to post-burial practices. It has been noted, at Brougham for example (Cool 2004, 42), that burial grounds attracted an element of ritualistic behaviour that is not associated with any individual act of interment. In particular, the deposition of a vessel within an upper fill of a feature (as in this case) may be associated with its closure, and/or that it functioned as a 'special pot deposit' (Cool 2004, 42; Weekes 2008, 154ff).

Three further sherds of Severn Valley ware were recovered from a fill of the memorial stone setting (*112*) and, although uncertain, it is possible that these are fragments of the vessel from feature *09*. The likelihood that all the sherds are from the same vessel is supported by the stratigraphic relationship between the two features, as both ditch *09* and pit *112* were cut into deposit *11* and date from the same stratigraphic group phase. It is possible (if somewhat speculative) that this denotes a shared ritual between the two features, wherein a complete pottery vessel was deliberately broken and sherds deposited within the stone setting and the ditch, perhaps as part of the ritual associated with the relocation of the memorial stone from the first setting pit, *18*.

A few fragments of burnt oak were discovered in a fill (*114*) within pit (*112*); these might perhaps have been associated with a cremation rite. Using Cool's typology of cremation burial forms from Brougham (Cool 2004, 284), this would conform to the 'pyre debris' type. In this form the whole, or more usually a small part, of the unsorted pyre remains was gathered and placed within the burial deposit. The virtual complete absence of cremated bone suggests that this possibility is, however, unlikely. Alternatively, and perhaps more convincingly, the memorial stone and its setting could be identified as Cool's 'cenotaph/memorial' type, that is, sepulchral monuments without a burial (Cool 2004, 306). This can perhaps be viewed as a substitute for a formal burial where circumstances dictated that the remains of the individual were either deliberately disposed of outside of the confines of the cemetery or were unavailable for burial. The former may have occurred when the remains were transferred to another resting-place, possibly even the individual's homeland (Cool 2004, 307), the latter when, for military or practical reasons, the body could not be recovered. Parallels for such a practice can be found in the cenotaph discovered at Chester (*RIB* 526).

A group of three postholes, all subsequently recut (*148/152*, *153/154* and *155/156*), surround the stone setting, pit *112*. What they supported or contained is a matter of conjecture. It is tempting to assume that they housed timber uprights, supporting a roof or shelter that covered the memorial stone. The remarkably good condition of the carving on the stone could suggest that it was sheltered from the weather, but unfortunately an assessment of the geometry of the postholes would make this unlikely. A conventional ridged roof with two gable ends (echoing the design of a household shrine or *aedicula*) would have been much more simply supported by posts at each of the four corners than by the three recorded here. It could be that there was a structure supported by the front pair of postholes and propped diagonally from behind, which would explain why the rear posthole (*148*) appears to be cut at an angle rather than vertical. It is worth noting, however, that any substantial posts erected in features *153/154* and *155/156* would probably have partially obscured the memorial stone itself, detracting from the prominence of position intended for it and thus implying that they served some other purpose.

It is also possible that these postholes have something to do with the erection or support of the memorial stone itself, which weighs in the order of 700kg. The Roman army undertook a considerable amount of construction, and the erection of a simple set of sheer-legs (a tripod of three strong poles, tied together at the top and with a pulley attached to the apex for a lifting rope to run through) to lift the stone into position and hold it whilst it was secured in place would have been a simple task. Such sheer-legs would, however, not normally require their legs to be set into substantial postholes, nor does it explain why the postholes appear to have been recut. Parallels for these features require further research.

A medieval plough-soil (*02*) sealed the Romano-British activity across the site. This soil contained artefacts from the thirteenth to fourteenth centuries, and also a stratum of stones that probably represent the plough-damaged upper surface of the Roman road. Documentary evidence points to this area being part of Lancaster's medieval open fields, and later ditch *78* cut into soil *02* would appear to represent a substantial field boundary, perhaps associated with the later strip-field system portrayed in this area on the Ordnance Survey first edition 1:10,560 mapping of 1848 (Fig. 4.16). The slightly sinuous morphology of the field boundaries shown there strongly suggests that they originally defined strips in an open-field system that had its origins in the medieval period. These fields are noted as 'arable' on Kenneth Docton's recreated map of 1684, although they seem rather straight and wide when compared to later maps, such as that by Stephen Mackreth, dated 1778, and Binns' map of 1821 (White 2003, 47–55), as well as the 1848 Ordnance Survey mapping. It is interesting to note the alignment of the field boundaries with the Roman road, but this does not necessarily imply any survival of the road as a landscape feature.

Gradual expansion of the city during the seventeenth to mid-eighteenth centuries accelerated considerably in the nineteenth century, as Lancaster's industries expanded (see, for example, Dalziel 1993). As part of this the site underwent substantial development, with the house represented by cellar *119*, present by 1778, being followed by the construction of a row of houses along Aldcliffe Road (foundation walls *04* and *05*) before 1821. To the north, infilling occurred along Henry Street, and a series of cellared buildings around four courtyards was completed by 1848 (Fig. 4.16). These houses were subsequently demolished, and the site given over to industrial development.

There exist numerous strong parallels between the Romano-British enclosure discovered upon this site and that excavated at the Streamline Garage site (chapter 3). These include the general design, the apparently deliberate nature of their infills, the intrusion of second-to third-century ritual deposits within the already-filled ditches, and the probability that both underwent substantial modifications before reaching their final form. The principal difference between these two enclosures lies in the nature of the ritual expressed within them, with cremations dominating the Streamline Garage site. At the Arla Foods Depot site, the enclosure area appears to have been devoted to the housing of the memorial stone, with later ritual depositions within the recut road zone ditch perhaps being associated with its relocation; if there were any other funerary acts, they were not detected and must be presumed to have lain outside the area of excavation. It would seem reasonable to suppose, if the earlier pit setting was for the memorial stone, that the burials discovered on the Streamline Garage site to the north could have been attracted to this area by its existence, and thus that the two sites represent at least part of a cemetery area. The converse is also true, in that the resiting of the memorial stone may have been prompted by the expansion of the cemetery into the adjacent area, and resulted in the re-dedication of its setting. The discovery of an enclosure on each of these sites does not, however, suggest that this area was divided into individual cemetery plots, as they were apparently disused before burials occurred. This contrasts with the site excavated at 79–81 Penny Street (chapter 3, pp.21ff), which appears to have been a plot that was used and re-used over a considerable period. It may be, of course, that it was this 'crowding' that led to the expansion of the cemetery into the Streamline Garage and Arla Foods Depot sites.

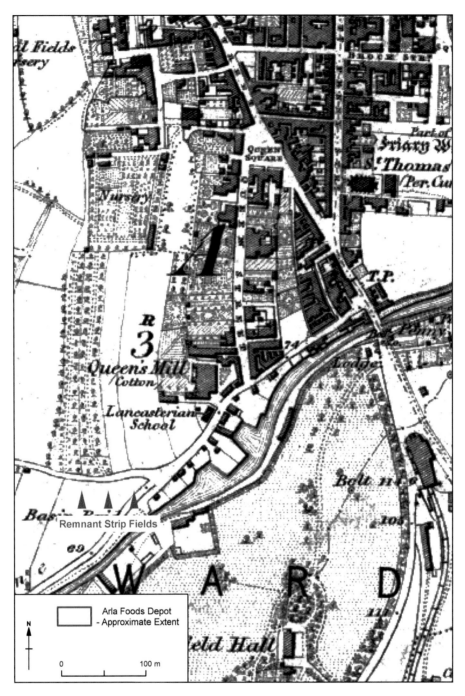

Figure 4.16   Extract from OS 1:10,560 mapping; sheet Lancashire XXX (1848)

CHAPTER 5

Lancaster's Roman Cemeteries in Context

(This chapter has been compiled by the editors, but is drawn largely from material supplied by all of the contributors to the present book during the course of discussions held in 2008)

The settlement of the site of Rome originated in the form of separate villages on the tops of the group of hills that flanked the River Tiber (Gjerstad 1962). At first, the form of these villages was essentially simple, as is demonstrated by surviving funerary urns and by the hut-dwelling, the postholes of which may still be seen cut into the living rock of the Palatine Hill, and which was 'remembered' as the 'House of Romulus' (Boethius and Ward-Perkins 1970, 20f). In the earliest days the valleys between the hills were swampy, hazardous and unhealthy and, for that reason, given over to the cemetery-sites of the early settlers. Even in those early days, however, the dead were envisaged as continuing their existence after life, and many of their cremation-urns took the form of miniature ceramic or bronze huts (Keller 1975, 16–19).

Eventually these hill-top settlements came together into an urban entity; the catalyst for this process was probably provided by the engineering skills of Etruscan settlers who by that time clearly formed a dominant group in central Italy (Ogilvie 1976). These skills were put to use in schemes to drain the marshy valleys and to construct on the reclaimed land the first of the city of Rome's monumental buildings. Dominating and guarding this newly-unified city was Jupiter, the Greatest and Best, in his Temple on the summit of the Capitoline Hill.

Care for the dead was clearly a characteristic of the early settlers: in the countryside, there were always suitable secluded places in which people might lay their dead to rest and mark the spot with a monument if they so desired. The law did not in these circumstances prescribe what made, or did not make, a suitable place for a burial. However, as villages in Rome and elsewhere developed to form towns and cities, in the matter of the burial of the dead, more notice had to be taken of such factors as public health, physical order and the risk of accidental defilement of earlier graves through subsequent building-works. Thus, in the earliest legal codification, The Law of the Twelve Tables, which was laid down in the fifth century BC, *Tabula X* forbade the cremation or interment of the dead within the areas defined by the walls or other boundaries of a city

(Cicero *On the Laws* 2. 23, 58 and 2. 24, 61; Toynbee 1971, 39; 48); this ruling was re-enacted as late as the reign of Antoninus Pius and, in the case of Rome itself, it appears to have been generally observed at least until the later fourth century (Writers of the Augustan History *Life of Antoninus Pius* 12, 3).

Some exceptions were, however, evidently permitted: Gaius Julius Celsus Polemaeanus, the founder of the great library at Ephesus, was allowed burial within the precincts of his library inside the city (Boethius and Ward-Perkins 1970, 397). Roman Emperors, too, were allowed a dispensation: Trajan, for example, was buried in a vault at the base of his Column in the heart of Rome (Dio Cassius *Roman History* 68. 16, 3; 69. 2, 3; Rossi 1971, 14; Coarelli 1999, 23; Plate 5.1).

Plate 5.1 Rome: Trajan's Column: burial vault
(photograph: David Shotter)

Generally, therefore, the dead were laid to rest outside their towns, in sites which flanked the roads which ran in and out of them. Some cemeteries, following the Etruscan model, as can be seen at the Etruscan site of *Caere* (Cerveteri; Plate 5.2), were set out as 'Cities of the Dead' (*nekropoleis*); the fact that they were conceived as 'cities' emphasises that the dead were still regarded, in some sense at least, as integral to the civilised life of a Roman city. However, just as it has been suggested that the location of amphitheatres in these boundary-areas symbolised the struggle between civilised life and uncivilised nature (Wiedemann 1992, 90ff), in the same way the extramural position of the cemeteries also emphasised the battle for civilisation fought by the living.

The physical proximity of the living and the dead was emphasised by two festivals in particular – the *Parentalia* (in February) and the *Rosalia* (in May/June) – when Roman families took the opportunity to visit their ancestral tombs and leave offerings (Toynbee 1971, 63f; Potter 1987, 173f). The purpose of this was to placate the Spirits of the Underworld (*Manes*), and thus to 'persuade' them not to do harm to, but to protect, the living. Parallels for such activity could be drawn from across the globe and for all of recorded history.

The use of the roads as focal points for tombs is well illustrated by the remains surviving, for example, along the *Via Appia Antica* (outside Rome's southern limit) and the *Via dei Sepolcri* (outside Pompeii; Plate 5.3). Whilst this type of arrangement was relatively common in the Empire, the construction of Etruscan-inspired *nekropoleis* was limited to Italian cities (Toynbee 1971, 18ff). In either case, families might buy a plot of land on which to erect a tomb, or they might purchase a site upon which a speculator had already built a 'ready-to-use' tomb. Usually, rules were put in place to set a limit to the length of street-frontage that a tomb might occupy, as well as the permissible depth back from the frontage (Toynbee 1971, 75, citing Horace *Satires* I. 8, 12f). Further, families were able to

Plate 5.3 Pompeii: Via dei Sepolcri (photograph: David Shotter)

exact penalties from and/or place curses upon any person invading and alienating their tomb-space (Toynbee 1971, 76, citing *CIL* 14. 850; see also *RIB* 754 from Watercrook).

The existence of these rules suggests that a limit needed to be placed on over-ostentatious display and the wasteful use of precious burial-space. Certainly the linear nature of most such cemeteries strongly suggests that tombs were to be seen and thus that there was an element of social status associated with the possession of a splendid family-tomb. In common with the carrying of family-busts in funeral processions and the creation of family-trees in the *atria* of the houses of the nobility, this highlighted the pride that Roman and Romanised families derived from the deeds of their ancestors, and the importance to the living of ancestral custom (*mos maiorum*; Tacitus *Annals* 3.76, 2). As well as this, a case could also be made for the rôle of a memorial as a *memento mori* for the traveller, though we have yet to find such graphic representations of inevitable death as the fifteenth-century 'Cadaver' or Transi Tombs (Cohen 1973).

Thus, graves could be marked by impressive monuments, such as that of Marcus Nonius Macrinus, recently uncovered on the banks of the River Tiber (*The Times*, 17 October 2008), or they might be as simple as holes in the ground marked by a border of stones. The Roman biographer, Suetonius, describes the Emperor, Nero, preparing such a simple grave for himself shortly before committing suicide (*Life of Nero* 49). Edward Champlin (2003, 49–51) has offered an ingenious re-interpretation of Nero's famous dying remark, 'What an artist dies in me' (*qualis artifex pereo*), seeing it as an ironic and self-deprecating observation on Nero's part on the poor grave that he felt forced to construct for himself. As well as differences between burial sites, grave goods might or might not be part of the funerary process, and their nature can also vary considerably (Philpott 1991; Cool 2004, 333ff). Such matters were, presumably, influenced by families' perception of tradition and status, as well as their physical

Plate 5.2 Cerveteri: street of house-tombs (photograph: David Shotter)

circumstances and, no doubt, the length of time that they had been dwelling or intended to dwell in a particular location.

It should also be noted that, whilst the majority of tombs, to facilitate access to the living, were to be found in relatively close proximity to the boundaries of towns, groups of tombs or mausolea might be found anywhere, though most seem to cluster along the lines or in the vicinity of roads (Charlton and Mitcheson 1984, Fig. 1). For this reason, it is an attractive suggestion that the earthwork on Burrow Heights, some three miles south of Lancaster's city-centre and in close proximity to the road from Lancaster to Walton-le-Dale, may have been a mausoleum (Edwards 1971; see further below on pp.103ff).

How far burial practices in Roman Britain followed 'normal' Roman rules is hard to say, for, although a number of cemetery-sites have been excavated and published in recent years, the volume and geographical spread of evidence remain limited (for example, Wenham 1968; Cool 2004). It has been noted that circular (or 'tumulus') tombs are frequent in Britain (Toynbee 1971, 179ff); this, however, seems to have less connection with the circular tombs to be found in cemetery-sites in Italy than with local pre-Roman custom in Britain and elsewhere in north-western Europe, as noted at both Colchester (Pooley *et al.* 2006) and Petty Knowes (Charlton and Mitcheson 1984).

It is evident that, in general, Roman law requiring the burial of human remains beyond the boundaries of a settlement was respected in Roman Britain; the most obvious exception to this appears to have concerned infant burials. It is clear from Classical references that, until the age of teething (Pliny *Natural History* 7. 15), an infant was not regarded as a separate individual with a soul, and that, therefore, the usual rites to 'placate the gods of the afterlife … were neither necessary nor appropriate' (Philpott 1991, 101). Infants were generally inhumed rather than cremated and are frequently found within houses or under the eaves of buildings (Pliny *Natural History* 7. 54).

Adult burials within settlements, on the other hand, may simply reflect the growth and movement of the settlement within and beyond its original boundaries. For example, alongside Botchergate in Carlisle (McCarthy 2002, 77f), the earliest activity appears to have been represented by a cremation-cemetery. This area was, however, subsequently covered by strip-buildings which, in their turn, were demolished and the site returned to use as a burial-area. Alternatively, adult burials within settlements may also point to deaths of a suspicious (or plainly illegal) nature: this appears to have been the case with a body from the Lanes, Carlisle, which had suffered traumatic head injuries and was then concealed in a third-century well (John Zant *pers. comm.* 2009). In another example two skeletons were found

buried under the floor of a house in the civilian settlement at Housesteads on Hadrian's Wall, one of which had a blade embedded in it (Crow 1995, 69f). As we have seen, a further possibility may be that, as appears to be the case with the Church Street interments in Lancaster (above on p.14f), late burials have occurred in areas of extramural settlements that had shrunk or had been abandoned in the later years, as appears to have been the case at Wroxeter (Wacher 1974, 374).

In the early imperial period, until the late second to early third centuries, cremation was the normal method of disposal of human remains. Ashes might be placed in a grave in a ceramic vessel, normally of an everyday domestic type, or in a glass receptacle; alternatively, they might be deposited without a container, a practice which has been thought to derive in Britain from pre-Roman traditions (Philpott 1991, 47). The presence of nails (as distinct from hobnails) in some cases indicates also the possibility of burial in a wooden box.

In the North West it appears that cremation remained in use until well into the third, and even into the fourth century, along with a higher than normal proportion of deposits without evident containers and fewer than usual grave-goods (Philpott 1991, 47; Hair and Howard-Davis 1996). However, from the third century, an increasing use of inhumation can often be detected. It may be assumed that this was due to a growing belief in the notion of the importance of bodily survival which, of course, owed much to the spread of Christianity. Such an attitude to the continuity represented by belief in an afterlife can be seen perhaps in the elaborate tombstones which depict the dead person engaged in feasting, as on a fragmentary tombstone recently discovered at Heronbridge, to the south of Chester (Mason 2004, 19ff; *cf. RIB* 1064 from South Shields). However, the fact that, in the North West at least, cremation appears, in its turn, to have been overtaken only slowly by inhumation may represent a comment on the speed and depth of the spread of the new religion in Roman Britain.

In the case of inhumations, the body was usually placed at full length on its back, although not lying in any specific direction. It is clear, however, that this was not a universal practice: for example, excavations at the Bath Gate site in Cirencester (Viner and Leech 1982, 76ff) found a significant proportion of burials where the individuals lay prone or on their sides. In later years, when presumably increasing numbers of people were touched by Christianity, it became more common in an inhumation for the arms to be crossed over the chest and for the feet to point in an easterly direction.

It should, however, be borne in mind that a particular form of inhumation – in the 'crouch' or 'womb' position, with the knees drawn up to the chin – was observed in the cemetery at Low Borrowbridge (Hair and Howard-Davis 1996, 103f). It was clear at that site that these burials pre-dated most of the cremations, and may, therefore, be assumed to represent the persistence of a native tradition. Although the fort at Low Borrowbridge was integrated into the Roman road-network, the remoteness of its location may go some way towards explaining this persistence. It is, of course, possible that, in some cases at least, the onset of *rigor mortis* or the effects of a disease in life may have made it difficult to lay the bodies in any other posture (Viner and Leech 1982, 81; see also above on pp.17ff for the burials at the Westfield War Memorial Village in Lancaster).

In the cases of both cremations and inhumations, the recovery of hobnails suggests that the dead were equipped with shoes for the onward journey to the Underworld. Similarly, burials are sometimes found to have been provided with a coin (or coins) with which to pay Charon, the dreaded ferryman, for the journey across the river Styx into Hades (Virgil *Aeneid* 6, 295–336; Juvenal *Satire* 3, 264–7; Toynbee 1971, 49; Philpott 1991, 208). In the case of inhumed bodies, such coins, when present, were generally placed in the mouth, or occasionally over the eyes. However, few coins were recovered from the burials at Brougham (Cool 2004, 381f) or Low Borrowbridge (Hair and Howard-Davis 1996, 113), and none from those at Lancaster. It may be that, despite the risks that failure to provide 'the fare' were thought to entail, this particular custom did not prove attractive in the North West.

In some cases it appears that the 'graves' were cenotaphs – a plot marked by a memorial stone, though lacking significant bodily remains (see above on p.44). One particular stone (*CIL* 13. 8648) – that of Marcus Caelius, a centurion in Legion XVIII, who perished in the Varus-disaster in Germany in AD 9 – specifically states that it had not been possible to recover the remains of the deceased. The absence from the excavations on the Arla Foods Depot site of any sign of material relating to either cremation or inhumation would lead us to regard the memorial to the auxiliary soldier, Insus, as probably being a cenotaph; indeed, Insus may well have been killed in battle and his remains buried elsewhere. It is equally possible, however, given his obvious pride in his Treveran origins (Shotter 2007) and the 'nationalism' that appears to have characterised some of the Treveri in the late first century AD, that his physical remains were returned to his tribal homeland for burial. This practice is not unknown in the modern world, with a number of religious and ethnic groupings placing great importance on returning remains to their original homeland after death.

In most cases, the existence of a cenotaph will become clear only through excavation, although the absence from a stone of a formula such as **H S E** (*hic situs est* – 'here lies') or **S T T L** (*sit tibi terra levis* –

'may the earth lie lightly on thee') may lead us to suspect the absence of cremated ashes or a body-burial. In the case of a stone from Chester (*RIB* 544; Wright and Richmond 1955, 40, no. 92; Plate 5.4) commemorating an unknown *Optio*, who had perished in a shipwreck, the fact that the site was a cenotaph was marked by a change to the normal formula, **H S E**, which had been altered by the omission of the **H** ('here'). Although only a relatively small number of *Reiter*-stones survive with their inscriptions sufficiently intact, it is clear that the majority of those that do are inscribed with one of the formulae which should indicate the presence of a burial (Schleiermacher 1984, 66–153 and 176–200 for the German and British examples). The memorial of Insus, however, notably lacks it, or, indeed, the space for it to be present.

Plate 5.4 Chester: memorial stone for a ship-wrecked *Optio* (*RIB* 544; photograph by courtesy of the Grosvenor Museum, Chester)

It has already been noted that we still do not have a substantial body of evidence from cemeteries of the Roman period in north-west England (Fig. 5.1); few large-scale excavations have taken place, and only those from Low Borrowbridge and Brougham (Hair and Howard-Davis 1996; Cool 2004) have resulted in major publications. However, a number of other cemetery-sites, such as Brough-under-Stainmore, Birdoswald and Beckfoot, have yielded information which has been published and discussed (Jones 1977, 18–45; Wilmott 1993, 79–85; Caruana 2004, 134–73). A certain amount of information has also come to hand regarding other Roman cemeteries in the North West through

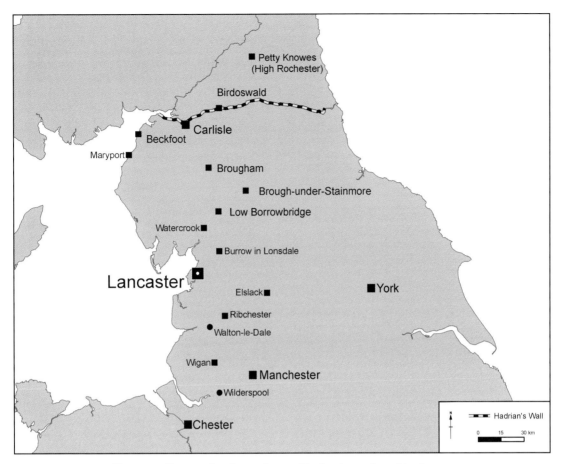

Figure 5.1 Roman sites in north-west England mentioned in the text

antiquarian and casual reporting, such as that collected by the late Dorothy Charlesworth (1978) for Carlisle, which inevitably lacks the detail that the recent excavation-reports have shown to be so significant to our understanding of burial-practices.

The fully-published sites have produced rather different pictures: in the case of Low Borrowbridge, which was excavated in the early 1990s (Hair and Howard-Davis 1996), the site produced evidence, as we have seen, of both inhumations and cremations, with the latter representing a clear majority; this may seem surprising in view of the fact that the dating placed these burials securely in the third and fourth centuries. In the river-gravels which characterised the site differential drying allowed clear sight of individual grave-plots, which were surrounded by shallow ditches which may have represented bedding-trenches for low hedges (Hair and Howard-Davis 1996, 98–102 (Figs 5.6 and 5.7) and 122; Plate 5.5). All of the graves, with a single exception, lacked a surviving marker, and it could be seen that, in some cases, plots had been cut into one another, presumably because of ignorance of an already-existing grave – unless, of course, a family connection provides an explanation. It is, however, worth noting that the physical integrity of the grave was supposedly guaranteed by the fee which serving soldiers contributed from their pay into a burial-club (Webster 1985, 279f); this does not appear to have been universally observed either there or at some other sites (see, for example, Viner and Leach 1982).

The majority of cremations at Low Borrowbridge had been placed in cooking-pots, although a considerable number lacked a container. There was some evidence of pyre-debris in the burials, although in such small quantities as to suggest that the pyre-sites were not immediately adjacent to the burials. Indeed, in view of the very close setting of the grave-plots, it is difficult to see how pyres could have been easily set up in the areas under excavation. Grave-goods were virtually absent, with the exception of a few nails (including hobnails), which would indicate that shoes and perhaps boxes may have been present in the cremations themselves or in the burials. It was impossible to tell whether any particular characteristic linked those buried at the site – whether military, civilian or both – although the single tombstone recovered was that of a thirty-five year old woman (Shotter 1996, 115–18).

The cemetery area excavated at Brougham in the mid-1960s by the late Dorothy Charlesworth lay adjacent to the road leading eastwards from the fort in the direction of the Stainmore Pass, at a distance of some 500m from the fort's east gate (Cool 2004, 1ff). Set on a low hill, it will have been clearly visible from the fort, and a reminder, if that were needed, of ever-present mortality. The evidence from Brougham is

Plate 5.5 Low Borrowbridge: cemetery-area with enclosure ditches (photograph: Oxford Archaeological Unit Ltd)

altogether more complex than that from Low Borrowbridge, both regarding the nature of the cremation-ritual itself and the deposition of the remains. However, as at Low Borrowbridge and against the normal trend in the Roman world, cremation seems to have been preferred to inhumation throughout the third century.

Men, women and children were buried in the Brougham cemetery, although there was no sign of infants who, we may presume, were buried closer to where they had lived (see above on p.91). Pyre-goods and grave-goods were common, and there is every sign in both cases that the assignment of such goods was in no way haphazard, but may have related to the gender, age and status of the deceased (Cool 2004, 460f). Pyre-goods and grave-goods bear evidence of families of considerable wealth and, presumably, status. Pottery and glass vessels of various types, beads and hob-nails were present in the graves, whilst pyre-goods included not only biers decorated with carved bone, but also cremation with items of jewellery, with food – for example, a joint of pork on a platter in one case – items of military equipment, including sword-scabbards, and the whole or parts of horses, one of which at least was associated with a female cremation. Was this an honour derived from a dead husband, or did such items mark status that crossed the gender-boundary? Further, many of the burials were marked by inscribed tombstones (Fitzpatrick 2004, 407–21), which indicated an age-range of 6 to 80 years.

Overall, the evidence points to a cemetery area for military personnel and their families; further, the presence of certain items of metalwork and the names

of some of those cited on the inscriptions (Fitzpatrick 2004, 434–5) suggest that these people may have had an eastern European origin. Indeed, it seems very likely that the unit concerned was mounted (a *numerus* or *cuneus equitum*), and that, in this case, the unit may have been the *Numerus Equitum Stratonicianorum* from the Danube-region (*RIB* 780; Holder 1982, 126); the prevalence of cremation in the Brougham cemetery, however, is seen as ruling out any connection with the Sarmatians sent to Britain by Marcus Aurelius in AD 175 (Dio Cassius *History of Rome* 72.16, 2).

The evident closure of this cemetery at the end of the third century prompts two observations: first, since the excavated cemetery seems to be related to a single unit, there must be other cemetery areas in the vicinity of Brougham; secondly, it would seem possible that the exclusivity noted in this Brougham cemetery may be applicable to other northern sites, such as Lancaster. Although the only known military memorial stones from Lancaster were of men from the same unit, their evident findspots were separated by a considerable distance, and it has been suggested (chapter 2, above) that the tombstone of Lucius Julius Apollinaris had been moved from its original setting. The closure of this cemetery at Brougham may imply the transfer of the unit that used it (Cool 2004, 466); the wholesale reform of the Roman army carried out at that time by Diocletian in the late third century may provide a context for this.

Material eroding from the coast at Beckfoot, Cumbria, apparently from a Roman cemetery, has been collected and reported during much of the twentieth century (and, indeed, continues to appear, Plate 5.6); as

Plate 5.6 Beckfoot: two views of an intact cremation burial, complete with urn and cover (photograph: Stuart Noon, Portable Antiquities Scheme)

noted above, an inventory of this material has recently been compiled (Caruana 2004, 136–53). Formal excavations, however, did not take place until 2007 (OA North 2007). As with the other north-western cemeteries discussed above, the site appears to have been in use from the late second and perhaps into the fourth century, but to have consisted largely of cremation burials. It remains uncertain whether the cemetery related to Milefortlet 15 of the coastal sequence (Bellhouse 1989, 38) or to the Beckfoot fort itself – or possibly both.

Many of the cremation-burials were contained in cooking-pots (black burnished ware fabric I), and within some of the graves other ceramic drinking-vessels were present as grave-goods, together with hobnails and occasional items of jewellery. The condition of many of these suggested that they had been on the pyre, whilst the pots containing the ashes showed signs of burning, mostly on one side, as if they had perhaps stood alongside the pyre – unless, of course, previous usage had led to their condition. Two pyre-sites have been reported (Hogg 1949, 32–7; Caruana 2004, 137), one of which – unusually – contained a number of items of military equipment (Caruana 2004, 147–53). In the latter case, a funeral bed was also recognised, together with nails, some of which were said to have been gilded; it is a plausible conjecture that, in this case, the pyre-site (*bustum*) became the place of burial (Caruana 2004, 156); two sites of this nature have also been excavated at Botchergate in Carlisle (Giecco *et al.* 2001; Zant *et al.* in prep). The other pyre-site at Beckfoot displayed a less striking

assemblage; remains of what may have been woollen cloth were present, but no suggestion is offered as to its origin (Caruana 2004, 137). In contrast to the sites at Brougham and Low Borrowbridge, a considerable number of Roman coins have been recovered from Beckfoot, many in recent years from the beach by metal-detectorists. These, although generally badly worn and corroded, have not exhibited obvious signs of burning (Shotter 1990, 49; 2000b, 30; 2010 forthcoming).

The cemeteries excavated at Beckfoot, Brougham and Low Borrowbridge have certain features in common: most cremation-pots appeared to contain only a small amount of burnt bone; all three sites revealed the presence of hobnails (from shoes) and ordinary nails (presumably from pyre-furniture or interment boxes); all three sites highlighted the continuing resilience in the North West of cremation through the third and into the fourth centuries, although at Low Borrowbridge, as we have seen, inhumation was practised at an early date. Whilst the pyre-sites and graves uncovered at Brougham appear to have been more elaborately furnished, the grave-goods at Beckfoot – albeit with certain exceptions – were less impressive, and those at Low Borrowbridge and Lancaster decidedly meagre – none exhibiting the level of elaboration observed, for example, in the cemetery at London Road, Carlisle (Ferguson 1893; Patten 1974). There, at various times in the nineteenth century, sites adjacent to what is now the A6 road produced evidence of cremations, glass vessels, numerous coins (Shotter 1990, 184f), inscribed tombstones (*RIB* 955, 956, 959), coffins in lead, stone, and one formed from *tegulae*, some of which bore the stamps LEG II AVG and LEG XX VV (*RIB* 2459.1,i-v; 2463. 1,i), and a mausoleum-like structure containing a coffin. The elevated status of Carlisle as a *civitas*-capital, with its citizens of status and wealth, presumably offers an explanation for the obvious wealth represented by such cemetery-finds. There were, however, earlier graves, found during excavations on Botchergate; although some of these were far less lavishly appointed, two appear to have been of the *bustum*-type (for references, see above on p.95; also McCarthy 2002, 85f; Zant *et al.* forthcoming).

So, how far can the practices outlined above and the evidence that has been accumulated from excavation and casual reporting help to inform our understanding of the townscape of Roman Lancaster and its relationship with its cemetery-sites? Until the excavations to the west of King Street in 2001, Lancaster was one of those sites whose Roman cemetery-remains were known largely from isolated and fortuitous discoveries and antiquarian reports (see above in chapter 2).

As a site consisting of a fort with an extramural settlement, Roman Lancaster will not have had town-walls or gates; the points at which the cemeteries began, therefore, will have been somewhat arbitrary, although they must have lain beyond the perceived extent of the initial settlement. However, neither the extent of Lancaster's civilian settlement nor the course of its development are as yet properly understood, although it is assumed, on the basis of antiquarian reports and of the excavations that have taken place over the last 30 years or so, that the main focus of settlement will have been in an area between Common Garden Street (in the south) and the River Lune (in the north), and eastwards perhaps as far as Stonewell (Fig. 5.2). Market Street and Church Street were evidently linked by a series of medieval 'lanes' which, as in Carlisle, had predecessors in the Roman period (Howard-Davis *et al.* in prep; McCarthy 2000).

Beyond Common Garden Street to the south (Drury in prep), excavation has failed to reveal signs of Roman settlement; although there has been some confusion over the dating of some of the burials which have been located in this area (see above in chapter 2; Fig. 2.1); antiquarian reports suggest that some of these may have been of prehistoric date. Settlement in the Lancaster-

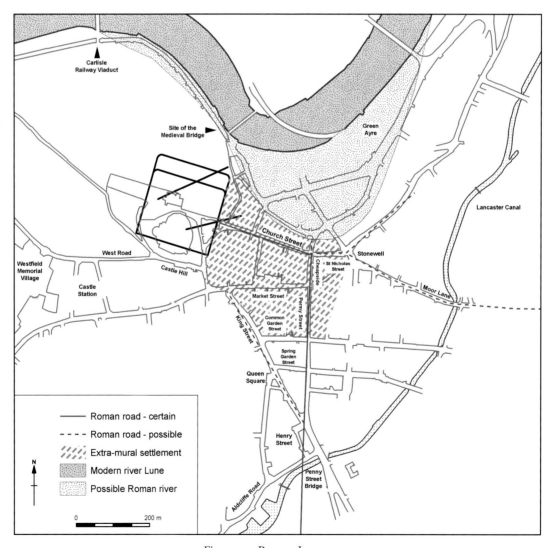

Figure 5.2 Roman Lancaster

area in prehistory is not in any way surprising in view of the obvious defensive and strategic significance of Castle Hill and the potential food-resources available in the Lune valley. It has, in fact, been suggested (above in chapter 3) that the large ditched enclosure recognised on the site of Streamline Garage may have related to pre-Roman settlement, although later utilised for burials. It is equally possible, however, that it may have been connected with burials from the late pre-Roman Iron Age; unfortunately, the absence of artefactual evidence effectively precludes conclusive discussion of both the date and the purpose of this ditch-feature. It is, however, worth noting that the excavations on the site of the Arla Foods Depot (above in chapter 4) also demonstrated the presence of Neolithic activity in this area and that none of the prehistoric burials in the city have been subject to modern scientific dating methods. It is possible, therefore (although perhaps unlikely), that some of the antiquarian reports of 'Bronze Age' material discussed in chapter 2 are actually of Iron Age, or even Romano-British origin.

It may be, therefore, that Common Garden Street marks the southern end of the Roman civilian settlement and the beginning of an area in which some burials may have already taken place in the pre-Roman period, but which was used more coherently as a cemetery area after the arrival of the Romans in the early 70s. This would have sent out a message which was at the same time powerful, but conciliatory, proclaiming a 'new era', but emphasising some continuity with what had gone before. This recalls the observation of the third-century historian, Dio Cassius (*History of Rome* 56.18, 2–3), regarding the economic and social impact of the Roman presence on German tribesmen in the time of the Emperor, Augustus – that they 'became different without knowing it'.

In broad terms, the routes of the main roads leading in and out of Roman Lancaster from the south are tolerably well-known: the roads approaching from Ribchester and Walton-le-Dale appear to have converged somewhere in the vicinity of the present village of Galgate, some four miles to the south of Lancaster (Fig. 5.3; Graystone 1996, 41ff). From there, the road proceeded northwards and to the west of the modern A6, by way of Burrow Heights; indeed, it is the proximity of this road to the visible earthwork on

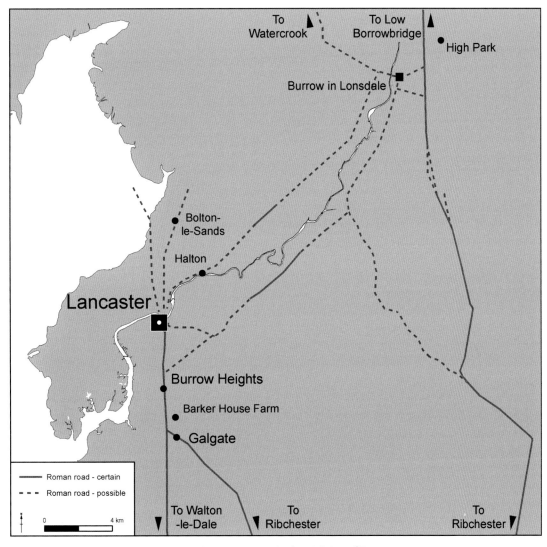

Figure 5.3 Roman routes in the vicinity of Lancaster

Burrow Heights that has prompted the suggestion that this may have been the site of a roadside mausoleum of the Roman period. The site has yielded Roman copper coins of the second and third centuries (Shotter 2000b, 28), as well as a palstave of the middle to late Bronze Age. Further possible support for this suggestion has come from a group of statuary which was evidently found in 1794, when the Lancaster Canal was being dug (Watkin 1883, 180ff; Edwards 1971; see below on pp.103ff).

From Burrow Heights, the road approached Lancaster probably by way of Ripley Heights (LUAU 2000b; 2001b), and across the site where the Royal Lancaster Infirmary now stands. It is worth noting that it appears that a collection of Roman copper coins, recently presented for examination (Shotter 2000b, 141f), contains hoard-material which was probably found during the construction of the hospital in the late nineteenth century. The course of the road ran just to the west of the present Penny Street Bridge, where its line was revealed in the excavations of 2005 (see above in chapter 4). In the centre of Lancaster itself, this road is then represented by the modern lines of Penny Street and Cheapside. The precise location of the Roman crossing-point of the River Lune at Lancaster itself remains unknown, although the site later used for the medieval bridge or that beneath the Carlisle railway-viaduct appear to be possibilities, as at these points the bedrock is exposed in the river.

The Roman fort itself was probably served by a 'spur' leaving the north-south line near Penny Street Bridge and leading in a north-westerly direction to the south gate of the fort on Castle Hill, perhaps reflected in the line of King Street. It has to be remembered, however, that no traces of such a 'spur' or, indeed, of the fort's south gate itself have ever been reported, and the line of King Street (*via regia*) may be of medieval date (Penney 1981a, 16f). It has also been speculated above (on p.7f) that a burial on Queen Square may be of Roman origin; this, in its turn, may serve to leave open the debate concerning the origin and date of King Street.

As we have seen, two other exit-roads from the Roman fort have yielded suggestions of possible cemetery-material – to the west in the region of West Road and eastwards in the lower Church Street area. In the former case, evidence of burials was reported from the site of Westfield War Memorial Village in the mid-1930s, although the interpretation of this material is not without difficulties (see above in chapter 2). Nor can it now be confirmed whether the substantial collection of finds mentioned in connection with the construction of a railway station in 1849–50 (Watkin 1883, 186) in fact came from Lancaster Castle Station to the west of the fort or from that at Green Ayre, which lay on the bank of the River Lune to the north east. In any case, this seems not to have been the site of a burial as assumed

by later authors (above p.7f). Furthermore, it remains uncertain how far this westward-leading road would have been viable in the estuarine conditions that must have prevailed, or indeed what its destination would have been, unless there was a beaching-point further down the estuary (as at Kirkham on the Ribble estuary; see Howard-Davis and Buxton 2000).

In the case of the lower Church Street area, proximity to the fort has led to doubts about its use for burials; it is, of course, possible that some burials may have been placed there in the very early years prior to the growth of the extramural settlement, or alternatively much later following the evacuation of this settlement, which on present evidence appears to have been taking place from the mid-fourth century (Howard-Davis *et al.* in prep). Whilst the inhumations on St Nicholas Street (above on p.15) cannot be confirmed as Roman, it may be that burials lay further out along Moor Lane, which was effectively the continuation of Church Street in the direction of Lancaster Moor and Quernmore, where kilns of the Roman period have been located (Shotter and White 1995, 65–8). Indeed, one of the burials from Lancaster Moor is assigned to the Roman period (above in chapter 2). Finally, if, as seems possible, the River Lune was crossed at some point upstream of the present Carlisle railway-viaduct, there may be further cemetery-sites awaiting discovery in the Ryelands Park area.

For the present, however, it is clear that what seems to have been an extensive cemetery area on the southern and south-eastern flanks of Roman Lancaster provides our best evidence for funerary activity relating to the Roman settlement. The first – and most obvious – point to note is the great contrast that exists between the social and economic implications of the memorial stone of Insus and of most of the other burial sites that lie in the vicinity of Penny Street and King Street. It has already been suggested (above in chapter 4) that not only may the stone of Insus have been repaired and moved, presumably to provide it with a more prominent position in the cemetery, but also that it may be inferred from the excellent preservation of the carvings on the memorial stone that it may have had a protective superstructure; however it should be noted again that attempts to recreate such a superstructure from the archaeological evidence have not led to a satisfactory outcome. We have also seen that the absence of bones or cremated material, together with the obvious omissions from the text of the inscription, make it very likely that it functioned as a cenotaph, rather than a gravestone; the possible reasons for this have already been discussed (above in chapter 4). It may be that these characteristics, together with the evident absence of other burials in the immediate vicinity of the memorial stone, point to a secondary use of the stone by the cemetery-authorities, perhaps as part of a 'refurbishment-phase', as an 'advertisement' for the cemetery itself. The known graves in this southern cemetery area appear to have fallen a long way short of Insus' memorial in terms of the wealth and social position that they represented. It should be remembered, however, that the tile tomb (although its site cannot now be located) is clearly another elaborate burial, which presumably also indicated a person of higher status in Roman Lancaster (see above in chapter 2).

The majority of excavated graves were urned or unurned cremations; most of those that were urned were deposited in pottery vessels dating to the mid-second to late third centuries. These were not distributed evenly across the ground, or set out in regular patterns (as would be expected in a modern cemetery), but occurred in clusters, as is reported elsewhere (for example, in Colchester: Pooley *et al.* 2006, 15). In all cases, the cremated material consisted mostly of burnt oak or alder from the pyre, with sometimes very little cremated human bone present. It has been suggested (above on p.45) that the difference in the species of burnt wood involved may have had a significance, as the contents of a burial with alder differed from another with oak, although both were recovered from the same burial pit. The overriding impression conveyed by these graves as a whole, however, is one of low social status and considerable, presumably involuntary, asceticism.

There were virtually no grave-goods present, such as appear to have differentiated gender, age and status in the cemetery at Brougham (Cool 2004), although occasional fragments of cremated animal bone (sheep and pig) on the Streamline Garage Site, suggest that in a few cases a meal may have been placed on the pyre for consumption by the deceased. There were a few nails, pointing to the possibility that in some cases wooden boxes may have been used to hold the cremated remains. However, the only objects that were present in any quantity in the burials were hobnails from shoes which had been placed either on the pyres or in the graves to facilitate the deceased's journey to the Underworld; no coins were recovered, such as are often found for payment of the dead person's journey across the River Styx (see above on p.92). Most of the graves appear to have been unmarked, although a few provided evidence of a posthole, as if perhaps a simple wooden marker had been inserted (as at Petty Knowes and elsewhere, Charlton and Mitcheson 1984, 21).

The fact that many of the burials were set within an enclosure ditch, which may, in fact, have been an already-existing feature of a settlement-site – perhaps a stock-pen – does not provide the impression of a military cemetery area, where payment into a burial-club should have guaranteed the integrity of the individual plot (although, as we have seen at Low Borrowbridge, this was not always the case). The

conclusion must surely be drawn that these were in all probability the graves of non-military personnel and their families from the extramural settlement.

Although pyre-material was present in the cremations, there were no indications of the presence of pyre-furniture within the areas most recently excavated, such as has been recognised at Brougham and Beckfoot, unless, of course, some of the sherds of burnt pot, which were found in some graves, derived from containers of food and drink which were either placed upon the pyres or possibly consumed nearby by the relatives and friends of the deceased. Indeed, the most likely piece of pyre-furniture recorded from Lancaster is the small fragment of carved bone veneer, which was recovered during excavations in 1973 in a completely different part of the city (see above on p.17). It would seem that, as at Low Borrowbridge, the pyre-sites were not immediately adjacent to the graves as they appear to have been at Beckfoot, Birdoswald and Brougham or, indeed, directly over the grave-plot as at Petty Knowes (Hair and Howard-Davis 1996; Hogg 1949; Caruana 2004; Wilmott 1993; Cool 2004; Charlton and Mitcheson 1984). We cannot, therefore, speculate on the relative significance of ritualistic activities at the pyre-side when compared to the limited evidence for such ceremonial within the burial-area itself.

Although the majority of the excavated burials were of cremated remains, there was some evidence that there may have also been a few inhumations; two of these, from the site at 77–79 Penny Street, were associated with calcite-gritted pottery of the late third to fourth centuries. The uppermost fill of the later grave yielded a calcite-gritted rim dated to *c.* 300–370; a build-up of soil above this contained further fragments of such wares and was cut by two probable unurned cremations placed in small pits. It is not possible to draw significant conclusions about the inhumations, as surviving bone was either absent or only barely present; further, these burials were in the main truncated by post-Roman activity. It is clear, however, that in fourth-century Lancaster cremation and inhumation were practised contemporaneously; this might be taken to point towards the reintroduction (or, indeed, the long-term persistence) of a northern European rite in the later years of the Roman period, perhaps derived from Germanic traditions. At Colchester, for example, rather more secure evidence of this has been detected (Pooley *et al.* 2006, 69).

The memorial to Insus has been dated to the late first or early second century, and would appear to provide the earliest evidence of funerary activity on this site within the Roman period. There is some evidence, from the infringement of the road upon this area, that it may have suffered a period of relative neglect in the early to middle years of the second century. The recutting of the road-zone ditch appears to indicate an end to this period perhaps coinciding with the start of the use of the adjacent site as part of a cemetery. At a later point, whilst burials were still being added, Insus' memorial stone is thought to have been lifted and moved to its final setting.

The significance of the excavation results are principally twofold. First, we have a Romano-British cemetery established on ground that was already in use, at least in part, for ritual purposes in the Roman period. The remains recovered from this offer an obvious and marked contrast, in terms of wealth and implied status, to those which have been found further north at Brougham (Cool 2004). This suggests a rather smaller reliance on elaboration of ritual; it also offers further evidence of the continuing predominance of cremation, with only minor indications of inhumation. This could possibly point to conservatism in parts of the North West regarding religious and funerary practice, manifesting itself in a resistance on the part of devotees of the familiar pagan rituals to the spread of new practices related to Christianity. We do find evidence elsewhere that public proclamations of Christianity remained decidedly muted until, at least, the second half of the fourth century (Shotter 1979). It is also the case that, in the single modern excavation of a Romano-British settlement in the Lancaster area (OA North 2004), a distinctly traditional lifestyle seems to have been chosen, on a site within a short distance of a major Roman road leading to a Roman fort and settlement. This also indicates an innate conservatism within at least some of the population; just how extensive such attitudes were, however, remains to be seen.

The second significance, of course, lies in the implications arising from the discovery of the memorial stone of the Treveran cavalryman, Insus, who belonged to a unit known as the *Ala Augusta* (Bull 2007; see also above on pp.79ff). The stone was located alongside the main approach to the settlement, indicating, as has recently been suggested by the discovery of two Roman stone sarcophagi at Newcastle upon Tyne, that it was of great importance to ensure its visibility (Richard Annis, Durham University, Department of Archaeology, Press Release dated 15 August, 2008). The presence on the rear of the stone of slots, intended for the insertion of brackets to reinforce the stone after it had evidently cracked, lends further weight to the suggestion that the cemetery may have suffered a period of neglect in the first half of the second century – perhaps following the transfer of the *Ala Augusta* to Hadrian's Wall (Holder 1982, 107 and 109). It seems likely that the stone was repaired and moved to a new position as part of a restoration of the cemetery. The imposing impression that this stone will have given will obviously have drawn attention to this cemetery area, although it contrasts sharply with the apparent simplicity of all the other burials excavated in the vicinity.

We now have evidence for two stones from Lancaster, which were set up, probably around the turn of the first and second centuries, as memorials for Treveran horsemen in this *ala*; this perhaps provides a small insight into the workings of Roman imperial management. As suggested above in chapter 4, it would not be at all surprising if these, and presumably other, Treverans were brought to Britain under the auspices of Quintus Petillius Cerialis, Rome's former commander in the Gallo-German war of AD 69–70, when he took up his new appointment in Britain in AD 71. Vespasian's and Cerialis' intention was presumably to benefit from lessons learned during the Gallo-German conflict by detaching auxiliary soldiers from their homelands, particularly at a time when Rome's relationships with the Treveri were especially sensitive. On the larger scale, Vespasian certainly did not yield to sentiment in his reorganising of the Roman army in Germany (Levick 1999, 152ff).

Insus' memorial stone provides its own gloss on that situation through its portrayal of the triumphant aftermath of the decapitation of an enemy on the battlefield; it dramatically demonstrates Insus' and his heirs' pride in his Treveran origin. As we have seen, the historian, Diodorus Siculus (*Library of History* 5.29), highlights the importance to the Treveri of the Celtic ritual of battlefield-decapitation – despite the fact that the Treveri are not universally regarded as having been of Celtic origin (Wightman 1970, 20; W.T.W. Potts *pers. comm.* 2008). Nonetheless, the attachment of the Treveri to the practice was sufficiently well-known in Rome for Cicero to have been able to make a wry and pointed joke about it (*Letters to his Friends* 7.13, 2; Shotter 2007).

In addition, this stone, which must be regarded as one of the finest of its type, will have made an impressive and striking spectacle in its raised position in the cemetery. This will have been greatly enhanced if, as seems likely, the letters of the inscription and perhaps features of the sculpture itself were picked out in bright paint (Bull 2007, 20). The stone also points to a degree of wealth on the part of Insus and his family, as well as the presence – even if only temporarily – in Lancaster of a craftsman capable of carrying out such a prestigious and complex commission. It has been suggested (Fred Broadhurst *pers. comm.* 2009) that the source of the stone might have been the coast at Heysham and that the raw material could then have been brought up to Lancaster by boat.

The absence of human remains associated with Insus' stone suggests that it was a cenotaph; this may have been the case also with a few of the grave-sites at the Streamline Garage site, although these did contain a very small amount of human remains together with pyre-debris. It is not difficult to infer the circumstances that might have led to the creation of a cenotaph, especially in the early days of Roman campaigning in Britain.

There are not likely to be further opportunities in the near future to examine substantial areas of the southern cemetery of Roman Lancaster, although we need to remain aware of the disposition of the recently-published cemetery area at Brougham (Cool 2004), which highlights the distance that might separate a fort from an area of its cemeteries, and shows that cemeteries might occur well beyond the accepted edges of settlements. In other words, areas adjacent to the known or inferred lines of Roman roads should not be ignored simply because of their distance from settlements; for example, recent work at Vindolanda (Burnham, Hunter and Fitzpatrick 2006, 391f.; Burnham, Hunter and Booth 2007, 261ff) and at Binchester (County Durham: Burnham, Hunter and Booth 2008, 283ff) has served to emphasise the fact that impressive burials might well be situated at a considerable distance from the fort-sites to which they related. Whilst it does not appear on present evidence that the *Ala Augusta* had a segregated cemetery at Lancaster, it is still not impossible that the *Ala Sebosiana* and the *Numerus Barcariorum* did, particularly since the only recorded tomb of a man who may have been a member of the *Ala Sebosiana* cannot be allotted a findspot.

Overall, our knowledge of Lancaster's Roman cemeteries continues to leave a number of unanswered questions – beyond those regarding the extent of the southern cemetery and the possible locations of other major cemetery areas: for example, could the skull recovered outside the fort's east gate at the western end of Church Street have belonged to a victim of crime? Why were there burials at the eastern end of Church Street so close to the fort's east gate? How are we to interpret the finds made in Cheapside, especially the lost tombstone of Lucius Julius Apollinaris? What should be inferred from so striking a tomb as that constructed of *tegulae* bearing the stamp of the *Ala Sebosiana*?

In view of the divergencies observed in the various cemetery-sites noted in the North West, care has to be exercised before assuming that wide-ranging conclusions can be drawn from what we presently know of sites in Lancaster. Whilst it is clear that a well-funded research programme would be very desirable, it is remarkable how much has emerged from a series of small developer-funded excavations and how they have advanced our knowledge of Roman Lancaster. The results are even more welcome when it is realised that all of the work described above was undertaken before the publication of *An Archaeological Research Framework for North West England* (Brennand 2007), and that a specific research agenda for Lancaster remains an idea rather than a plan.

This volume has brought together the sum of all that is *currently* known of Lancaster's Roman cemeteries; it is, however, very unlikely that the sites and finds reported here represent the total of the information potentially available. The significance of the extramural settlement has already been realised and a report on the important site of Mitchell's Brewery, Church Street (Howard-Davis *et al.* in prep) is awaited, but other sites

Plate 5.7 Lancaster: re-enactment of a Roman funeral procession, honouring Insus
(Participants: *Deva Victrix* of Chester; photograph: Peter Iles)

within the city have not been examined with such thoroughness. It is crucial, therefore, however difficult it may be within a modern urban environment, that every opportunity provided by development projects is taken to extend, broaden and deepen our knowledge.

What is written here must surely illuminate only a very small proportion of the cemetery areas of Roman Lancaster that were integral elements of the relationship which was so important in Roman culture – that between the living and the dead (Plate 5.7).

The Burrow Roman Sculptures, with a Hypothetical Reconstruction of a Mausoleum

By Ben Edwards

The sculptures

Among the many pieces of information about the Roman period in Lancashire which were collected by W. Thompson Watkin for his book *Roman Lancashire* (Watkin 1883) was the discovery in 1794 of a number of apparently Roman sculptures in the area known as Burrow, in Ashton-with-Stodday. These he published (Watkin 1876; 1883, 180–1) and included engravings of all seven of them. They came to Lancaster City Museum, and were brought together from dispersal around the museum's premises about 1970 by the then Curator, Mrs Edith Tyson. A publication appeared soon afterwards to assess their significance (Edwards 1971); this was illustrated with the photographs reproduced here as Plates 5.8 and 5.9, and incorporated the suggestion that the sculptures had come from a tomb or mausoleum. Whether or not this idea is acceptable depends on the reader's opinion, since it was not possible to be certain that the interpretation was correct. Nevertheless, the apparently funerary nature of the sculptures makes further consideration of them appropriate.

Whatever the status and derivation of the sculptures as a whole, one thing is certain – they included four stone heads carved at about double life-size. Watkin chose to illustrate three of them by reproducing the engravings made 60 years before for Thomas Dunham Whitaker (Whitaker 1823, 215), saying that they were 'much worn (probably through being for some time in a carpenter's yard at Lancaster)' and that Whitaker's engravings '[were] the best criterion of their original appearance' (Watkin 1883, 180). Comparison of the engravings with the photographs published in 1971 suggests that very little damage had in fact occurred. That is not to say that the engravings were completely accurate. The same comparison with the photographs shows that Whitaker's engraver made all three too narrow, that he failed to observe the block-like base or plinth on which one of them at least is depicted, and that he gave the same head – Watkin's no.2 and Edwards Plate 5.8a – a soulful upward gaze by placing the drilled pupils at the top of the eyeballs, while they are, in fact, central.

The fourth head Watkin illustrated with an engraving from Clark (1811, 122), and here there is more of a problem. Clark's illustration shows a possible female head with no neck, base or other support. The face is surrounded by a rope-like band or plait of hair, and is shown with eyes having large pupils, a nose with somewhat distended nostrils and a 'cupid's bow' mouth. The fourth surviving head, however (Edwards Plate 5.8b), is rather different from Clark's engraving. It is, in fact, very similar to Edwards Plate 5.8a, but the front, that is the face itself and the front of its block-like base, have been removed. It is now impossible to say whether or not this damage is the result of maltreatment in a carpenter's yard, of damage in the Roman period, or indeed of damage by the navvies of 1794. There is a hint that some of the damage to this head did indeed occur at some time in the nineteenth century. Very crude engravings of all the sculptures were published by Gregson (1869, 238), with the head under discussion shown as having the eyes and most of the nose undamaged, although the lowest part of the nose, the mouth and the chin had all been lost. By 1970 no facial details at all survived. This head bears comparison with a head from Corbridge (Phillips 1977, no. 130), there dated on the basis of the hairstyle to the third century.

An additional minor problem results from the fact that Watkin (1883, 180) reported the discovery, in 1872, of a fifth stone head from the same field as those found in 1794. This had been 'supposed to be' of Jupiter Ammon, but Watkin rejected this identification and he himself, working from a drawing, considered the head to be a 'medieval corbel'. Because of the element of doubt, he submitted this drawing to no less an authority than Charles Roach Smith, who confirmed the medieval identification, thereby perhaps raising more questions than he answered. A field which has yielded seven Roman sculptures can produce an eighth without undue surprise; but what a medieval corbel might be doing in a rural field well away from any known medieval buildings is much less easily explained. The significance of this other head must remain a mystery unless and until it, or an illustration of it, appears. It had been taken to Clifton Hall by 'Mr.

Plate 5.8 Burrow Heights, Lancaster: sculpted heads (photographs: Ben Edwards)

Plate 5.9 Burrow Heights, Lancaster: sculpted figures (photographs: Ben Edwards)

Dalzell'. The combination of name and owner shows that this particular Clifton Hall was that near Workington, although no trace of this head was found during a search in 1970.

Correspondence with Professor Jocelyn Toynbee, then the foremost authority both on Roman art and, particularly, on death and burial customs in the Roman world, showed that she was perfectly happy with the idea that the Burrow statuary had been derived from a tomb or mausoleum, and considered that the small female statue found at the same time as the other pieces (now, and apparently when discovered, headless) might well have represented the deceased. It was she, too, who identified the object in the hands of that figure as a scroll, and suggested that it might have been either the Scroll of Destiny or the deceased person's will. Again, comparison with the 1970 photograph (Plate 5.9) shows that Whitaker's engraver depicted the drapery of the figure to be complete down to its hem, which drapes over the toe of the right foot, and the whole figure mounted on a block base. Today, the drapery stops short, the base is a modern addition, and the sculpted figure has suffered a major break. If Watkin's statement (1876) that the figure was 2 feet (610mm) high is accurate, its present height of *c.* 1 foot 10 inches (560mm) might explain the discrepancy, though it is more probably the result of the common practice in the nineteenth century of silently 'improving' objects illustrated. The lack of a base on Whitaker's illustration of head 2 (= Edwards Plate 5.8a) is a case in point.

The connection of the whole group with a funerary monument was supported by the presence of two animal sculptures (Plate 5.9), of which Watkin (1883, 181) wrote '. . . animals, whose *genus* I will not attempt to determine. By some they have been called 'sea-lions'; I however leave the reader to form his own opinion of them . . .'. Despite the fact that Watkin appears to have forgotten that a sea lion is a kind of seal, they seem quite certainly to be lions, though perhaps allowance should be made for a sculptor who had never seen such an animal at close quarters! At any rate, the association between lions and death is frequently found. As Toynbee (1964, 113) put it, when discussing a funerary group from London, 'Here we have an allegory of the all-devouring jaws of death, one that is familiar on carved sarcophagi and other funerary monuments throughout the Roman Empire'.

The association between sculpted lions and death already alluded to is generally accepted, and the analogy with the lion-and-stag groups at Shorden Brae (Northumberland) is used in the hypothetical reconstruction (below on p.106f). Much the best-known of such creatures in Roman Britain, however, is the Corbridge lion (Phillips 1977, no. 82), which ended its working days as a fountain spout, but almost certainly derived originally from a funerary context. Corbridge has also produced two other such lions (Phillips 1977, nos 81 and 83). Nearer geographically, but much less well known, is the sculpture in the British Museum from Kirkby Thore (Bruce 1875, no. 759; Plate 5.10), which depicts a lion with the head of a ram between its fore-paws. This is particularly interesting in the context of Burrow Heights in that its sculptor's first-hand experience of lions was probably little greater than that of the Burrow sculptor. The same could certainly be said of the Cramond lioness, recovered in 1997 from the waters of the river Almond, not far from the eastern end of the Antonine Wall, though the sculpture itself has been dated to the time of Septimius Severus (Burnham, Keppie and Esmonde Cleary 1998, 380). The lioness is a crouching feline having between her fore-paws a naked bearded human torso, while two snakes emerge from beneath her body. The teeth with which she is threatening to devour her prey, however, would better have endowed a shark. Other such lions from Roman

Britain represent better attempts at depicting the beast. At Chester, for example, there is both a lion-and-stag group and a relief sculpture of a lion (Wright and Richmond 1955, nos 168 and 167).

What, however, the four heads represent has not been resolved; that they are personifications is a strong possibility. There are two obvious groups of four which are known to have been represented in Roman art – the Four Winds and the Four Seasons. Interpretation must depend on the detail of the sculptures themselves: first, they are solely heads; that is to say that they were so intended by their sculptor, and are not derived from statues. In this they resemble the well-known head from York which carries the letters **D M C E** (D(is) m(anibus) c(onsecratus) e(st) – *RIB* 701), though this is somewhat different from the Burrow Heights heads in that the head itself is at 45 degrees to its plinth, and two letters appear on adjacent faces of the plinth. The York head, therefore, was clearly placed on the corner of something. Other heads on plinths also exist from both Roman Britain and other parts of the Empire and these are discussed by Toynbee (1964, 111–12). Second, the Burrow heads fall into two groups; the first pair appear

Plate 5.10 Kirkby Thore: lion devouring a ram (photograph by courtesy of the Trustees of the British Museum)

to be female (Plate 5.8a, b) and, given the damaged state of head (b), very similar, with the hair dressed in a circle of ringlets round the face and the rest of the hair covered by some form of cap.

In contrast, the third head (Plate 5.8c) is certainly male, for it has a beard, whilst the last (Plate 5.8d), although unbearded, also appears masculine. The former also appears to be wearing a Phrygian Cap. This form of headgear derives from Phrygia, in central Anatolia, and is sometimes used to indicate its wearer's generic easternness. Thus, the Magi, when not shown with crowns, are sometimes endowed with Phrygian Caps to show their derivation from the east, as can be seen on a Byzantine ivory plaque of the early sixth century in the British Museum (Medieval and Modern European 1904, 7–2, 1). Another familiar group of figures who wear the Cap are Mithras and his attendants, Cautes and Cautopates (Ferguson 1970, 63). Mithraic ceremonial is not suggested in general as an explanation of the Burrow heads, though it may have its place, as will become apparent. Apollo, too, sometimes wears the Phrygian Cap. Head (d) also wears a cap, though it is not as obviously a Phrygian Cap. It should be noted that the two male heads do not have drilled pupils, while head (a) does and head (b) probably had, if we accept the evidence of Clark's engraving (1811).

These factors still do not allow us to differentiate between the two groups already mentioned. To have the colder winds (north and east) represented by males and the warmer (west and south) by females would make sense. It is difficult to differentiate further within each of the two pairs, except for the inclusion of the obvious eastern cap. Toynbee (1964, 115) notes that '[the] Wind Gods ... were conceived of as wafting the souls of the departed to paradise', which strengthens the case for that identification. On the other hand, in mosaics at least, Wind Gods usually have either wings in their hair or carry conch shells. The seasons, though perhaps a less probable identification, could also be seen in two pairs, with autumn and winter possibly male and spring and summer female. However, personifications of the seasons as busts are almost always female (Ling 1983, 18). It may also be significant that Cautes, the Mithraic attendant symbolising light, occasionally represents spring, with Cautopates, the bringer of darkness, autumn (Ferguson 1970, 121). No helpful indications of identity were supplied by a somewhat similar head from Towcester (Northamptonshire), in the British Museum (Brailsford 1951, 54, IV, b, 1); nor was information supplied by Watkin (1883, 180–1) helpful in this respect.

If we leave aside the idea that they are personifications, we may presume they represented actual people associated with the person commemorated – perhaps family members. Toynbee (1964, 247), in discussing the mosaic from Lufton in Wiltshire, is happy to suggest that it carried busts with 'no attributes ... to suggest that [they] depict a Wind or a Season or a god', and might therefore be 'stylized portraits of members of the family that owned the villa'. If the Burrow monument commemorated a husband and wife, then the two pairs might have been the parents of both persons. No immediate parallel for this idea is forthcoming, and ultimately we have to say that the problem is probably not resolvable, unless some further evidence emerges from the ground in the Burrow area.

Hypothetical reconstruction of a mausoleum on Burrow Heights

The drawing (Fig. 5.4) represents an attempt to suggest the type of structure which might have existed on Burrow Heights, the site from which the sculptures found in 1794 probably came. The reconstruction is, it must be stressed, purely hypothetical; but what is suggested is generally in accord with what is known of such monuments elsewhere in the Roman Empire, and it also finds a place for all the surviving statuary (Toynbee 1971, 164–72). As stated above, the notion that the Burrow Heights statuary might have been associated with a mausoleum was first proposed in the 1960s by Mrs Edith Tyson, then Curator of the Lancaster City Museum. Strongly in its support was the fact that the lions recalled the sculptured animal groups recovered in the excavation of a mausoleum on Shorden Brae, a little to the west of Corbridge (Gillam and Daniels 1961). There, the groups consisted of lions attacking deer, and had been found in positions which made it seem likely that they had been mounted on the corners of the temenos (enclosure) wall. It is also worth noting the recent identification of portions of sculptured friezes, now built into the structure of the Anglo-Saxon crypt at Hexham Abbey, as having been derived from the Shorden Brae mausoleum (Paul Bidwell pers. comm. 2009; Hodgson 2009, 105–7).

A consideration of monuments such as that at Igel, near Trier (Wightman 1970, 239ff), that at St Rémy-en-Provence (Rivet 1988, 200) and a variety of similar monuments in North Africa (particularly, though not exclusively, in Libya) suggested, as a starting point, a rectangular, tower-like structure for the funerary monument itself. Although the Igel and St Rémy examples have extensive relief sculpture, by no means all such monuments carry sculpture, either in relief or three-dimensional. There was no evidence for relief sculpture at Burrow Heights, obviating the need to incorporate it into the reconstruction; but any speculative design would have to accommodate four over-life-sized human heads on block-like bases, at least two lions, and a human figure at a much smaller scale.

Certain aspects of the sculptures were crucial to their disposition on the monument as a whole. The large scale of the stone heads, for instance, suggested that

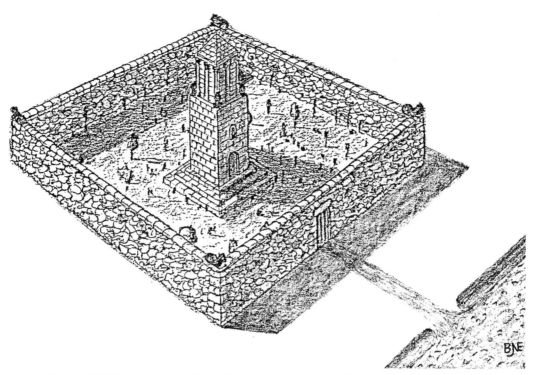

Figure 5.4 Burrow Heights, Lancaster: a hypothetical reconstruction of a mausoleum (drawing: Ben Edwards)

they had been sited some distance from the ground, perhaps at the point at which an offset reduced the dimensions of a tower at the commencement of a smaller upper stage. As noted above (on p.105f), their actual significance was not obvious, and they could not be assigned to a particular group of four. The fifth head, discussed above (p.103f), has been omitted from the reconstruction because of doubts about its origin. After consideration of all the factors, it was decided to place one head at each of the four corners of the base of the upper section of a two-stage tower. The location seemed appropriate: the heads would be surveying the surrounding scene, on watch on high, as it were.

The siting of the lions in the overall scheme required much consideration. The ferocity of the creature makes it a suitable symbol of the ultimate triumph of death over life. Only two lion sculptures were recovered, as at Shorden Brae; they therefore might be aptly placed on the plinth of the monument tower, on the front, one on each side of the door. However, following the suggestion made in the case of Shorden Brae, the final drawing indicates four such creatures, positioned at the corners of the enclosure (Gillam and Daniels 1961). If, in fact, the monument featured only the two lions recovered in 1794, then they might well have been sited on the two corners of the enclosure which faced the road.

Finally, the smaller scale of the headless human figure made it seem likely to have been positioned nearer the ground. The figure wears flowing garments which emphasise civilian, rather than military, activities; the fact that it is holding, and possibly reading, a scroll (above p.104), may imply that this figure represented the deceased. Whatever its symbolism, a single figure at this scale might well have been placed in a niche over a doorway, as illustrated. The monument is depicted as standing beside the road leading south from the fort at Lancaster, and connected to it by a path which leads through a gap in the roadside ditch.

While there do not seem to be any obvious parallels in Roman Britain to the suggested Burrow monument other than that at Shorden Brae, other sites have produced evidence of tomb structures outside the fort, notably those known as Petty Knowes near the fort of *Bremenium* (High Rochester), in Northumberland (Charlton and Mitcheson 1984). There does not seem to be any suggestion, however, that these were as elaborate as that at Shorden Brae (or that suggested for Burrow), that they carried sculpture, or that they were placed in any form of enclosure.

The recent discovery of the foundations of several mausolea near the fort at Binchester, in County Durham, shows that such funerary monuments might occur both in numbers and close to a fort (Burnham, Hunter and Booth 2008, 283ff). It is worth bearing in mind, however, that the Shorden Brae mausoleum was sited in countryside at some distance from Corbridge. Perhaps the position afforded by Burrow Heights was chosen for the same reasons as those prompting, centuries later, the choice of the site of the Ashton Memorial of 1906–9 in Williamson Park, high above the City of Lancaster.

APPENDIX 2

The Conservation of the Roman Memorial Stone

By Emily Somerville and Jenny Truran

From the excavation in November 2005 until March 2008, the two main pieces and the smaller fragments of the memorial stone were placed on pallets in the store of Lancashire Museums, to enable the sandstone to dry out under controlled conditions. This lengthy process was undertaken to ensure the stability of the sandstone. During this period, a considerable amount of time was dedicated to the assessment of potential methods of treatment and to the options for displaying the repaired memorial stone.

At the completion of the drying process the stone sections were transported to the adjacent Lancashire Conservation Studios, where a large amount of mud and ingrained dirt covering the surfaces was removed using dry methods of cleaning. The thicker areas of mud were removed with more abrasive techniques, including the careful use of a brass-bristle brush, whilst more-thinly encrusted areas and ingrained dirt were cleaned using bamboo carving tools and ordinary brushes. No attempt at wet cleaning was made now the stone was dry, as its porosity and the consequent possibility of salt migration could have led to damage.

Following cleaning, the weights of the main parts of the stone were calculated and a hydraulic engine-lifting crane was assessed as the most appropriate and versatile equipment available. This was used both to raise the stone to an upright and secure position, and to lift, lower and support the upper portion whilst the two main parts were joined together. The main part of the stone was lifted using slings around its centre, carefully rotated and then secured upright into a temporary wooden stand and fastened against a wall, using Plastazote padded steel brackets on either side. This provided the necessary vertical support, allowing this part of the stone to stand securely whilst the upper portion was re-attached.

Consultation with the York Archaeological Trust and the National Conservation Centre at Liverpool indicated that the best method of joining the two large pieces was to use two 16mm stainless steel dowels fixed in place with a polyester resin. This ensures a high degree of stability and is a widely-used practice. Two holes, 20mm wide and 120mm deep, were drilled into the stone across the central section of the main horizontal break. One of the holes was in line with the

cavalryman's head and the other with the horse's head. At this point, six of the smaller pieces were also attached to the central section using a polyester resin. Dowels were not used on these pieces, as they were too small to drill, and resin alone was considered to be sufficiently secure.

The upper section was lifted using the engine lifting crane and slings, and test-fitted before the adhesive was applied. Polyester resin was then generously applied to the dowel and joint faces and the top part slowly lowered into position. The resin was left to set completely and then two further small pieces were fixed into place on the front face of the stone, again using polyester resin. No attempt was made to re-attach the basal stub to the main portion of the stone, as the junction between the two sections was incomplete due to damage and loss in antiquity. Any such join would have required speculation as to the relative positions of the two parts and have been mechanically weak, requiring substantial further intervention to provide adequate support to facilitate display.

Where there were large gaps at the exterior edges of the joins, filling was carried out to give added support and for aesthetic reasons, the voids being filled with

Plate 5.11 Reiter memorial stone during conservation
(photograph: Emily Somerville)

plaster applied by means of a syringe, ensuring penetration of the cracks (Plate 5.11). The filled areas on the front and sides were subsequently retouched so that they did not stand out from the original surface. This was achieved using ground-up sandstone adhered via an archival PVA glue and acrylic paints.

Following the completion of the process of conservation, the complete memorial stone (less the detached basal stub) was packed and transported to Lancaster City Museum, where, due to its size and weight, it had to be lifted by crane through a window on the first floor (Plate 5.12). It is now on display adjacent to the Burrow Heights Sculptures, where it is the major feature of the newly-refurbished Roman gallery.

Plate 5.12 Reiter memorial stone arriving at Lancaster City Museum (photograph: Emily Somerville)

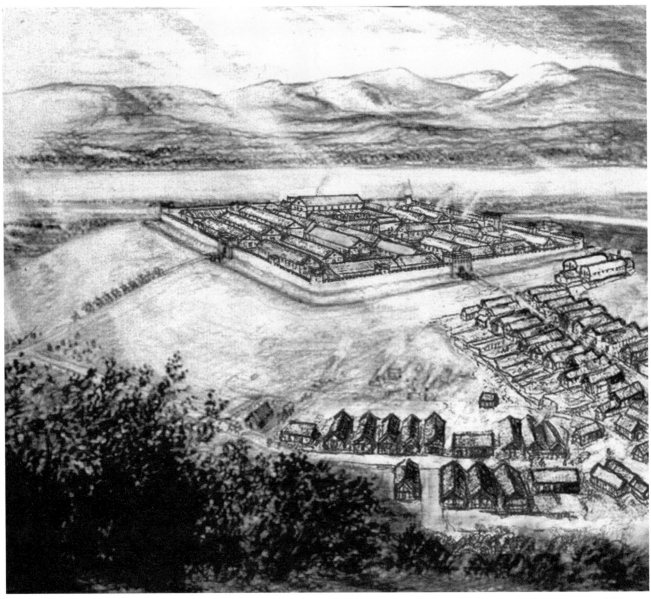

Plate 5.13 Impression of Roman Lancaster by David Vale M.B.E. (reproduced by kind permission of Mrs Mary Vale)

Abbreviations

AE	L'Année Epigraphique
Arch. Ael.	Archaeologia Aeliana
Arch. Journ.	Archaeological Journal
CBA	Council for British Archaeology
CIL	*Corpus Inscriptionum Latinarum*
CSIR	*Corpus Signorum Imperii Romani*
CW	Transactions of the Cumberland and Westmorland Antiquarian and Archaeological Society
GMAG	Greater Manchester Archaeology Group
HSLC	Transactions of the Lancashire and Cheshire Historic Society
ILS	H. Dessau, *Inscriptiones Latinae Selectae*, Berlin 1892
JBAA	Journal of the British Archaeological Association
JRS	Journal of Roman Studies
LCAS	Transactions of the Lancashire and Cheshire Antiquarian Society
LUAU	Lancaster University Archaeological Unit
MoLAS	Museum of London Archaeological Service
OA North	Oxford Archaeology North
PME	H. Devijver, *Prosopographia Militiarum Equestrium*, Leuven 1976–
PPS	Proceedings of the Prehistoric Society
RCHME	Royal Commission on the Historical Monuments of England
RIB	R.G. Collingwood and R.P. Wright, *The Roman Inscriptions of Britain: Inscriptions on Stone*, Oxford 1965
RIC	H. Mattingly *et al.*, *The Roman Imperial Coinage*, London 1923–2007
RMD	M. Roxan and P. Holder, *Roman Military Diplomas, 1–5,* London 1978–2006
Tab. Luguval	*Tabulae Luguvalenses* in R.S.O. Tomlin, 'Roman Manuscripts from Carlisle: The Ink-Written Tablets', *Britannia* **29** (1998), 31–84
Tab. Vindol.	*Tabulae Vindolandenses* in E.B. Birley, R. Birley and A.R. Birley *Reports on the Auxiliaries, The Writing Tablets, Inscriptions, Brands and Graffiti*, Vindolanda Research Reports **2**, Hexham 1993
UMAU	University of Manchester Archaeological Unit
ZPE	Zeitschrift für Papyrologie und Epigraphik

The superscript numbers attached to *Arch. Ael.* and *CW* indicate first, second, etc. series. In the case of *RIC*, they signify editions.

Bibliography

Ambrose T. and Henig M., 1980: 'A New Rider-Relief from Stragglethorpe, Lincolnshire', *Britannia* 11, 135–8

Anderson A.C., 1980: *A Guide to Roman Fine Wares*, Highworth

Anderson A.S., 1984: *Roman Military Tombstones*, Aylesbury

Anon., 1908: *Catalogue to 'The Old Lancaster Historical, Antiquarian and Picture Exhibition, 2 July, 1908'*, Lancaster City Reference Library (Unpublished)

Bagshawe R.W., 1979: *Roman Roads*, Princes Risborough

Baines E., 1836: *The History of the County Palatine and Duchy of Lancaster*, London

Baines E. (Ed. Croston J.), 1893: *The History of the County Palatine and Duchy of Lancaster*, Manchester

Barber B. and Bowsher D., 2000: *The Eastern Cemetery of Roman London: Excavations 1983–1990*, Museum of London Archaeol. Service Monog. 4, London

Bass W.M., 1995: *Human Osteology, a Laboratory and Field Manual* (fourth edition), Missouri Archaeol. Soc., Springfield (MO)

Bellhouse R.L., 1989: *Roman Sites of the Cumberland Coast*, Cumberland and Westmorland Antiq. Archaeol. Soc., Research Ser. 3, Kendal.

Bellis R. and Penney S.H., 1980: 'The Lancaster *Vicus*: Excavations in Church Street, 1978', *Contrebis* 7, 1–31

Biggins A.J. and Taylor D.J.A., 2004: 'The Roman Fort and *Vicus* at Maryport: Geophysical Survey, 2000–2004', pp. 102–33 in R.J.A. Wilson and I.D. Caruana (Eds), *Romans on the Solway: Essays in Honour of Richard Bellhouse*, Cumberland Westmorland Antiq. Archaeol. Soc., Extra Ser. 31, Kendal

Birley A.R., 1973: 'Petillius Cerialis and the Conquest of Brigantia', *Britannia* 4, 173–90

Birley A.R., 2002: *Garrison Life at Vindolanda: A Band of Brothers*, Stroud

Birley A.R., 2008: '*Cives Galli de(ae) Galliae concordesque Britanni*: a Dedication at Vindolanda', *L'Antiquité Classique* 77, 171–87

Birley E.B., 1936: 'A Roman Altar from Bankshead: *CIL* VII. 802', *CW²* 36, 1–7

Birley E.B., 1939: 'The Beaumont Inscription, the *Notitia Dignitatum* and the Garrison of Hadrian's Wall', *CW²* 39, 190–226

Boethius A. and Ward-Perkins J.B., 1970: *Etruscan and Roman Architecture*, Harmondsworth

Brailsford J.W., 1951: *Antiquities of Roman Britain*, British Museum, London

Braithwaite G., 1984: 'Romano-British Face Pots and Head Pots', *Britannia* 15, 99–131

Brears P.C.D., 1971: *The English Country Pottery: Its History and its Techniques*, Newton Abbot

Breeze D.J., 2006: *J. Collingwood Bruce's Handbook to the Roman Wall* (fourteenth edition), Newcastle upon Tyne

Brennand M. (Ed), 2007: 'Research and Archaeology in North West England: An Archaeological Research Agenda for North West England: Volume 2 Research Agenda and Strategy', *Archaeology North West* 9

Brooke G.C., 1950: *English Coins from the Seventh century to the Present Day* (third edition), London

Brothwell D.R., 1972: *Digging up Bones* (second edition), London

Bruce J.C., 1875: *Lapidarium Septentrionale; or a description of the monuments of Roman rule in the north of England*, Newcastle upon Tyne

Buikstra J.E. and Ubelaker D.H. (Eds), 1994: *Standards for Data Collection from Human Skeletal Remains*, Arkansas Archaeol. Survey Res. Ser. 44, Fayetteville (AR)

Bull S., 2007: *Triumphant Rider: The Lancaster Roman Cavalry Tombstone*, Preston

Burnham B.C., Hunter F. and Booth P., 2007: 'Roman Britain in 2006: I. Sites Explored', *Britannia* 38, 241–302

Burnham B.C., Hunter F. and Booth P., 2008: 'Roman Britain in 2007: I. Sites Explored', *Britannia* 39, 263–336

Burnham B.C., Hunter F. and Fitzpatrick A.P., 2006: 'Roman Britain in 2005: I. Sites Explored', *Britannia* 37, 370–428

Burnham B.C., Keppie L.J.F. and Esmonde Cleary A.S., 1998: 'Roman Britain in 1997: I. Sites Explored', *Britannia* 29, 365–432

Campbell D.B., 1986: 'The Consulship of Agricola', *ZPE* 63, 197–200

Carrington P., 1985: 'The Roman Advance into the North-West Midlands before AD 71', *Chester Arch. Journ.* 6, 5–22

Caruana I.D., 1997: 'Maryport and the Flavian Conquest of North Britain', pp. 40–51 in R.J.A. Wilson (Ed),

Roman Maryport and Its Setting: Essays in Memory of Michael G. Jarrett, Cumberland and Westmorland Antiq. Archaeol. Soc., Extra Series **28**, Kendal

Caruana I.D., 2004: 'The Cemetery at Beckfoot Roman Fort', pp. 134–73 in R.J.A.Wilson and I.D. Caruana (Eds), *Romans on the Solway: Essays in Honour of Richard Bellhouse*, Cumberland Westmorland Antiq. Archaeol. Soc., Extra Ser. **31**, Kendal

Cave A.J.E., 1935: 'Report on Romano-British Remains from Cist-Burials at Westfield, near Lancaster', Lancaster City Museum, Unpubl. Report

Champlin E., 2003: *Nero*, Cambridge (MA)

Chandler C., 1982: 'Excavations at Fairfield Road/West Road, Lancaster', *Contrebis* **9**, 11–14

Charlesworth D., 1978: 'Roman Carlisle', *Arch. Journ.* **135**, 115–37

Charlton B. and Mitcheson M., 1984: 'The Roman Cemetery at Petty Knowes, Rochester, Northumberland', *Arch. Ael.*[5] **12**, 1–31

Cheeseman G.L., 1914: *The Auxilia of the Roman Imperial Army*, Oxford

Clark C., 1811: *An Historical and Descriptive Account of the Town of Lancaster* (second edition), Lancaster

Clarke A. and Fulford M.G., 2002: 'The Excavation of Insula IX, Silchester: The First Five Years of the "Town-life" Project', *Britannia* **33**, 129–66

Clarke G., 1979: *Pre-Roman and Roman Winchester. Part II: The Roman Cemetery at Lankhills*, Winchester Studies **3**, Oxford

Coarelli F., 1999: *La Colonna Traiana*, Rome

Cohen K., 1973: *Metamorphosis of a Death Symbol: the Transi Tomb in the Late Middle Ages and the Renaissance*, Berkeley (CA)

Cool H.E.M. (Ed), 2004 : *The Roman Cemetery at Brougham: Excavations 1966–67*, Britannia Monograph Series **21**, London

Crow J., 1995: *Housesteads*, London

Crummy P., 1997: *City of Victory*, Colchester

Cunliffe B.W. and Fulford M.G., 1982: *Corpus Signorum Imperii Romani: Great Britain I. 2: Bath and the Rest of Wessex*, Oxford

Dalziel N.R., 1993: 'Trade and Transition, 1690–1815', pp. 91–144 in A.J. White (Ed) *A History of Lancaster, 1193–1993*, Keele

Dames H., 2000: *An Electrical Resistivity Survey at Burrow Heights Earthwork, Lancaster*, B.Sc. Dissertation (Unpublished), Lancaster University

Darling M.J., 2004: 'Guidelines for the Archiving of Roman Pottery', *Journ. Roman Pottery Stud.* **11**, 67–75

Davey P.J., 1978: *Rainford Clay Tobacco Pipes, 1650–1750*, Archaeological Survey of Merseyside **3**, Liverpool

Davies H., 2002: *Roads in Roman Britain*, Stroud

Devijer H., 1976–2001: *Prosopographia Militiarum Equestrium Quae Fuerunt ab Augusto ad Gallienum I-VI*, Leuven

Dixon K. and Southern P., 1992: *The Roman Cavalry*, London

Druce D., 2007: 'The Plant Remains', pp. 360–77 in F. Brown *et al.*, *The Archaeology of the A1(M), Darrington to Dishforth: DBFO Road Scheme*, Lancaster Imprints **12**, Lancaster

Drury D., in prep.: *Excavations during the Development of Lancaster Market Hall*

Edwards B.J.N., 1969: 'Lancashire Archaeological Notes: Prehistoric and Roman', *HSLC* **121**, 99–108

Edwards B.J.N., 1971: 'Roman Finds from "Contrebis"', *CW*[2] **71**, 17–34

Edwards B.J.N., 2000: *The Romans at Ribchester*, Centre for North-West Regional Studies, Occasional Paper **40**, Lancaster

Edwards B.J.N., 2006: 'The *Caput Carvetiorum* and the Putative God of the Tribe', *CW*[3] **6**, 221–6

Ellis M., 1986–7: 'A Roman Cremation Burial from Lancaster', *Contrebis* **13**, 32

Ellis M., 1987: '80 Church Street, Lancaster, 1985', *Contrebis* **14**, 18–19

Esmonde Cleary A.S., 1987: *Extra-Mural Areas of Romano-British Towns*, Brit. Arch. Reports (British Series) **169**, Oxford

Evans J., in prep.: 'The Roman Pottery', in P. Gibbons† and C.L.E. Howard-Davis, in prep., *Excavations at Walton-le-Dale, 1981–83 and 1996*

Farrer J. and Brownbill W. (Eds), 1914: *The Victoria History of the County of Lancaster* **8**, London

Ferguson J., 1970: *The Religions of the Roman Empire*, London

Ferguson R.S., 1893: 'On the Roman Cemeteries of Luguvallium', *CW*[1] **12**, 365–74

Fitzpatrick A.P., 2004: 'The Tombstones and Inscribed Stones', pp. 405–35 in H.E.M. Cool (Ed), 2004

Flouest J-L., 1993: 'L'Organisation Interne des Tombes à Incinération de IIème au Ier Siècle av J–C: Essai de Description Mèthodique', pp. 201–9 in D. Cliquet, M. Remy-Watt, V. Guichard and M. Vaginay (Eds), *Les Celtes en Normandie. Les Rites Funéraires en Gaule IIème au Ier siècle av J–C. Actes du 14éme Colloque de l'Association Française pour l'Etude de l'Age du Fer, Evreux – Mai 1990. Revue Archéologique de l'Ouest*, Supplément **6**, Rennes

Fox G.M., n.d.: *Roman Lancaster*, Lancaster City Reference Library (Unpublished)

Giecco F.O., 2000: *Report on an Archaeological Watching Brief at Syke Road, Wigton, Cumbria*, Carlisle Archaeology Ltd, Unpubl. Report

Giecco F., Zant J., Craddock G. and Wigfield N., 2001: *Interim Report on Archaeological Excavations between Mary Street and Tait Street, Botchergate, Carlisle, Cumbria*, Carlisle Archaeology Ltd, Unpubl. Report

Gillam J.P., 1970: *Types of Roman Coarse Pottery Vessels in Northern Britain*, Newcastle upon Tyne

Gillam J.P. and Daniels C.M., 1961: 'The Roman Mausoleum on Shorden Brae, Beaufront, Corbridge, Northumberland', *AA*[4] **39** 37–62

Gjerstad E., 1962: *Legends and Facts of Early Roman History*, Lund

GMAG, 1980: *Excavation of a Cairn at Windhill, Heywood, Lancashire, and Reports of Recent Work by the Bury Archaeological Group*, Publications **1**

Goodburn R., 1978: 'Roman Britain in 1977: I. Sites Explored', *Britannia* 9, 404–72

Grahame R., 1999: *Report on an Archaeological Evaluation at Tiffenthwaite Farm, Syke Road, Wigton, Cumbria*, Carlisle Archaeol. Ltd, Unpubl. Report

Graystone P., 1996: *Walking Roman Roads in the Fylde and the Ribble Valley*, Centre for North-West Regional Studies, Occasional Paper **31**, Lancaster

Greep S., 2004: 'Bone and Antler Veneer', pp. 273–82 in H.E.M. Cool (Ed.), 2004

Gregson M., 1869: *Portfolio of Fragments relative to the History of the County and Duchy of Lancaster* (third edition), Liverpool

Hair N. and Howard-Davis C.L.E., 1996: 'The Roman Cemetery at Low Borrowbridge, near Tebay', pp. 87–125 in J. Lambert (Ed), *Transect through Time: the Archaeological Landscape of the Shell North-Western Ethylene Pipeline*, Lancaster Imprints **1**, Lancaster

Halstead P. and Collins P., 1995: *Sheffield Animal Bone Tutorial: Taxonomic Identification of the Principal Limb Bones of Common European Farm Animals and Deer: A Multimedia Tutorial*, Glasgow

Harker J., 1865: 'British Interments on Lancaster Moor', *JBAA* **21**, 159–61

Harker J., 1877: 'British Interments at Lancaster', *JBAA* **33**, 125–7

Harrison J.E., 1922: *Prolegomena to the Study of Greek Religion* (second edition), London

Harrison W., 1894: 'Archaeological Finds in Lancaster', *LCAS* **11**, 184–6

Harrison W., 1896: *An Archaeological Survey of Lancashire*, Manchester

Hartley K.F., 1981: 'Painted Finewares made in the Raetian Workshops near Wilderspool, Cheshire', pp. 471–80 in A.C. Anderson and A.S. Anderson (Eds), *Roman Pottery Research in Britain and North-West Europe. Papers presented to Graham Webster: Part II*, Brit. Arch. Reports (Int. Series) **123** (ii), Oxford

Hartley K.F. and Webster P.V., 1973: 'The Romano-British Pottery Kilns near Wilderspool', *Arch. Journ.* **130**, 77–103

Haselgrove C., 1996: 'The Iron Age', pp. 61–73 in R. Newman (Ed), *The Archaeology of Lancashire*, Lancaster

Hassall M.W.C. and Tomlin R.S.O., 1978: ' Roman Britain in 1977: II. The Inscriptions', *Britannia* **9**, 473–85

Hassall M.W.C. and Tomlin R.S.O., 1979: 'Roman Britain in 1978: II. The Inscriptions', *Britannia* **10**, 339–56

Hassall M.W.C. and Tomlin R.S.O., 1986: 'Roman Britain in 1985: II. The Inscriptions', *Britannia* **17**, 428–51

Hayward K.M.J., 2006: 'A Geological Link Between the Facilis Monument at Colchester and First-Century Army Tombstones from the Rhineland Frontier', *Britannia* **37** pp. 359–63

Higham N.J. and Jones G.D.B., 1985: *The Carvetii*, Stroud

Hillson S., 1992: *Mammal Bones and Teeth: An Introductory Guide to the Methods of Identification*, London

Hird L. and Howard-Davis C.L.E., in prep.: 'The Roman Pottery (1988 and 1992)', in C.L.E. Howard-Davis *et al.*, in prep

Hodgson J. and Brennand M., 2007: 'The Prehistoric Research Agenda', pp.31–54 in M. Brennand. (Ed), *Research and Archaeology in North-West England*, Archaeology North West **8**

Hodgson N. (Ed), 2009: *Hadrian's Wall 1999–2009*, Kendal

Hogg R.A., 1949: 'A Roman Cemetery Site at Beckfoot, Cumberland', *CW*[2] **49**, 32–7

Holden J.L., Phakley P.P. and Clement J.G., 1995a: 'Scanning Electron Microscope Observations of Incinerated Human Femoral Bone: A Case Study', *Forensic Sci. Int.* **74**, 17–28

Holden J.L., Phakley P.P. and Clement J.G., 1995b: 'Scanning Electron Microscope Observations of Heat-Treated Human Bone', *Forensic Sci. Int.* **74**, 29–45

Holder P.A., 1982: *The Roman Army in Britain*, London

Holder P.A., 2006: *Roman Military Diplomas 5*, London

Howard-Davis C.L.E., 1996: 'The Ironwork', pp. 114–5 in N. Hair and C.L.E. Howard-Davis, 1996

Howard-Davis C.L.E. and Buxton K.M., 2000: *Roman Forts in the Fylde: Excavations at Dowbridge, Kirkham*, Centre for North-West Regional Studies, Lancaster

Howard-Davis C.L.E., Miller I., Newman R.M. and Hair N., in prep.: *Excavations at the Mitchell's Brewery Site, Church Street, Lancaster*

Huntley J.P., 1993: *Caythorpe Gas Pipeline – CGP92: The Plant Remains*, Archive Report to Northern Archaeological Associates, Barnard Castle, Durham

Jackson J.J., 1935: 'The Prehistoric Archaeology of Lancashire and Cheshire', *LCAS* **50**, 63–106

Jecock M., 1998: *High Park and Cow Close, Lancaster and South Lakeland, Lancashire and Cumbria*, RCHM(E) (Unpublished)

Jones G.D.B., 1988: 'The Mitre Yard, 1973: The Early Buildings', pp. 59–60 in G.D.B. Jones and D.C.A. Shotter (Eds), 1988

Jones G.D.B. and Leather G.M., 1988a: 'Bath House II', pp. 72–6 in G.D.B.Jones and D.C.A. Shotter (Eds), 1988

Jones G.D.B. and Leather G.M., 1988b: 'The Late Coastal Fort', pp. 80–4 in G.D.B.Jones and D.C.A. Shotter (Eds), 1988

Jones G.D.B. and Shotter D.C.A. (Eds), 1988: *Roman Lancaster: Rescue Archaeology in an Historic City, 1970–75*, Brigantia Monographs 1, Manchester

Jones G.D.B., Leather G.M. and Shotter D.C.A., 1988: 'Bath House I and the Courtyard Building', pp. 61–71 in G.D.B. Jones and D.C.A. Shotter (Eds), 1988

Jones M.J., 1977: 'Archaeological Work at Brough-under-Stainmore, 1971–72', *CW²* 77, 17–47

Keller W., 1975: *The Etruscans*, London

Leather G.M., 1972: *Roman Lancaster: Some Excavation Reports and Some Observations*, Preston

Leather G.M. and Webster P.V., 1988: 'The Quernmore Kilns', pp. 85–93 in G.D.B. Jones and D.C.A. Shotter (Eds), 1988

Levick B., 1999: *Vespasian*, London

Ling R., 1983: 'The Seasons in Romano-British Mosaic Pavements', *Britannia* 14, 13–22

LUAU, 1995: *MFI Site, Aldcliffe Road, Lancaster: An Archaeological Assessment*, Unpubl. Report

LUAU, 1996: *77–79 Penny Street, Lancaster, Archaeological Excavation Assessment Report*, Unpubl. Report

LUAU, 1997: *Streamline Garage, Lancaster: An Archaeological Assessment*, Unpubl. Report

LUAU, 2000a: *Streamline Garage, King Street, Lancaster, Evaluation Report*, Unpubl. Report

LUAU, 2000b: *Former Royal Albert Hospital, Lancaster: Evaluation Report*, Unpubl. Report

LUAU, 2001a: *Streamline Garage, King Street, Lancaster: Post-excavation Assessment Report*, Unpubl. Report

LUAU, 2001b: *Former Royal Albert Hospital, Lancaster: Archaeological Evaluation and Watching Brief*, Unpubl. Report

Lukis W.C., 1883: *Stukeley's Diaries and Letters, Volume 2*, Surtees Society 76, Durham

Mack R.P., 1964: *The Coinage of Ancient Britain*, London

MacKintosh M., 1986: 'The Sources of the Horseman and Fallen Enemy Motif on the Tombstones of the Western Roman Empire', *JBAA* 139, 1–21

Margary I.D., 1955: *Roman Roads in Britain* (volume 1), London

Margary I.D., 1957: *Roman Roads in Britain* (volume 2), London

Mason D.J.P., 2003: *Roman Britain and the Roman Navy*, Stroud

Mason D.J.P., 2004: *Third Interim Report on Archaeological Investigations at Heronbridge, Chester, Cheshire: Excavation and Survey 2004*, Chester

McCarthy M.R., 2000: *Roman and Medieval Carlisle: The Southern Lanes*, Carlisle Archaeology Ltd, Research Report 1, Carlisle

McCarthy M.R., 2002: *Roman Carlisle and the Lands of the Solway*, Stroud

McKinley J.I., 1993: 'Bone Fragment Size and Weights of Bone from Modern British Cremations and its Implications for the Interpretation of Archaeological Cremations', *Int. J. Osteoarchaeol.* 3, 283–7

McKinley J.I., 1994a: *The Anglo-Saxon Cemetery at Spong Hill, North Elmham, Part VIII: The Cremations*, East Anglian Archaeol. 69, Norwich

McKinley J.I., 1994b: 'Bone Fragment Size in British Cremation Burials and its Implications for Pyre Technology and Ritual', *J. Archaeol. Sci.* 21, 339–42

McKinley J.I., 1996: 'The Cremated Human Bone', pp. 118–21 in N. Hair and C.L.E. Howard-Davis, 1996

McKinley J.I., 1997: 'The Cremated Human Bone from Burial and Cremation-related Contexts', pp. 55–72 in A.P. Fitzpatrick, *Archaeological Excavations on the Route of the A27 Westhampnett Bypass, West Sussex, 1992, Volume 2*, Wessex Archaeol. Rep. 12, Salisbury

McKinley J.I., 2000a: 'The Analysis of Cremated Bone', pp. 403–21 in M. Cox and S. Mays (Eds), *Human Osteology*, London

McKinley J.I., 2000b: 'Cremated Human Remains, Cremation Burials, and Cremated Remains', pp. 61–7, 264–77 and 360–5 in B. Barber and D. Bowsher, 2000

McKinley J.I., 2000c: 'Phoenix Rising; Aspects of Cremation in Roman Britain', pp. 38–44 in M. Millett, J. Pearce and M. Struck (Eds), *Burial, Society and Context in the Roman World*, Oxford

McKinley J.I., in prep.: 'Mitchell's Brewery, Lancaster: Report on the Cremated Bone', in C.L.E. Howard-Davis *et al.*, in prep

McKinley J.I., 2004: 'The Human Remains and Aspects of Pyre Technology and Cremation Rituals', pp. 283–309 in H.E.M. Cool (Ed.), 2004

McMinn R.M.H. and Hutchings R.T., 1985: *A Colour Atlas of Human Anatomy*, London

McWhirr A., Viner L. and Wells C., 1982: *Romano-British Cemeteries at Cirencester*, Cirencester Excavations 2, Cirencester

Miller I., 2004: 'Pottery and Fired Clay', pp. 63–72 in Northern Archaeological Associates, *Samlesbury to Helmshore Natural Gas Pipeline: Post-Excavation Report*, Unpubl. Report

MoLAS, 2000: *A Romano-British Cemetery on Watling Street: Excavations at 165 Great Dover Street, Southwark, London*, Museum of London Archaeol. Stud. Ser. 4, London

Moore P.D., Webb J.A. and Collinson M.E., 1991: *Pollen Analysis* (second edition), Oxford

Nash-Williams V.E., 1930: 'Further Excavations at Caerwent, Monmouthshire, 1923–5', *Archaeologia* 60, 229–88

OA North, 2003a: *81 Penny Street, Lancaster: Excavation Assessment Report*, Unpubl. Report

OA North, 2003b: *Gardners Tiles, 99–101 Penny Street, Lancaster: Evaluation Report*, Unpubl. Report

OA North, 2004: *South-West Campus, Lancaster University: Post-excavation Assessment Report*, Unpubl. Report

OA North, 2005: *Gardners Tiles, 99–101 Penny Street, Lancaster: Watching Brief Report*, Unpubl. Report

OA North, 2007: *Beckfoot Roman Cemetery and Milefortlet, Cumbria, Archaeological Evaluation and Assessment Report*, Unpubl. Report

OA North, 2008: *Electricity Substation, Spring Garden Street, Lancaster: Watching Brief*, Unpubl. Report

OA North, forthcoming: *Electricity Substation, Spring Garden Street, Lancaster: Excavation Report*

Ogilvie R.M., 1976: *Early Rome and the Etruscans*, London

Olivier A.C.H., 1987: 'Excavation of a Bronze Age Funerary Cairn at Manor Farm, near Borwick, North Lancashire', *PPS* **52**, 129–86

Ostridge J.H., 1954: 'Ordnance Survey Record Card for Antiquity, SD46SE54', Unpubl. Doc.

Oswald A., 1967: *English Clay Tobacco Pipes*, London

Patten T., 1974: 'The Roman Cemetery on London Road, Carlisle', *CW*² **74**, 8–13

Penney S.H., 1975: 'Gazetteer', *Contrebis* **3** (2), 92

Penney S.H., 1978: 'A Mortlake Bowl from Lancaster', *Lancs. Arch. Journ.* **1**, 5–8

Penney S.H., 1981a: *Lancaster: The Evolution of its Townscape to 1800*, Centre for North-West Regional Studies, Occasional Paper **9**, Lancaster

Penney S.H., 1981b: 'Excavations at 41 Church Street, Lancaster', *Contrebis* **9**, 1–10

Penney S.H., 1982: 'Gazetteer', *Contrebis* **10**, 55

Phillips E.J., 1977: *Corpus Signorum Imperii Romani: Vol. 1, fasc. 1: Corbridge [and] Hadrian's Wall East of the North Tyne*, Oxford

Philpott R.A., 1991: *Burial Practice in Roman Britain: A Survey of Grave Treatment and Furnishing, AD 43–410*, Brit. Arch. Reports (British Series) **219**, Oxford

Pooley L., Holloway B., Crummy P. and Masefield R., 2006: *Assessment Report on the Archaeological Investigations carried out on the Alienated Land, Colchester Garrison*, Colchester Arch. Trust Report **361**, Colchester

Potter T.W., 1987: *Roman Italy*, London

Potts W.T.W., in prep.: 'The Human Bone' in C.L.E. Howard-Davis *et al.*, in prep

RCHME, 1962: *Eburacum, Roman York: An Inventory of the Historical Monuments in the City of York*, London

Richmond I.A., 1954: 'Queen Cartimandua', *JRS* **44**, 43–52

Rivet A.L.F., 1988: *Gallia Narbonensis: Southern Gaul in Roman Times*, London

Robertson A.S., 1988: 'Romano-British Coin Hoards: Their Numismatic, Archaeological and Historical Significance', pp. 13–38 in P.J. Casey and R. Reece (Eds), *Coins and the Archaeologist* (second edition), London

Rogers J. and Waldron T., 1995: *A Field Guide to Joint Disease in Archaeology*, Chichester

Ross A., 1974: *Pagan Celtic Britain*, London

Rossi L., 1971: *Trajan's Column and the Dacian Wars*, London

Roxan M., 1978: *Roman Military Diplomas 1, 1954–1977*, London

Roxan M., 1985: *Roman Military Diplomas 2, 1978–1984*, London

Roxan M., 1994: *Roman Military Diplomas 3, 1985–1993*, London

Roxan M. and Holder P.A., 2003: *Roman Military Diplomas 4*, London

Salisbury C.R. and Coupe J., 1995: *Report on the Archaeological Potential of the Site of the Former Premises, 77/79 Penny Street, Lancaster*, Unpubl. Report

Salway P., 1981, *Roman Britain*, Oxford

Schleiermacher M., 1984: *Römische Reitergrabsteine: Die Kaiserzeitlichen Reliefs des Triumphierenden Reiters*, Bonn

Schmid E., 1972: *Atlas of Animal Bones for Prehistorians, Archaeologists and Quaternary Geologists*, London

Shotter D.C.A., 1973: '*Numeri Barcariorum*: A Note on *RIB* 601', *Britannia* **4**, 206–9

Shotter D.C.A., 1976: 'A Newly-Discovered Fragment of a Roman Inscription from Lancaster', *Contrebis* **4**, 22–3

Shotter D.C.A., 1977: 'Tacitus and Antonius Primus', *Liverpool Classical Monthly* **2**, 23–7

Shotter D.C.A., 1979: 'Gods, Emperors and Coins', *Greece and Rome* **26**, 48–57

Shotter D.C.A., 1988a: 'The Roman Garrisons at Lancaster', pp. 212–9 in G.D.B. Jones and D.C.A. Shotter (Eds), 1988

Shotter D.C.A., 1988b: 'Inscriptions and Stamps on Tiles and Bricks', pp. 186–8 in G.D.B. Jones and D.C.A. Shotter (Eds), 1988

Shotter D.C.A., 1988c: '*RIB* 605 and the Lancaster Bath-Houses', pp. 208–11 in G.D.B. Jones and D.C.A. Shotter (Eds), 1988

Shotter D.C.A., 1990: *Roman Coins from North-West England*, Centre for North-West Regional Studies, Lancaster

Shotter D.C.A., 1994: 'Rome and the Brigantes: Early Hostilities', *CW*² **94**, 21–34

Shotter D.C.A., 1996: 'The Tombstone', pp. 115–18 in J. Lambert (Ed), 1996: *Transect Through Time*, Lancaster Imprints **1**, Lancaster

Shotter D.C.A., 2000a: 'Petillius Cerialis in Northern Britain', *Northern History* **36**, 189–98

Shotter D.C.A., 2000b: *Roman Coins from North-West England: Second Supplement*, Lancaster

Shotter D.C.A., 2001a: 'Roman Lancaster: Site and Settlement', pp. 3–31 in A. J. White (Ed), *A History of Lancaster* (second edition), Edinburgh

Shotter D.C.A., 2001b: '"Agricolan" is an Overworked Adjective', pp. 75–83 in N.J. Higham (Ed), *The Archaeology of the Roman Empire: A Tribute to the Life and Work of Professor Barri Jones*, Brit. Arch. Reports (Int. Series) **940**, Oxford

Shotter D.C.A., 2002: 'Chester: Early Roman Occupation', pp. 25–31 in P. Carrington (Ed), *Deva Victrix: Roman Chester Re-assessed*, Chester

Shotter D.C.A., 2004: *Romans and Britons in North-West England* (third edition), Centre for North-West Regional Studies, Occasional Paper **51**, Lancaster

Shotter D.C.A., 2005: 'The Romans in North-West England: Conquest and Occupation', *LCAS* **101**, 1–23

Shotter D.C.A., 2007: 'Cicero and the Treveri: New Light on an Old Pun', *Greece and Rome* **54**, 106–9

Shotter D.C.A., 2010: *Roman Coins from North-West England: Third Supplement*, Lancaster, in prep

Shotter D.C.A. and White A.J., 1990: *The Roman Fort and Town of Lancaster*, Centre for North-West Regional Studies, Occasional Paper **18**, Lancaster

Shotter D.C.A. and White A.J., 1995: *The Romans in Lunesdale*, Centre for North-West Regional Studies, Occasional Paper **31**, Lancaster

Simmonds A., Marquez-Grant N. and Loe L., 2008: *Life and Death in a Roman City: Excavation of a Mass Grave at 120–122 London Road, Gloucester*, Oxford Archaeol. Monog. **6**, Oxford

Simpson R., 1852: *History and Antiquities of Lancaster*, Lancaster

Sommer C.S., 1984: *The Military Vici of Roman Britain*, Brit. Arch. Reports (British Series) **129**, Oxford

Spaul J.E.H., 1994: *Ala 2: The Auxiliary Cavalry Units of the pre-Diocletianic Imperial Roman Army*, Andover

Spence J.E., 1935: *Excavations at Westfield Memorial Village*, Lancaster City Museum (Unpublished)

Stace C., 1997: *New Flora of the British Isles* (second edition), Cambridge

Swan V., 1975: *Pottery in Roman Britain*, Princes Risborough

Taylor H., 1903: 'The Ancient Crosses of Lancashire: The Hundred of Lonsdale', *LCAS* **21**, I–III

Tildesley M.L., 1934a: *Report on Human Remains from Lancaster*, Lancaster City Museum (Unpublished)

Tildesley M.L., 1934b: *Report on Human Remains dug up in Lancaster*, Lancaster City Museum, Unpubl. Report

Todd M., 1977: 'Germanic Burials in the Roman Iron Age', pp. 39–43 in R. Reece (Ed), *Burial in the Roman World*, CBA Research Reports **22**, London

Tomber R. and Dore J., 1998: *The National Roman Fabric Reference Collection. A Handbook*, Museum of London Archaeol. Service, Monog. **2**, London

Tomlin R.S.O., 1998: 'Roman Manuscripts from Carlisle: The Ink-Written Tablets', *Britannia* **29**, 31–84

Tomlin R.S.O., 2008: 'Roman Britain in 2007: II.The Inscriptions', *Britannia* **39**, 369–89

Tomlin R.S.O. and Hassall M.W.C., 2006: 'Roman Britain in 2005: II. The Inscriptions', *Britannia* **37**, 467–88

Tomlin R.S.O. and Hassall M.W.C., 2007: 'Roman Britain in 2006: II. The Inscriptions', *Britannia* **38**, 345–65

Toynbee J.M.C., 1964: *Art in Britain under the Romans*, Oxford

Toynbee J.M.C., 1971: *Death and Burial in the Roman World*, London

Turnbull P., 1984: 'Stanwick in the Northern Iron Age', *Durham Arch. Journ.* **1**, 41–9

Tyers P.A., 1999: *Roman Pottery in Britain*, London

UMAU, 1996: *Davenport Road, Broadheath: An Archaeological Excavation*, Unpubl. Report

UMAU, 2003: *Arla Foods Depot, Aldcliffe Road, Lancaster: An Archaeological Assessment*, Unpubl. Report

UMAU, 2005: *Arla Foods Depot, Aldcliffe Road, Lancaster: An Archaeological Evaluation*, Unpubl. Report

UMAU, 2007: *Arla Foods Depot, Aldcliffe Road, Lancaster: An Archaeological Excavation of a Romano-British Cemetery*, Unpubl. Report

Van Arsdell R.D., 1994: *The Coinage of the Dobunni*, Oxford

Van Beek G.C., 1983: *Dental Morphology: an Illustrated Guide*, Bristol

Viner L. and Leech R.H., 1982: 'Bath Gate Cemetery, 1969–76', pp. 69–109 in A. McWhirr, L. Viner and C. Wells, 1982: *Romano-British Cemeteries at Cirencester*, Cirencester Excavations **2**, Cirencester

Wacher J., 1974: *The Towns of Roman Britain*, London

Watkin W.T., 1876: 'Roman Lancaster', *HSLC* **28**, 95–120

Watkin W.T., 1883: *Roman Lancashire*, Liverpool

Watson W.G., 1987: 'Excavations at Cheapside, Lancaster, 1984', *Contrebis* **13**, 18–19

Webster G., 1985: *The Roman Imperial Army* (third edition), London

Webster G., 1986: *The British Celts and Their Gods under Rome*, London

Webster J., 1988: 'The Small Finds', pp. 146–52 in G.D.B. Jones and D.C.A. Shotter (Eds), 1988

Webster P.V., 1976: 'Severn Valley Ware: A Preliminary Study', *Trans Bristol and Gloucestershire Archaeol. Soc.* **94**, 18–46

Webster P.V., 1988: 'The Coarse Pottery', pp. 103–45 in G.D.B. Jones and D.C.A. Shotter (Eds), 1988

Webster P.V., 1996: *Roman Samian Pottery in Britain*, CBA Practical Handbook **13**, York

Weekes J., 2008: 'Classification and Analysis of Archaeological Contexts for the Reconstruction of

Early Romano-British Cremation Funerals', *Britannia* **39**, 145–60

Weiss, P., 2006: 'Neue Militärdiplome für deu Exercitus von Britannia', *ZPE* **156**, 245–54

Wellesley K., 1988: *The Long Year: AD 69* (second edition), London

Wenham L.P., 1968: *The Romano-British Cemetery at Trentholme Drive, York*, Ministry of Public Buildings and Works Archaeol. Report **5**, London

West T., 1778: *A Guide to the Lakes in Cumberland, Westmorland and Lancashire,* London

Wheeler H., 1985: 'The Racecourse Cemetery', *Derbyshire Arch. Journ.* **105**, 222–80

Whitaker T.D., 1823: *An History of Richmondshire in the North Riding of the County of York*, London

White A.J., 1974: 'Excavations in the *Vicus*, Lancaster, 1973–4', *Contrebis* **2** (2), 16–20

White A.J., 1975a: 'Excavations at No. 1 Penny Street, Lancaster, 1975', *Contrebis* **3** (1), 30–3

White A.J., 1975b: 'Kiln Sites and Documentary Evidence in North Lancashire', p. 121 in P.J. Davey (Ed.), *Medieval Pottery from Excavations in the North West*, Liverpool

White A.J., 1987: *Roman Lancaster: A Survey*, Lancaster Museum Monograph **4**, Lancaster

White A.J., 1993a: 'Setting the Scene', pp. 9–48 in A.J. White (Ed), 1993: *A History of Lancaster, 1193–1993* (first edition), Keele

White A.J., 1993b: 'A Medieval Pottery Kiln at Ellel, Lancashire', *Contrebis* **18**, 5–18

White A.J., 1997: 'Evidence for Roman Burials in Lancaster', *Contrebis* **22**, 9

White A.J., 2000: 'Pottery Making at Arnside and Silverdale', *CW*² **100**, 285–91

White A.J. (Ed), 2001: *A History of Lancaster* (second edition), Edinburgh

White A.J., 2003: *Lancaster: A History*, Chichester

White A.J., in prep.: 'The Medieval and Post-Medieval Pottery', in C.L.E. Howard-Davis, I. Miller, R.M. Newman and N.J. Hair, *Excavations at Mitchells Brewery, Church Street, Lancaster*, in prep

Wiedemann T.E.G., 1992: *Emperors and Gladiators*, London

Wightman E.M., 1970: *Roman Trier and the Treveri*, London

Wightman E.M., 1985: *Gallia Belgica*, London

Wilkinson J.L., 1997: 'The Cremated Skeletal Remains', pp. 204–19 in E. Evans and D.J. Maynard, 'Caerleon Lodge Hill Cemetery: the Abbeyfield Site, 1992', *Britannia* **28**, 169–243

Williams D.F., 1977: 'The Romano-British Black-Burnished Industry: An Essay on Characterisation by Heavy Mineral Analysis', pp. 163–220 in D.P.S. Peacock (Ed), *Pottery and Early Commerce. Characterisation and Trade in Roman and Later Ceramics*, London

Wilmott T., 1993: 'The Roman Cremation Cemetery in New Field, Birdoswald', *CW*² **93**, 79–85

Wilmott T., 2001: *Birdoswald Roman Fort: 1800 Years on Hadrian's Wall*, Stroud

Wilson D.R., 1964: 'Roman Britain in 1963: I. Sites Explored', *JRS* **54**, 152–77

Witteyer M., 2000: 'Grabgestaltung und Beigabenausstattung in der Gräberstraße von Mainz-Weisenau', pp. 319–43 in A. Haffner and S. von Schaurbein (Eds), *Kelten, Germanen, Römer im Mittelgebirgsraum zwischen Luxemburg und Thüringen*, Römisch-Germanische Kommission des Deutschen Archäologischen Instituts, Bonn

Wood P.N., Bradley J. and Miller I., 2008: 'A Pottery Production Site at Samlesbury, near Preston, Lancashire', *Medieval Ceramics* **30**, 21–47

Worley F., 2008: 'The Animal Bone', pp. 119–22 in A. Simmonds *et al.*, 2008

Wright R.P., 1959: 'Roman Britain in 1958', *JRS* **49**, 102–39

Wright R.P. and Richmond I.A., 1955: *Catalogue of the Roman Inscribed and Sculptured Stones in the Grosvenor Museum, Chester*, Chester

Zant J.M. *et al.*, in prep: *Excavations in a Roman and Medieval Suburb: 53–55 Botchergate, Carlisle*

A Note on the Classical texts cited
This Report contains references to the works of a number of Classical authors –

Penguin Classics
Caesar, *On the Gallic War*, (in *The Conquest of Gaul*), translated by S.A. Handford, Revised and Introduced by Jane F Gardner (1982)

Cicero, *Letters to His Friends*, translated by D.R. Shackleton Bailey (1978)

Dio Cassius, *History of Rome: The Reign of Augustus*, translated by Ian Scott-Kilvert (1987)

Horace, *The Satires of Horace and Persius*, translated by Niall Rudd (1973)

Juvenal, *The Sixteen Satires*, translated by Peter Green (1967)

Suetonius, *The Twelve Caesars*, translated by Robert Graves (1957)

Tacitus, *On the Life of Agricola*, (in *On Britain and Germany*), translated by Harold Mattingly (1948)

Tacitus, *Germania,* (in *On Britain and Germany*), translated by Harold Mattingly (1948)

Tacitus, *The Histories*, translated by Kenneth Wellesley (1995)

Tacitus, *The Annals of Imperial Rome*, translated by Michael Grant (1996)

Virgil, *The Aeneid*, translated by W.F. Jackson Knight (1956)

Writers of the Augustan History, *Lives of the Later Caesars*, translated by Anthony Birley (1976)

Loeb Classical Library

Cicero, *On the Laws*, translated by C.W. Keyes (1928)

Dio Cassius, *History of Rome* (Books 68, 69 and 72), translated by Earnest Cary (1925) in volume 8 of the Loeb translation

Diodorus Siculus, *Library of History* (Books 4 and 5), translated by Charles H. Oldfather (1935) in volume 3 of the Loeb translation

Pliny, *The Natural History* (Book 7), translated by Harris Rackham (1942) in volume 2 of the Loeb translation

Strabo, *Geographia* (Book 4), translated by Horace L. Jones (1923) in volume 2 of the Loeb translation

Maps and Plans:

Binns J., 1821: *Map of the Town and Castle of Lancaster*

Docton K., 1952: *Map of Lancaster 1684*

Harrison and Hall, 1877: *Plan of Lancaster, including part of the townships of Scotforth and Skerton in the County of Lancaster*

Mackreth S., 1778: *A Plan of the Town of Lancaster*

Ordnance Survey, 1848 1:10,560 Lancashire Sheet XXX, Southampton

Ordnance Survey, 1892 1:500 Lancashire Sheet XXX.15.3, Southampton

Ordnance Survey, 1893 1:2,500 Lancashire, Sheet XXX.11, Southampton

Ordnance Survey, 2004: 1:2,500 Outdoor Leisure 41

Newspapers:

Lancaster Gazette 12 September 1812

Lancaster Gazette 21 November 1840

Lancaster Guardian 15 April 1854

Lancaster Guardian 23 May 1857

Lancaster Guardian 9 June 1894

Lancaster Guardian 25 May 1907

Lancaster Guardian 12 October 1934

Also Consulted:

Petts D., n.d., 'Burial on Hadrian's Wall': http://www.dur.ac.uk/resources/archaeological.services/research_training/hadrianswall_research_framework/project_documents/Burial.pdf Accessed 28/11/2009

Lancaster Museum Records: LMA 92 and 271

Index of People

Index of Places

Index of Subjects